Of Thee We Sing
IMMIGRANTS AND
AMERICAN HISTORY

Of Thee We Sing

IMMIGRANTS AND AMERICAN HISTORY

Dale R. Steiner
California State University, Chico

HARCOURT BRACE JOVANOVICH, PUBLISHERS
San Diego   New York   Chicago   Austin
London   Sydney   Tokyo   Toronto

for my father and my mother

Acknowledgments

I owe a great deal to a large number of people. Without the cooperation of Jose and Magdalena Reveles, Jamie Nguyen, Elly Weinmann, and Frank and Moira Steiner, who generously shared memories that were often painful, this book could not have assumed its present form. They have my deep appreciation. Professors Robert Griswold of the University of Oklahoma, Stephan Thernstrom of Harvard University, and Francesco Cordasco of Montclair State College read portions of the manuscript, offering valuable advice and information. Several of my colleagues at California State University, Chico, also contributed enormously. Joseph Conlin read much of the manuscript and suggested ways it could be improved. In addition, he shared his insider's knowledge of the publishing world and shepherded me into the Harcourt Brace Jovanovich fold. Jacqueline Barnhart, Joanna Cowden, Don Lillibridge, and Kirk Monfort pored over the entire manuscript, contributing much in the way of substance and cohesion. Their moral support was no less important to me. Charles Geshekter brought insight and humor to his critique of several chapters. Carl Peterson, Cliff Minor, and Murray Markland commented upon portions of the manuscript as well. The interest which Karen Puccetti showed and the suggestions which she made regarding several chapters proved very important to me. Jan Geer assisted with research. Special thanks go to Sylvia Jones and Lorraine Mosley of the Meriam Library. Nancy Riley typed the manuscript with her usual speed, accuracy, and grace. There were many helpful people at Harcourt Brace Jovanovich, but I'm particularly grateful to Drake Bush for his encouragement, patience, and advice; Jack Thomas for sharpening my prose; Maggie Porter for her careful selection of illustrations; and Merilyn Britt for her elegant design. The collective efforts of these and other people notwithstanding, I am solely responsible for any errors of fact or interpretation which may exist in the text.

DALE R. STEINER

Contents

1

Italian Immigrants, 1905

Lewis Hine photo courtesy of George Eastman House.

1

A Nation
Of Immigrants

Americans Are Immigrants

ALL AMERICANS ARE EITHER immigrants themselves or the descendants of immigrants. There are no exceptions. Even the Indians, despite being called "native Americans," are not as a people truly indigenous to America. Their distant ancestors were immigrants who crossed a now-vanished land bridge from Siberia to Alaska during the most recent ice age, 10,000 to 40,000 years ago. There are, of course, several differences which separate these first Americans from those to whom we customarily attach the label "immigrant." The time of their arrival is perhaps the most obvious of these. The fact that all later immigrants were required, in some way, to adjust to a host society while the Indians did not, also sets the first Americans apart. The gradual, incremental nature of their movement to America, a process spanning generations and consuming centuries, clearly distinguishes the Indians from other immigrants, as does the fact that the Indians were not really aware that they *were* immigrating—they were entirely ignorant of their ultimate destination.

But they were nonetheless immigrants. And because all Americans are immigrants, or descended from immigrants, the study of immigration is an integral part of any inquiry into American history. Immigration has been a continuous and constant factor in America's economic growth, political change and cultural development. It is not something which can properly be compartmentalized neatly like "the Age of Jackson" or "the Progressive Era" and dispensed in a single chapter of a book which purports to survey American history. Yet that is precisely how the subject is handled in almost every instance. The standard procedure is to ignore immigration until the tidal wave of European arrivals in the late nineteenth and early twentieth centuries. After a few remarks about their impact upon urban and industrial growth, with perhaps an even briefer discussion of previous immigrants provided for the sake of "perspective," the subject is shelved again.

This approach distorts our understanding of American history. It obscures the nature of colonial society, for example, by referring to "colonists" and "indentured servants" without acknowledging that the settlers of Jamestown, the Pilgrims of Plymouth Plantation, and the Puritan founders of Massachusetts were in fact immigrants, and that indentured servitude was not merely a system of bonded labor but also a mechanism which facilitated the immigration of thousands of Europeans eager to link their destiny to the New World. Likewise, it would be foolish to examine slavery without at the same time attempting some analysis of Africans as immigrants—that is, the slave trade.

A definition of the immigrant experience that is so broad as to incorporate the African slaves brought to America against their will may seem, at first consideration, to be *too* inclusive, even contrived. Yet immigration was not always a voluntary process. Criminals, paupers, and other "undesirables" were shipped to America without their consent. Those who sailed for the colonies as indentured servants were sometimes the victims of trickery or violence, denied the opportunity of exercising any choice over their fate. Nor could children who accompanied their parents be considered in all cases to have been free agents. Choice, in other words, was not a necessary precondition for immigration.

The advantage of the study of immigration, particularly when it is defined in such a broad fashion, is that it promotes the consideration of American history from a non-traditional perspective. Such an approach may prove illuminating in the way it necessarily challenges the assumptions we make about our society and its history. For example, American blacks are often portrayed as outsiders engaged in a constant struggle to achieve a place in the social mainstream. Yet in terms of how deeply their roots extend into our nation's soil, they are more "American" than are most of their white countrymen. The great majority of black Americans are descended from Africans who were brought to America prior to the prohibition of the slave trade in 1808. Most white Americans, on the other hand, trace their ancestry to Europeans who came to the United States between 1815 and 1914, when immigration swelled to a flood tide. Although Africans certainly brought with them to America no less in the way of cultural baggage than did other immigrants, some of it was obliterated upon their arrival: the slave system aimed consciously at the suppression of their past as a means of discouraging organization and forestalling rebellion. One result of this was the creation of a culture among slaves that was a uniquely *American* amalgamation of many African peoples. In contrast, other immigrants often clung desperately to their past in an effort to cushion the shock of exposure to a new way of life.

To ignore the study of immigration, then, is to discard out of hand a valuable instrument for assessing the American past. The great irony of our nation's experience is that although America is a nation of immigrants, it has exhibited throughout its history a strong undercurrent of suspicion toward them. New arrivals have frequently been held at arm's length by more established Americans—overlooked, despised, rejected. At the same time, however, those immigrants were being woven into the nation's social fabric. To examine their experience is to study the evolution of American society, but from the vantage point of its underside.

However, the mere fact that America is a nation of immigrants does not stamp it as unique among the family of nations. Other societies—including, most obviously, the hemispheric neighbors of the United States—can make a similar claim. Even if we adopt a more limited—and more conventional—definition of the term "immigrant," one which includes only the relatively recent arrivals of the past four hundred years, there remain numerous other nations whose histories were shaped by immigrants in much the same way that America's has been. Yet in two fundamental respects the United States is distinct from these other nations of immigrants: the complexity of its ethnic formula and the overall number of the immigrants involved.

Other countries peopled by immigrants tend to be the products of relatively few cultures. The British Isles, for example, furnished about 75 percent of the immigrants to Australia and nearly 90 percent of the immigrants to New Zealand. About one half of Argentina's immigrants came from Italy and another one third from Spain. Of the emigrants who went to Brazil of their own volition, almost two thirds came from just two countries, Italy and Portugal.

In contrast, American society is a conglomeration of literally dozens of nationalities, none of which is numerically dominant. According to the 1980 census, only 26.34 percent of the American population claimed even partial descent from English stock, although this was a higher figure than for any other national group. Nearly as many, 26.14 percent, cited German ancestry. But these figures provide only the vaguest indication of America's ethnic diversity; many of those surveyed listed more than one national group, yielding a total percentage greatly exceeding one hundred. We must also recognize the unscientific nature of a survey based upon the respondents' unproven claims or assertions of ethnicity, for many Americans simply are not certain about the nationality of their ancestors.

A more reliable illustration is offered by the official statistics on immigration compiled by the federal government. Since 1820, when dependable records began to be kept, nearly fifteen percent of the immigrants to the United States have come from Germany, the highest figure for any national group. More than eleven percent have come from Italy, ten percent from Ireland, nine percent from Austria (including the pre-1919 Austro-Hungarian Empire), eight percent from Canada, seven percent from Russia, seven percent from England, as well as lesser numbers from a variety of other countries. There are, admittedly, still problems with these figures. The omission of pre-1820 arrivals of course reduces the proportion of English immigrants shown in the survey. And the inclusion of undocu-

Ellis Island, c. 1905

Photo courtesy of Culver Pictures, Inc.

mented aliens, if they could be counted, would certainly increase Mexico's share beyond the four percent indicated by the official records. Such imperfections aside, however, the basic point emerges with dramatic clarity: Americans are people from many nations, no one of which is statistically preeminent.

No less striking a characteristic of American immigration is its sheer volume. During the four centuries since the colonial foundations of the United States were laid, upwards of fifty million immigrants have poured in, from all over the globe. That is approximately ten times the number of immigrants to Australia and fifty times the volume of immigration to New Zealand. Perhaps three million immigrants have moved to Argentina. No more than ten million went to Brazil, including well over four million Africans taken there against their will. During this period, the greatest shift in population has been from Europe to other parts of the world—and of the eighty million emigrants who left Europe in the past four centuries, more went to the United States than to *all* of the other nations of immigrants combined!

Immigrants Are Emigrants

This last point suggests something else, obvious, but nonetheless important. That is, in order for immigrants to come to America, they had to depart from somewhere else. In other words, immigrants are emigrants.

These two words, similar in appearance and in meaning, in fact describe the same social and historical process, but from different perspectives. The **immigrant** migrates *into* a country; the **emigrant** *leaves* his homeland for some other place.

Perhaps the most effective way to arrive at the meaning of that tremendous movement of humanity to America is to consider its participants as emigrants: to attempt to understand where they came from, why they left home, what they sought. Only then can we begin to evaluate and appreciate where they settled, how they were received, what they found. If we view the migration process as a whole, from beginning to end, the act of emigration emerges in some respects as its most important part. At least it required more in the way of effort and conscious decision than anything else connected with immigration. Although scientific laws are rarely capable of explaining the complexities of human behavior, a Newtonian principle, the Law of Inertia, seems peculiarly relevant to this point. According to the Law of Inertia objects in motion tend to remain in motion, while those at rest tend to remain at rest. The difficulty with which most of us embark upon projects suggests the validity of this law as a guide to human action. Leaving home is an active endeavor, requiring effort and setting in motion a process of events. Once underway, however, the immigrant is carried forward by a sort of momentum, swept along in a current. This is not to say that immigration, once begun, is an easy experience. The trauma involved in adjusting to an alien culture—just one aspect of immigration—can be enormous. But unlike emigration, subsequent acculturation may proceed with or without the immigrant's conscious participation.

People too readily take for granted the necessity, the *compulsion*, to emigrate: of course Irish peasants fled the potato famine; naturally Russian Jews escaped czarist oppression! Who would not have done the same? What could possibly have held them back? We sometimes fail to recognize that such acts *were* extraordinary. Despite the prospect of starvation, compounded as it was by a cholera epidemic, political oppression and religious persecution, five people remained in Ireland for every one who came to America around the time of the famine. Despite the terror and brutality to which they were subjected, more Jews chose to stay in Russia than fled to the United States at the beginning of the twentieth century.

Why? How could so many people have failed to do what appears to us so easy and logical? The answer to that question lies in a fuller grasp of what emigration entails. Perhaps no better illustration exists than that which is offered by Oscar Handlin's classic study of immigrants, *The Uprooted*. The very title of the book suggests that emigration represented an almost violent act of separation from everything that people knew or held dear—family, friends, home, culture, landscape. It was, in most cases, a tremendous sacrifice, producing enormous trauma. To choose to leave home, even for the vague promise of America, was by no means a painless decision.

William Shakespeare, no less a genius in his understanding of human nature than in his literary craftmanship, commissioned the irresolute Hamlet to spell out the awful dimensions of choice. In his famous soliloquy which begins "To be, or not to be," Hamlet asks:

> . . . who would . . . grunt and sweat under a weary life,
> But that the dread of something after death,
> The undiscovered country, from whose bourn
> No traveller returns, puzzles the will,
> And makes us rather bear those ills we have,
> Than fly to others that we know not of?

In other words, it is often easier to face familiar horrors than to venture into the unknown. And immigration was almost invariably an excursion into the unknown. Recognition of that fact in turn makes it clear that the "typical" immigrant was not typical at all, but was instead—by definition—a rather exceptional person. For us to extract full value from whatever lessons their experiences may afford us, it is essential that we not lose sight of the fact that the immigrants who came to America from other societies were extraordinary people.

History Is People

For most of those who do not take the trouble to consider it, history appears to be nothing more than an endless procession of events—depressions and wars, inventions and achievements—marching by in rank upon rank. If anything, this impression is reinforced by the majority of history books, whose generalized, narrative approach renders the past too abstract, or even too boring, for very many people to appreciate. It is therefore little wonder that historical works, once a staple in the diet of anyone considered educated, are today consumed primarily by professional and amateur historians themselves, or by their students.

Biography, the personal account of an individual life, offers a means to broaden the appeal of the past, while at the same time increasing its utility. The publishers of those magazines and tabloids which clog the check-out lanes in supermarkets have recognized the attraction of biography much more readily than have most scholars. People are curious about other people; they are interested in learning the details of other lives. That holds true not only for the present, but for the past as well. Viewing history through the lens of an individual's life brings clarity and focus to the events which occurred during that lifetime. Biography enlivens history; it personalizes the abstract and animates the boring. And it reminds us that history is, after all, nothing more nor less than the record of the aggregate of humanity—that history is people.

But which people, out of the anonymous masses who flooded into America, should we examine? The choice is far from infinite. In a sense, only a relative handful nominated themselves as candidates for our consideration by leaving some evidence of their existence upon the historical record. Most of the people who immigrated to America have been inarticulate, illiterate peasants who disappeared into the shadows of history, leaving little or no trace. But a few left letters which they wrote home, or diaries in which they revealed their thoughts, or else achieved such prominence that they became the objects of comment by others. It is these few who must, of necessity, be our instruments for exploring America's past.

By definition, however, they are exceptional rather than typical. No one could sensibly argue that an African who was held in slavery in a northern colony, who purchased his freedom and that of his family, who learned how to write and left behind him an autobiography, is typical of his people. But Venture Smith, the individual in question, is in terms of his experiences representative of much which befell Africans victimized by the slave trade. At those points where his life diverges from the larger pattern, he merely becomes the exception which proves the rule. The characters in other chapters similarly deviate sometimes from what is usually perceived as the norm; but the subjects of our study need not be typical in order for us to profit from their investigation. The fact that their lives are open to our inspection at all suggests that they *cannot* be typical. Their stories nonetheless illuminate the lives of millions of other immigrants. And those lives, in a nation of immigrants, add up to its history.

FURTHER READING

ARCHDEACON, THOMAS. *Becoming American: An Ethnic History.* New York: The Free Press, 1983.

GORDON, MILTON M. *Assimilation in American Life: The Role of Race, Religion, and National Origins.* New York: Oxford University Press, 1964.

GREELEY, ANDREW M. *Ethnicity in the United States: A Preliminary Reconnaissance.* New York: John Wiley and Sons, 1974.

HANDLIN, OSCAR. *Race and Nationality in American Life.* Boston: Little, Brown and Co., 1957.

MANN, ARTHUR. *The One and the Many: Reflections on the American Identity.* Chicago: University of Chicago Press, 1979.

SOWELL, THOMAS. *Ethnic America, A History.* New York: Basic Books, 1981.

STEINBERG, STEPHEN. *The Ethnic Myth: Race, Ethnicity, and Class in America.* New York: Atheneum, 1981.

2

John Winthrop

Courtesy of American Antiquarian Society.

2

John Winthrop

THE SOCIAL FABRIC of John Winthrop's England seemed to be unraveling. Political turmoil, religious persecution, and economic ruin added their weight to the island kingdom's woes. Still worse trials, he believed, were yet to come. Deeply troubled by the prospect, he poured out his anxieties to his wife. "My dear wife," Winthrop wrote, "I am verily persuaded, God will bring some heavy affliction upon this land, and that speedily: but be of good comfort. . . . If the Lord sees it will be good for us, he will provide a shelter and a hiding place for us and ours." Less than one year after penning those prophetic words, John Winthrop sailed for the New World, leader of an expedition charged with establishing that "hiding place" in the wilderness of Massachusetts.[1]

The tiny fleet which John Winthrop commanded in the spring of 1630 signalled the beginning of an unparalleled transfer of populations and culture from one world to another. In the next three and a half centuries, over fifty million other immigrants would duplicate his journey. The earliest immigrants had much in common with those who came later—their reasons for leaving home, the anxieties they suffered, the hardships they endured. But in other respects Winthrop and his associates were unique. Unlike later immigrants, they were not required to adjust to a dominant host society: the Indians who inhabited America were scattered, divided, relatively few in number and, as a consequence, ultimately overwhelmed by the newcomers. In the process, the Great Migration of English men and women in the first half of the seventeenth century would create a nation where none had previously existed. Even though dozens of other ethnic groups would make up the flood which followed, the English—by virtue of their early arrival—left their indelible stamp upon the society which emerged.

[1]For the sake of twentieth-century readers, the archaic spelling and capitalization employed by Winthrop have been modernized.

In 1642, when the Great Migration ended, the population of England (including Wales) stood at nearly 5,500,000. During the preceding quarter century about 80,000 people—about one and one half percent of the total population—had left the island. Most of the emigrants sailed to the New World. This exodus coincided with a tremendous population increase: in the half century between 1570 and 1640, the number of England's inhabitants grew by about 30 percent. This was all the more remarkable in view of the high mortality rate—people born during this period could expect to live, on average, thirty to thirty-five years. Life was indeed, as the philosopher Thomas Hobbes observed in 1651, "nasty, brutish and short."

John Winthrop's life spanned the years in question: he was born in 1588 and died sixty-one years later, in 1649. During that period he married four times and fathered fourteen children, although only eight of them survived to adulthood. The size of Winthrop's family and the loss of six of his children—neither of which was unusual for the time—help explain the apparent contradiction of rapid population growth and limited life expectancy.

Not only were England's people increasing in number, many of them were also moving from the countryside to towns. This was in part the result of a reorganization taking place in English agriculture. Landlords bent on profiting from the burgeoning trade in textiles converted their fields from the cultivation of crops to the grazing of sheep. Tenants who had farmed the land were evicted. "Enclosure," fencing in lands that once stood open for all to use, likewise displaced peasants. Deprived of the means for making a livelihood, many of those thus driven from the soil migrated to the towns and cities—particularly London—and collected there.

Of course, not all of those who abandoned rural England were forced by agricultural reorganization to do so. The life of poor English farmers, tenants and farm laborers, never easy, was made especially hard in the early 1600s by a number of factors. Shortages of rural housing and firewood caused widespread physical discomfort. Crop failures and limited food supplies periodically raised the specter of starvation, a threat that became reality for some during the winter of 1623 and again from 1630 to 1633. Undoubtedly, many English men and women fled from the countryside to the city to escape such conditions. In addition, the growth of a commercial economy, centered in the city, lured the rural poor with its promise of economic improvement. By the time Winthrop sailed for Massachusetts, about a quarter of his countrymen were urban dwellers.

City life posed problems of its own sort. The rapid and haphazard growth of towns created crowded conditions. These, in turn, spawned almost unimaginable health hazards: outbreaks of deadly diseases, especially smallpox and bubonic plague, were common. The plague ravaged England in 1624–25, 1630–31 and 1636–40. During one week in July 1625, more than 5,200 Londoners died of the plague; over the entire year there

were 35,428 victims—more than ten percent of the city's entire population![2] Urban congestion also amplified problems of sanitation and waste
disposal. Uncontaminated drinking water was rare and food shortages not
uncommon. Ramshackle construction aggravated an already severe fire
hazard.

Throughout England about half the population had incomes at, or
slightly *below*, the subsistence level. There is little to suggest that this
proportion varied much from country to city. Such widespread poverty led
to further social ills. Drunkenness was rampant, more so in the cities than
in rural areas. And crime of all sorts, from petty to major, escalated alarm-
ingly. Accompanying these distressing developments was a loosening of
morality and decay in the quality of family life. The cumulative effect of
all of this was to place an unprecedented strain upon the bonds which had
in the past held English society together.

Hastening the process of disintegration were religious divisions stem-
ming from the Protestant Reformation of the previous century. The attack
upon Catholicism by theologians like Martin Luther in Germany and John
Calvin in Switzerland had echoed in England as well, encouraging King
Henry VIII in 1534 to reject papal authority and renounce the Catholic
Church. In its stead he had created the Church of England, or the Anglican
Church, with himself at its head. Henry's motives had not been entirely
religious. Overthrowing the Catholic Church in England had permitted
him to seize its extensive and valuable property, swelling his treasury.
And replacing the pope's authority with his own had solved, at least for
the time being, Henry's marital and dynastic problems: the Catholic pon-
tiff had refused to grant an annulment of Henry's marriage to Catherine of
Aragon, to enable him to marry Anne Boleyn. Under the rules of his new
church, Henry had faced no such obstacle.

Many Englishmen, though not all, were caught up in the spirit of the
Reformation and approved secession from a religious institution which
they regarded as corrupt and spiritually remote. Quite a few, in fact, desired that the process of reform be carried even further. They believed that
the Anglican Church did not represent enough of a departure from Catholicism. There was, in their view, still too much ritual and ceremony in
the Anglican service. To them the new institution seemed plagued by the
same unnecessary hierarchy of priests, bishops, and archbishops. These
dissenters advocated instead a simplified ecclesiastical structure and lit-
urgy. The religious dissidents were called "Puritans," a label which reflected their desire to purify the Church of England from within. In fact,
however, their differences over church structure were so deep that the
Puritans and Anglicans represented distinct Protestant denominations. By
1620 the Puritan leadership was working assiduously to gain control of
the Church of England, an effort strongly opposed by the religious and
civil authorities.

[2]The maximum reliable estimate of London's population in 1634 is 339,824. Other estimates
range from 225,000 to 320,000.

East Anglia, the stronghold of Puritanism, was also the home of John Winthrop.³ A member of the landed gentry, Winthrop was born and brought up at Groton Manor, which had been purchased by his grandfather from Henry VIII. Reared in a Puritan household, Winthrop early on manifested a serious attitude toward religion. He later recalled that at the age of twelve "I had more understanding in Divinity than many of my years." Shortly after his admission to Cambridge University's Trinity College at fourteen, Winthrop contracted "a lingering fever." "Being deprived of my youthful joys," he would write, "I betook myself to God . . . as I took pleasure in drawing near to him." But it was through his 1605 marriage to Mary Forth, at age 17, that Winthrop learned he "could no longer dally with religion." His commitment became total:

> I had an insatiable thirst after the word of God and could not miss a good sermon, though many miles off. . . . I also had a great striving in my heart to draw others to God.

As Winthrop's religious involvement deepened, his temporal responsibilities increased as well. At eighteen he became a father. By the time his wife died in 1615, they had had six children together, although only four outlived their mother. Needing a mother for his children, Winthrop soon remarried, but his new bride, Thomasine Clopton, died in childbirth little more than a year later. After another brief courtship the thirty-year-old widower in 1618 married Margaret Tyndal. John Winthrop was, by this time, a man of considerable substance. He was the squire of Groton Manor. Moreover, each of his marriages had increased his estate. Winthrop had, in addition, begun a law practice which required him to spend increasing amounts of time in London. As a consequence of this last development, John Winthrop came into extensive—and troubling—contact with a commercial world which contrasted sharply with the pastoral one he knew at Groton Manor.

The crowded, bustling city exposed Winthrop to the social problems described earlier, confronting him with political values in direct conflict with those he held dear. The English ruling class, of which he was a member, was being polarized into two distinct factions, the Court and the Country. The former represented the dynamism of the city, the latter reflected the traditions of a rural society. The Court party was oriented primarily toward the king, symbol of centralized national government, while the Country faction focused more upon local interests and their representation in Parliament. And, while the Country group remained unwavering in its commitment to Protestantism, those of the Court not only exhibited less concern about religious matters, they appeared to tolerate and, at times, even flirt with, Catholicism.

Events of the early 1620s did not augur well for the Country point of view. Parliament, which King James I had refused to summon since 1614,

---

³East Anglia consisted of the counties of Norfolk, Suffolk, and Essex. Winthrop's home, Groton Manor, was in Suffolk.

was called into session in 1621. But when that body attempted to challenge the king's absolutist notions, he dissolved it once more. Scarcely less disquieting was the crown's attempt to arrange a marriage for Prince Charles to a Catholic princess. Negotiations on this subject with Spain in 1623 failed to produce a match—a development John Winthrop reported with satisfaction in a letter to his wife. But the following year Charles contracted to marry a French princess.

The progress of the bloody Thirty Years War, which had broken out in 1618, offered even more dramatic evidence of the advance of Catholicism. Winthrop followed the news of the conflict closely and with obvious anxiety. His distress at Catholic success in driving the recently crowned Protestant King of Bohemia from his throne is apparent in another of his letters. Events at home and abroad suggested to Winthrop that the Protestant Reformation might yet be reversed by aggressive Catholicism. Pessimistic about the future, he remarked to his brother-in-law, "we might rejoice greatly in our own private good, if the sense of the present times, and the fear of worse did not give occasion of sorrow."

Winthrop's comments on these matters reflected a more active political role which he had begun to play. When Parliament reconvened in 1624 he attended sessions of its committees and, drawing upon his experience in the law, offered his recommendations on legislation. He also helped draft and circulate a rather extensive catalog of "Common Grievances Groaning For Reformation." Heading the list was one which complained of "the daily increase of the multitudes of papists." He proposed that the problem be met by passing a law "to remove all their children from them, to be trained up in the truth and sincerity of religion." Winthrop also criticized "the suspension and silencing of many painful learned ministers for not conform[ing] in some points of ceremonies"—clearly a protest against the suppression of Puritan clergymen. Another grievance resisted royal presumption by protesting "the removal of indictments" brought in local courts to the king's courts at Westminster. The rest of the grievances (twenty-three in all) further suggest the extent to which John Winthrop was distressed by the decay of traditional values and rights.

Those rights eroded even further under the pressures of protracted warfare. During the early 1620s King James sent troops to assist King Frederick of Bohemia, his son-in-law. The expense of this effort proved particularly burdensome, coming as it did at a time of already acute economic distress. And, over the next several years, England's foreign involvement increased rather than diminished. Upon his death in 1625, James was succeeded on the throne by his son Charles. Despite his marriage to a French princess, Charles I soon became embroiled in war with France as well as Spain. The inhabitants of English seaports were terrorized by press gangs forcibly recruiting for the royal navy. In rural areas similar measures were used to raise an army. The unwilling recruits, many of them vagrants or criminals, were then quartered in private homes, to the great dismay of the householders. Across the country widespread economic distress was magnified by the forced loans required to fund the crown's military ventures.

The reverses suffered by the English in the war made these burdens even less bearable. An expedition sent to attack a Spanish fleet at Cadiz in 1625 blundered fruitlessly before returning to England. Hundreds of soldiers and sailors died. An expedition sent to relieve the French Protestants besieged at La Rochelle in 1627 yielded even more ghastly results. Of the 8,000 troops who participated in the campaign, only about 3,000 returned, most of them stricken with disease. John Winthrop's anxiety over these events was heightened by the fact that his eldest child, John Jr., was part of the force which sailed to La Rochelle.[4] News of the disaster there "put us in great fear" for their son's life, according to Margaret Winthrop. In a pessimistic vein she wrote, "[May] the Lord fit and prepare us for whatsoever it shall please him to send to us."

The enormity of these problems for those of the Country was amplified by the fact that England was once more being administered without the consent of Parliament. Charles I proved no more able or willing to deal with that body than his father had been, so in 1626 he had ordered it dissolved once more. The methods Charles then used to raise money and recruit men for his military ventures were of questionable legality. They were also insufficient. Charles was, as a result, finally forced in 1628 to reconvene Parliament. Parliament, trading on the king's need, required that he accept the Petition of Right, which limited royal prerogatives. But Charles had not abandoned his absolutist beliefs. When Puritans in Parliament attempted to push through a resolution setting religious policy, the king ordered it dissolved again and had several of its members arrested. Underscoring his point, Charles declared that, as king, he was answerable "to none but God above." Winthrop received an excited account of these events from his brother-in-law.

Increasingly, Winthrop was in a position to observe for himself, reflect, and sometimes act upon much of what was happening. In early 1627 he was appointed to the Court of Wards and Liveries, a sign of his growing political importance. He also attempted, although unsuccessfully, to secure a seat in Parliament for Sir Robert Naunton, master of the Court of Wards and Liveries. Winthrop urged Naunton's candidacy on the grounds that his "favor and help" would be useful "in the causes of our county especially for our clothiers." This last point, Winthrop knew, was critical: the prosperity of Suffolk—indeed, of all East Anglia—was closely tied to the cloth trade. But because of the disruption of traditional markets by the war and, even more, due to government policy, the cloth trade was severely depressed.

---

[4]From his post, John Jr. assured his father, "I am (I thank God) hitherto in good health and our ship has been generally healthful." John Winthrop, Jr. (1606–1676) went on to become governor of Connecticut in 1657 and from 1659 to 1676. A physician and scientist, he was the first American elected to the Royal Society in England.

For Puritans like Winthrop, however, the most serious issue remained that which was implicit in the resolution which had led King Charles to close down Parliament: the direction of, and control over, religious life. During the 1620s, royal and church officials increasingly reflected Arminian inclinations. Among other things, Arminians asserted belief in the free will of man—that is, that people could of their own volition achieve faith and secure salvation. Not only did this run contrary to Puritan belief, it also represented a step backward toward Catholicism. Uneasily, the Puritans watched as Arminians became more and more entrenched in important positions. Among the most formidable of these was William Laud, whom Charles made Bishop of London in 1628. Bishop Laud immediately set about curtailing the influence of Puritan ministers within his diocese and setting an example for other Arminian churchmen.

It was this issue which weighed most heavily on John Winthrop, and in early 1629 it came to a head. The resolution, which had caused Charles to dismiss Parliament and imprison some of its members, defined as "a betrayer of the liberties of England, and an enemy of the same" anyone who attempted to "bring in innovation in religion, or by favour or countenance seek to extend or introduce popery or Arminianism." In the turbulent aftermath of these proceedings Winthrop abandoned London, resigning his position in the Court of Wards and Liveries. Depressed by events, he clearly expected divine retribution to strike England in the form of some calamity:

> In these so evil and declining times . . . the increasing of our sins gives us so great cause to look for some heavy scourge and judgment to be coming upon us. The Lord has admonished, threatened, corrected, and astonished us, yet we grow worse and worse, so as his spirit will not always strive with us. He must needs give way to his fury at last. He has smitten all the other churches before our eyes, and has made them drink of the bitter cup of tribulation, even unto death; we saw this, and humbled not ourselves, to turn from our evil ways, but have provoked him more than all the nations round about us. Therefore he is turning the cup towards us also, and because we are the last, our portion must be, to drink the very dregs which remain.

Just as clearly, too, it had occurred once more to Winthrop that such a disaster might be avoided by resettling elsewhere. Wrapping up his affairs in London at the end of June, 1629, he hinted at his thoughts to his wife. "I hope," he wrote, "we shall never part so long again, till we part for a better meeting in heaven. But where we shall spend the rest of our short time I know not."

Similar thoughts were on the minds of many of Winthrop's coreligionists who were affected by events in much the same manner as he. The options open to them were, however, limited. One possibility was Holland. For twenty years or more, small numbers of English Separatists—extremist Puritans who withdrew from the Anglican Church—had sought religious sanctuary in the Netherlands, including a part of that group which would later be known to American history as the Pilgrims. But the Pilgrims had, after all, then abandoned Holland for America. Although they had found religious freedom in the Netherlands, they had also been subjected to economic discrimination there. In addition, they discovered that as time passed their children became more Dutch than English. The fact that the Netherlands and Spain were, by the 1620s, at war with each other diminished Holland's attraction even further.

But America—already the home of the aforementioned Pilgrims— offered better prospects. Physically remote from Europe, the New World provided freedom both from intrusive authorities and from incessant warfare. Its inhabitants could, instead, shape their lives largely as they chose. Abundant wood, fertile soil, and unlimited land added to America's appeal.

The New World fired the English imagination well before John Winthrop's mind turned in its direction. There was by 1629 an extensive literature on America—the accounts of adventurers like Captain John Smith of the Jamestown colony, as well as promotional tracts, letters home, and the like. Casual references to the New World occurred in the works of John Donne and other popular writers. Moreover, the terms of these references were not merely favorable but effusive:

> Where every wind that rises blows perfume
> And every breath of air is like an incense.

The early history of English settlement in America contrasted rather grimly with this inviting image. Attempts to plant permanent colonies in the late 1500s and early 1600s had all failed disastrously until 1607. Even the establishment of Jamestown in that year can hardly be reckoned a success. Within six months of their arrival, two thirds of the hundred or so colonists were dead. The handful who survived owed their lives to the legendary John Smith. The progress of the tiny Virginia colony over the next several years was unsteady. Following the "starving time" of 1609, from a population of approximately 500, only sixty remained—some only because they had, in desperation, resorted to cannibalism. About a dozen years later, an Indian attack took the lives of 350 settlers, nearly one third of the struggling colony's population.

Jamestown was the creature of a group of investors organized as the London Company (also called the Virginia Company). Their primary purpose in establishing an overseas colony was economic profit, pure and simple. Much of the difficulty which the colonists encountered was directly attributable to a mentality which placed the Company's success above the welfare of individuals. The colonists were, for example, instructed to erect buildings for the Company's use before constructing shelter for themselves: "though the workmen may belong to any private persons, yet let them all work together, first for the company and then for private men." A further explanation for the difficulties suffered at Jamestown lies in the sort of men which the enterprise attracted: they were adventurers, not settlers. Their interest lay in quick riches, not in the hard work of colony-planting.

The expected substantial profits and sudden wealth did not materialize. Instead, the colonists suffered through starvation and Indian attacks while the Company's losses mounted. Finally, in 1619 the London Company shifted its orientation. It abandoned the Spanish model of extracting gold and silver from the New World, and instead resolved to turn a profit through the promotion of trade between Virginia and England. The larger the colony's population, the more extensive that trade would be. For the first time, then, the Company began actively to promote immigration to Virginia, bent on creating a real colony rather than merely an outpost of empire.

To accomplish that end the Company undertook several strategies. For the first time it began to import substantial numbers of women to James-town to insure that "the planters' minds may be faster tied to Virginia by the bonds of wives and children." In addition, it gave the colonists a share in the management of their society by creating the House of Burgesses, a legislative assembly open to all free adult males. Overnight Virginia be-came more democratic than England itself would be for another 250 years. The Company also attempted to lure immigrants by offering them the only thing which it had in abundance besides debts—land. All free adult males who settled in Virginia would receive "headrights" from the Com-pany—free grants of about fifty acres of land. Additional headrights for each servant were awarded to the persons responsible for bringing them. These measures accomplished the Company's initial objective. Although the number of immigrants to Virginia began to increase almost immedi-ately, it occurred too late to save the London Company. In 1623, burdened by debts and crushed by the recent Indian attack upon Jamestown, it went bankrupt. The next year Virginia became a royal colony: it was now the direct responsibility of the king.

By this time the Virginia colonists were no longer alone. Several fishing camps were scattered along the rocky coast of New England, although only a few fishermen actually wintered in them. Most of their comrades, instead, returned to England with the season's catch. In 1620 the afore-mentioned Pilgrims established Plymouth Plantation on Cape Cod in Massachusetts. Their early experience was scarcely less horrible than the Jamestown colonists' had been; in their first winter in America nearly half of them died. The survivors, however, stubbornly began to scratch out a living.

All of these early ventures, modest though their success may have been, encouraged other English men and women to view America with some hope. Among these was the Reverend John White, a Puritan minister instrumental in founding the Dorchester Company, a group of merchants who hoped to establish in Massachusetts a settlement that would serve as both a trading post and a center of religious activity. A village which would become Salem was established under its auspices. In 1628 White helped organize another group, the New England Company, which in effect superseded the Dorchester Company. The New England Company quickly laid plans for another group of colonists to sail to Salem.

This particular effort was of considerable interest to John Winthrop. For one thing, he knew most of the principals behind it, some of them quite well. More to the point, Winthrop's son, John Jr., announced his intentions to sail to its colony. Winthrop discouraged this plan, bluntly informing his son, "I am loath you should think of settling there." Yet barely a year later Winthrop would commit himself to a similar undertaking.

Early in 1629—at virtually the same moment that Charles I dissolved Parliament—the New England Company, reorganized as the Massachusetts Bay Company, obtained a royal charter and began to lay plans for establishing an overseas settlement. The motives behind its organization were a mixture of economic and religious aims. Most of the investors in the group were Puritans who intended that the colony not merely reflect their orientation but also serve as a Puritan refuge.

Although John Winthrop was not initially a part of this effort, his interest and that of the Company quickly converged. Already disposed by 1629 to think wishfully in terms of "a hiding place" that would shield him and his family from the punishment he expected God to unleash upon England, Winthrop was also increasingly pressured by economic concerns. His large family constituted an enormous drain upon his financial resources. His three eldest sons in particular, all of an age when Winthrop himself had already gone out on his own, continued to tax both his budget and his patience. John Jr., whom Winthrop had sent to Ireland's Trinity College, left school before obtaining his degree. Forth, Winthrop's third son, seemed similarly disinclined to please him. Supposedly studying for the ministry as his father desired, Forth was absent from college for so long that his tutor wrote to Winthrop complaining of it. Frustrated, Winthrop urged his wife: "I pray thee speak with him, . . . for if he intends not the ministry, I have no great mind to send him any more."

But it was Henry, Winthrop's second son, who posed the greatest problem. Henry's 1626 emigration to Barbados to become a tobacco planter produced little besides debts. To the extent that he was able, Winthrop covered his son's losses. But early in 1629 he reached his limit. Rejecting Henry's latest plea for help, Winthrop described his own sorry financial state:

> . . . in truth I have no money, and I am so far in debt already to both your uncles, as I am ashamed to borrow any more. . . . I can supply you no further. I have many other children that are unprovided [for], and I see my life is uncertain.

Henry's immediate return to England offered no relief to his father. He lodged in London with an uncle who soon wrote Winthrop to complain of Henry's behavior. The younger Winthrop had abused his uncle's hospitality by entertaining friends (including "a papist") and carrying on in such a manner that the house "was like an inn." Most alarming was the uncle's report to Winthrop that "your son has wooed and won my daughter Bess for a wife and they both pretend to have proceeded so far that there is no recalling of it." An embarrassed Winthrop hastily took in Henry and his new bride at Groton Manor.

The mounting weight of his personal problems, when added to the rapidly deteriorating political situation, persuaded Winthrop to move from thinking in abstract terms about leaving England to proceeding energetically in that direction. Once inclined toward emigration, he acted decisively. During the summer of 1629, Winthrop became actively involved with the principals of the Massachusetts Bay Company. Taking a leading role in their deliberations, he so impressed them with the quality of his mind and his ability to command that in October they selected Winthrop as governor of their yet-unfounded colony. Scarcely less important for the future welfare of their settlement was their decision to transfer both the Company and its charter to New England.

Once committed to the enterprise, Winthrop quickly emerged as its most forceful spokesman. In a tract entitled "Reasons to be Considered, and Objections with Answers" he attempted both to justify the Company's project and to encourage others to participate in it. Winthrop began by stressing the importance of halting the spread of Catholicism in the New World by establishing a Puritan mission there: "It will be a service to the Church of great consequence to carry the Gospel into those parts of the world . . . and to raise a bulwark against the kingdom of anti-Christ which the Jesuits labor to rear up in those parts." He next noted the "evil times . . . coming upon us" and claimed "God has provided this place to be a refuge for many whom he means to save out of the general calamity." In view of the turbulent state of religious affairs in England, "the Church has no place left to fly into but the wilderness." Winthrop alluded as well to the troubled economy—"all towns complain of the burden of their poor"—and compared the dismal prospects in England with those of the New World: "why then should we stand striving here for places of habitation etc. and in the mean time suffer a whole continent as fruitful and convenient for the use of man to lie waste without any improvement?"

Winthrop also addressed the objections which could—and would—be raised to the Puritan venture. Concern that "our church and country" would suffer from the departure of "the good people," making it even more vulnerable "to the judgment feared" was unfounded; "the departing of good people from a country does not cause a judgment but [foretells] it, which may occasion such as remain to turn from their evil ways, that they may prevent it." Those who predicted disaster for the enterprise, based on "the ill success of other plantations," failed to appreciate that those earlier expeditions suffered as a consequence of "their own sloth." Winthrop promised that the Massachusetts Bay Company would avoid its predecessors' "great and fundamental errors":

1. Their main end was carnal and not religious.

2. They used unfit instruments, a multitude of rude and misgoverned persons the very scum of the land.
3. They did not establish a right form of government.

In addition to his general remarks, Winthrop drafted a list of "Particular Considerations in the Case of J.W." They reveal how the confluence of personal needs and public pressures guided his judgment. The first of these "Personal Considerations" indicates that several of the principals of the Company made their ultimate participation contingent upon Winthrop's leadership of it: "It is come to that issue as (in all probability) the welfare of the plantation depends upon his going, for divers of the chief undertakers (upon whom the rest depend) will not go without him." But more than outward compulsion was involved: Winthrop acknowledged "a satisfactory calling, outward from those of the plantation, inwardly by the inclination of his own heart." His straitened economic circumstances also affected Winthrop's thinking: with "one half of [his worth] being disposed to his 3 elder sons, who are now of age, he cannot live in the same place and calling with that which remains." His personal ambition played a role in Winthrop's decision as well—he recognized his capacity to lead and desired to exercise it. But, he wrote, "if he should refuse this opportunity, that talent, which God has bestowed upon him for public service, were like to be buried." So for narrow reasons as well as grand ones, to answer private needs as well as public ones, John Winthrop prepared to leave England for America.

After his election as governor of the colony in October of 1629, John Winthrop's energies were devoted to preparing for the expedition. Under the terms of an arrangement undertaken in August, its departure was scheduled for the following March.[5] Time was short. Arranging for ships and supplies, answering curious inquiries, and encouraging prospective emigrants filled most of Winthrop's hours but could not completely distract him from the depressing fact that he would be leaving his wife behind when he sailed. Despite his assurances when he had given up his London practice a year earlier, that he and Margaret "shall never part so long again," her advanced pregnancy made it impossible for her to accompany Winthrop. That this weighed heavily upon them both, there can be no doubt. In his last letter to Margaret before departing—written while his ship rode at anchor, awaiting a break in the weather—Winthrop confided that he often read and reread her letters to him, finding "so much love and affection in them" that he could not "read them without tears." At last it was time for him to close. "O, how loath I am to bid thee farewell," he wrote, "but since it must be, farewell, my sweet love, farewell. Farewell my dear children and family, the Lord bless you all, and grant me to see your faces once again."

---

[5]The "Cambridge Agreement," as it was known, not only committed Winthrop and the other eleven signers to a March 1630 departure date, it pledged them all to join in the migration, in effect insuring transfer of the Massachusetts Bay Company to America.

That emigration fragmented the Winthrop family, if only temporarily, was not at all unusual in the larger scheme of immigration. Since 1607 a disproportionately large number of immigrants to America have been unaccompanied males—single men seeking their fortunes or family men hoping to establish a foothold before sending for wives or children. Only a few groups failed to conform to this pattern. Irish immigrants of the midnineteenth century included a relatively high proportion of young women, who were in some demand in the United States as household servants. The East European Jews who arrived in the late nineteenth and early twentieth centuries often travelled as family units. So did many of the English men and women whom Winthrop led in the Puritan Migration of the 1630s. This fact certainly set them apart from most other seventeenth century English immigrants. The expedition which founded Jamestown, for example, had been entirely composed of men.

Winthrop was not completely bereft of family on his journey. Two of his younger sons, Stephen and Adam, accompanied him. A third, the prodigal Henry, was supposed to go as well, but he characteristically missed the boat when it sailed early in April, 1630. Winthrop's ship, the *Arbella*, was accompanied by three others. Seven other vessels, not quite ready yet, would depart for America in two weeks' time.[6] In all, eleven ships carried about 700 passengers, according to Winthrop's count, as well as livestock, equipment and other supplies. It was the largest such expedition of the entire century. The day before they weighed anchor, Winthrop and six other leaders of the Massachusetts Bay Company signed a declaration titled "The Humble Request," designed to counter any "misreport of our intentions." In it they asserted their loyalty to "the *Church of England*, from whence we rise, our dear Mother," and to England itself.

Transatlantic travellers of the seventeenth century faced a variety of dangers which ran the gamut from bad weather to pirates.[7] Not surprisingly, the Winthrop fleet encountered several of these hazards. On the second day of the voyage, while battling "a merry gale," the voyagers sighted eight ships which they took to be Dunkirkers—Spanish privateers sailing out of the French port of Dunkirk. Grimly, passengers and crew alike cleared for action. Only after readying their guns, disassembling some temporary cabins that were in their way, and casting overboard some bedding which they feared might catch fire in a fight, did Winthrop and the rest learn that the eight ships were in fact friendly.

There were no further alarms on the two month voyage, but occasionally ships were sighted at a distance. The immigrants did, however, suffer

---

[6]The *Arbella*, formerly the *Eagle*, was named in honor of Lady Arbella Johnson, wife of Isaac Johnson, one of the driving forces behind the expedition. It displaced 350 tons and carried a crew of 52. The other ships in the fleet included the *Jewel*, the *Ambrose*, the *Talbot*, the *Charles*, the *Mayflower* (the same ship which ten years before had carried the Pilgrims to Massachusetts), the *William and Francis*, the *Hopewell*, the *Whale*, the *Success*, and the *Trial*.

[7]For a fuller description of transatlantic travel before the advent of the steamship, see Chapter 4.

other inconveniences. Their quarters were rude and makeshift, since all ships in those days were constructed to carry freight, not passengers. Food shortages occurred as supplies spoiled or ran out, although exchanges from one ship to another helped alleviate this difficulty. Still, many of the passengers aboard the *Success* would arrive in a state of near-starvation. The weather posed a continuing problem. After a week one of the three ships accompanying the *Arbella*, the *Talbot*, became separated from the rest during a squall, and had to make the crossing completely alone. The other two vessels, the *Jewel* and the *Ambrose*, got tangled together during another storm and suffered minor damage. Surging seas had a predictable effect upon the inexperienced travellers: on the first Sunday of the voyage, Winthrop noted "the sickness of our minister and people, put us all out of order this day so as we could have no sermon." During one particularly fierce storm which lasted ten days, seventy of the expedition's 240 head of cattle perished.

Despite all this, life—and death—proceeded in an approximation of normalcy aboard the floating colony. On the *Jewel* a child was born; a woman aboard the *Arbella* gave birth to a baby that was stillborn. Some people made love, others fought. The latter activity clearly posed more of a problem than the former. Winthrop worked hard to maintain order in the cramped world of his tiny ship. His journal details several instances in which people were punished for rowdy behavior. A servant who took advantage of a child in a minor transaction has "his hands . . . tied up to a bar and [we] hanged a basket with stones about his neck and so he stood for 2 hours." A young woman "drank so much strong water [liquor], that she was senseless, and had near killed herself." Sounding very much like an elder of any era contemplating the younger generation, Winthrop observed "it [is] a com[mon] fault in our young people, that they gave themselves to drink hot waters very immoderately."

After a little more than nine weeks at sea, the *Arbella* made port at Salem. The weary but excited voyagers scrambled ashore, gathered a "store of fine strawberries," dined on venison and "good beer" and socialized with the earlier settlers. Six days later the *Jewel* arrived. One by one, over the next three weeks, the other vessels which comprised the fleet straggled in. The New World adventure of the Puritan immigrants had begun.

The joy of the *Arbella*'s passengers at arriving in Salem was tempered by the disappointing conditions which they found there. Despite the fact that their arrival was expected, apparently nothing had been done by the earlier settlers to prepare for it. The store of food at the settlement was scarcely enough to carry the original inhabitants through two weeks. Because "Salem . . . pleased us not," as Thomas Dudley, deputy governor under Winthrop put it, the new arrivals relocated on the narrow Charleston peninsula, between the mouths of the Mystic and Charles rivers. Here, Winthrop believed, they would "be as a city upon a hill," as he had declared in a shipboard sermon. He had, of course, meant that figuratively; the Massachusetts Puritans, with "the eyes of all people . . . upon us," would serve as a model community, an example. But Winthrop's phrase was meant literally as well, at least to the extent that he envisioned all of the passengers in his fleet settling together as a group.

Almost immediately, however, circumstances forced abandonment of this plan. Due to an outbreak of disease in their encampment, as well as fear of an attack by the French, the immigrants were dispersed into a half dozen settlements. Despite these precautions, and despite the careful planning by Winthrop and others which had preceded the voyage, death soon began to make heavy inroads into the ranks of the colonists. By the end of December of 1630—after only half a year in the New World—200 or more of them were dead. Among the fatalities was Winthrop's ill-starred son Henry. Although he had missed sailing on the *Arbella*, Henry had taken passage on one of the later-sailing vessels of the fleet. The day after his arrival in Massachusetts he drowned while swimming in a creek, inept to the end. Several of Winthrop's servants were also among those who died. The effect of these losses was magnified by the fact that not all of the survivors remained in Massachusetts. As many as 100 returned to England, according to Dudley "partly out of dislike of our government, which restrained and punished their excesses, and partly through fear of famine."

Although disappointed by these setbacks, Winthrop extracted lessons from them as well. He recognized that the colony should not try to grow too quickly—it simply could not yet support a large population. More-over, it seemed clear that only those who could contribute directly to the settlement's welfare should immigrate there. Winthrop stressed these points in a letter to John Jr., functioning back in England as his father's agent: "people must come well provided, and not too many at once. Pease may come if he will, and such other as you shall think fit, but not many, and let those be good, and but few servants and those useful ones." Some immigrants that Winthrop *was* anxious to receive were his wife Margaret and their children, who eventually arrived late in 1631.[8] But in offering her advice on packing and preparing for the journey, he again made the point "be sure to bring no more company."

Winthrop's discouragement of further immigration contrasted sharply with the policy of Virginia, which actively attempted to recruit more settlers. Partly his stand on this matter was dictated by concern about adequate provisions for the colonists. But there were also political consid-erations. The Puritan mission necessitated rather strict control of the colony by its leaders—Winthrop had to insure that the "city upon a hill" set an example that was worthy of being followed. He was also aware that political turmoil could be seized upon as an excuse by the crown to inter-vene in the affairs of the Puritan colony. The hostility of royal authorities toward the Puritan effort was underscored by the fact that immediately after Winthrop's fleet had sailed an official proclamation prohibited any more passengers from departing seaports in western England without first

---

[8]Their baby, which Winthrop had never seen, died at sea.

obtaining licenses to do so. Mercantilist theory may have had as much to do with this pronouncement as religious considerations. Mercantilists, who advocated promoting national self-sufficiency through restrictive economic policies, regarded emigration as a drain upon national strength.[9]

Despite Winthrop's determination to maintain political tranquility in Massachusetts, controversy inevitably arose. Popular dissatisfaction with the restrictive system of government—only the governor, deputy governor, and a handful of "assistants," who constituted a sort of legislature, played any role—led in 1631 to the creation of a new political classification, the freeman. Free adult males who were also members of the Puritan Church were eligible to be freemen; their participation in government, however, was limited to electing the assistants. A few years later the structure of government changed again to permit two "deputies" elected from each town to make up what amounted to a lower legislative house. Further evidence of political ferment was offered by the steady trickle of emigration from Massachusetts. Some religious dissidents, like Roger Williams and Anne Hutchinson, were banished from the colony; the Puritans proved no more tolerant than the English officials who persecuted them! Other colonists departed voluntarily, like the congregation under the Reverend Thomas Hooker which founded Connecticut in 1636. Loss of the voluntary emigrants disturbed Winthrop, who attempted when possible to discourage them from leaving.

For all the turbulence which these events seem to suggest, the Massachusetts colony proved rather stable socially and was able to avoid the persistent internal conflicts which plagued Virginia. This reflected not so much the quality of the colony's administration as it did the social composition of its immigrants. The Puritans who came to Massachusetts, as already noted, often migrated in family units. The heads of households were often middle-aged males, in contrast to the younger, unaccompanied men who immigrated to other colonies. They were, in addition, more truly a cross section of English society in terms of social and occupational background than were the emigrants who journeyed to England's Chesapeake and Caribbean colonies. Of course their sense of religious mission further served to provide a stabilizing influence upon the Puritans' community.

Meanwhile, in England instability was increasing. William Laud, made Archbishop of Canterbury in 1633, promptly expanded the anti-Puritan campaign he had conducted while Bishop of London. In response to Laud's repression, the number of English Puritans seeking sanctuary in Massachusetts rose markedly. In 1633 alone, about twice as many immigrants entered the colony as had arrived in the two previous years combined. The number continued to increase steadily, producing a total of about 20,000

[9]Mercantilism was an economic theory which aimed at enlarging a nation's power by increasing its wealth through trade. One of the basic tenets of mercantilism was self-sufficiency, accomplished by conserving resources while restricting imports and encouraging exports. By the early 1600s English economic policies began to be influenced by mercantilist thought.

for the entire decade. This exodus disturbed English authorities, who consequently attempted to discourage it. Early in 1634, for example, Laud caused the Privy Council to hold up (but ultimately not prevent) twelve more shiploads of religious refugees from sailing. Later that year King Charles established the Lords Commissioners for Plantations, headed by Archbishop Laud, to prevent "such promiscuous and disorderly parting out of the realm" and to supervise England's overseas empire. In 1635 the king barred any of his subjects (except soldiers, sailors, and merchants) from leaving England without first obtaining royal permission, a measure designed specifically to prevent Puritans from emigrating.

But emigrate they nonetheless did. Given their swelling numbers, the immigrants could not help but have a considerable impact upon the Massachusetts colony. The political changes already described stemmed in part from their demand for a greater share of power. Their economic weight was, if anything, of even greater consequence. The thousands of Puritans pouring into Massachusetts brought with them their accumulated savings, providing the colony with a steady influx of capital and feeding an economic boom that lasted throughout the decade of the 1630s. Despite the need to import many items from England, the colony during this period enjoyed a favorable flow of economic exchange with its mother country.

In spite of the obvious economic benefits which immigration provided, Winthrop and the other leaders of the colony acted to control the process. Some new arrivals were judged unsuitable and sent back to England, while others were only accepted after a month's probation. A law was enacted which prohibited individuals or towns from entertaining strangers for longer than three weeks without special permission. The strict rules of the Puritan leaders antagonized some immigrants who returned to England, denouncing their treatment. Their complaints were seized upon by officials there, who attempted to use them as a pretext for rescinding the colony's charter. But the charter was in Massachusetts, where it was physically inaccessible to the authorities. This bit of luck and foresight, coupled with Winthrop's bulldog-like determination not to give the charter up, frustrated such efforts by the authorities. Nevertheless Archbishop Laud, in increasingly threatening tones, demanded that Winthrop yield the document to him.

Winthrop was able to outlast the Archbishop. Before the stubborn governor was forced to surrender the charter, events in England shifted attention away from Massachusetts. The crown's pressing financial difficulties, along with growing problems with Scotland, finally forced the King to reconvene Parliament in 1640, after an eleven-year hiatus. The Short Parliament, as it became known, was dismissed after only one month by the recalcitrant king. Half a year later, though, Charles bowed to the inevitable and summoned Parliament once more. The meeting of the Long Parliament, so named because it sat from 1640 until 1660, spelled the beginning of the end for King Charles. The Puritan-led Parliament began to gain the upper hand over the king, whose absolutist practices it declared illegal. William Laud was charged with treason and locked up in the Tower of London. In 1642 this tug of war became a war in earnest—a civil war which resulted in the execution of Charles I and a brief period of at least nominal rule by Parliament.

The impact of these developments upon the Massachusetts Bay Colony was enormous. For one thing, the flood of immigrants declined to a trickle in 1648. English Puritans, hoping for an improvement of religious and political conditions in their homeland, remained there instead of fleeing to America. In fact a sort of reverse migration began: "some among us began to think of returning back to England," observed Winthrop. Included in this movement was his son Stephen. So nearly complete was the cessation of immigration from England that Thomas Hutchinson, the eighteenth-century historian and governor of Massachusetts, calculated that more people emigrated from Massachusetts in the century following 1640 than immigrated to the colony![10]

The economic consequences of this pattern were immediate and painful. The colony's prosperity, propped up in the 1630s by the steady stream of immigrants, crumbled. Costly English imports rapidly reduced the supply of hard currency in Massachusetts, while prices of local products plunged by more than 50 percent.

The economic hardship suffered by the colony in general reflected Winthrop's own sorry circumstances. He spent freely of his own money on behalf of the colony. His financial situation was further eroded by the embezzlement of much of his English estate by a servant to whom he had entrusted its management. In economic terms, then, the twenty years which Winthrop spent in America, from 1630 until his death in 1649, were hardly rewarding.[11] But they were fulfilling in other respects. During that period Winthrop, more than any other individual, carried the weight of the colony upon his shoulders, setting its policies and shaping its future. He was active in government the entire time, serving as governor most of those years and as either deputy governor or as an assistant the rest of the time. Winthrop played a pivotal role in laying the foundation for an American nation to which millions more immigrants would come, following the trail which he had blazed.

FURTHER READING

BREEN, T. H. *Puritans and Adventurers: Change and Persistence in Early America.* New York: Oxford University Press, 1980.

BREMER, FRANCIS J. *The Puritan Experiment: New England Society From Bradford to Edwards.* New York: St. Martin's Press, 1976.

---

[10]The focus of English immigration during this period shifted to other American colonies.

[11]Margaret Winthrop died in 1647. About a year later Winthrop married Martha Coytmore, his fourth wife.

BRIDENBAUGH, CARL. *Vexed and Troubled Englishmen, 1590–1642.* New York: Oxford University Press, 1968.

DUNN, RICHARD S. *Puritans and Yankees: The Winthrop Dynasty of New England, 1630–1717.* Princeton: Princeton University Press, 1962.

MORGAN, EDMUND S. *The Puritan Dilemma: The Story of John Winthrop.* Boston: Little, Brown, 1958.

RUTMAN, DARRETT B. *John Winthrop's Decision for America: 1629.* Philadelphia: J.B. Lippincott Co., 1975.

_____. *Winthrop's Boston: A Portrait of a Puritan Town, 1630–1649.* Chapel Hill: University of North Carolina Press, 1965.

ZAGORIN, PEREZ. *The Court and the Country: The Beginning of the English Revolution.* New York: Atheneum, 1970.

3

James Logan

Courtesy of Historical Society of Pennsylvania.

3

James Logan

JAMES LOGAN WAS FURIOUS. The latest news from the Pennsylvania frontier indicated that some unruly immigrants had settled illegally on lands reserved for the Penn family. As Secretary of the province and the official guardian of the Penns' interests in America, Logan was obliged to report the incident. "This is the most audacious attack that has ever yet been offered," he complained to Thomas Penn. The identity of the squatters fueled the Secretary's fury—and perhaps excited his embarrassment as well. "They are," he noted, "of the Scotch-Irish (so called here) of whom . . . you seem'd to have a pretty good opinion but it is more than I can tho' their countryman."[1]

The disdain which the Scotch-Irish exhibited for the authority of James Logan and the Penns mirrored the low regard in which authorities tended to hold them. They were the descendants of people whom English officials viewed as mere pawns, to be moved from one part of the British Empire to another—or sacrificed—as policy demanded. The forebears of the Scotch-Irish had occupied the Scottish Lowlands—a bleak, violent area—their prospects blighted both by the region's infertility and its climate of lawlessness. William Shakespeare described it in 1606 as a place

> Where sighs and groans and shrieks that rend the air
> Are made. . . . and good men's lives
> Expire before the flowers in their caps.

[1]The term "Scotch-Irish" is an Americanism. The people it describes, Irish immigrants who were descended from Scottish forebears, regarded themselves simply as Irish, a designation which was reflected in most colonial-era references to them. It was not until the mid-nineteenth century that the term Scotch-Irish became widely used, as a means of distinguishing between these early arrivals and the flood of Catholic Irish which was then beginning to pour into the United States.

It is little wonder that when England's King James I offered the Lowland Scots a chance for a better life in a different place, thousands of them seized the opportunity. In the misery of his Scottish subjects James saw a means for solving his "Irish problem," the refusal of Ireland's Catholic population to accept either England's rule or its religion. He resolved to colonize Ireland with Lowland Scots, militantly anti-Catholic Presbyterians who could be counted on to crush Irish resistance. In 1607 James inaugurated the plantation of Ulster, the northernmost—and most rebellious—of Ireland's four provinces, by confiscating six of its nine counties. The native Irish were driven from their fields, taking refuge in bogs and mountains. The land was then awarded to wealthy "undertakers" on the condition that it be occupied by tenants from England or Scotland. According to one jaundiced observer, the plantation project attracted "the scum of both nations, who for debt, or breaking or fleeing from justice, or seeking shelter, came hither, hoping to be without fear of man's justice in a land where there was nothing."[2]

Between 1608 and 1618 as many as 40,000 Scots poured into Ulster, lured there by the availability of land and low rents. Thousands more followed in the 1620s and 1630s. The Irish resisted this invasion, mounting a campaign of guerrilla warfare. In 1641, taking advantage of England's preoccupation with the strife between Puritans and Anglicans, the Irish rose in rebellion. About a seventh of the Ulster Scots died in the eleven years that the struggle dragged on; Irish losses were even higher. An English army under Oliver Cromwell finally, and in bloody fashion, imposed order on the troubled island. Another wave of settlers then embarked for Ulster, spurred on by an English campaign in Scotland against dissenters from the Anglican Church.

Included in this group was the family of Patrick Logan, a one-time Anglican clergyman who had become a Quaker in 1671. The Logans settled in Lurgan, not far from Belfast, where Patrick Logan taught at a Latin school. In 1674 a son, James, was born, one of nine children, although only two would survive to adulthood. The meager earnings of a Quaker schoolmaster were reflected in the Logan family's poverty. Their distress was amplified by official harassment directed against Quakers, who for reasons of conscience refused to swear oaths, attend Anglican services, or pay tithes to support the established church. Their homes were frequently invaded by parish officials who seized goods usually worth several times the amount of the tithe or fine in question. Sometimes violence accompanied these expeditions as well.

Worse lay in store. The 1685 ascension of a Catholic, James II, to the English throne emboldened Ireland's Catholic population. Ireland was once more the scene of sectarian violence, as Catholic guerrillas attacked the homes of Protestants, looting and burning. Armed Protestants replied

---

[2]Many more Scots than English settled in Ulster, due both to the more proximate location of Scotland and the greater poverty of its inhabitants.

in kind. Ulster, with its concentration of Protestant Scots, was hard hit by the fighting. One witness reported that "it looked like a sudden famine, there was such great destruction." Understandably, childhood was a grim experience for James Logan. "In the days which should have been my gayest," he recalled later, "I knew nothing out of school but terror and horror."

In school, however, young James flourished, exhibiting a thirst for knowledge which a lifetime of study could not quench. He mastered Latin and Greek, as well as making a start in Hebrew, by the time he was thirteen. At that point, his parents apprenticed James to a linen merchant in Dublin. Their arrangement was disrupted within six months by the outbreak of full-scale warfare, and James went home to Lurgan.

Driven from the English throne by the Glorious Revolution of 1688, James II retreated with his army to Ireland. The army cut a devastating swath through Ulster, plundering a number of towns, including Lurgan. Many Protestants, the Logans among them, fled back to Scotland in early 1689. A year later Patrick Logan secured a position at a Quaker school in Bristol, England. James followed him there and resumed his education.

In Ireland, meanwhile, an English army under newly crowned King William had crushed that of James II in 1690, and imposed a harsh settlement upon the Catholics. The restoration of order and the confiscation of more land unleashed a flood of Scots into Ulster—at least 50,000 between 1690 and 1697. Although James Logan's parents were among them, he remained in Bristol, taking charge of his father's school at age nineteen. There he stayed for four years, advancing his own studies while overseeing those of others. Young Logan acquired more practical knowledge as well. Bristol was a bustling seaport—the second largest in the English empire— with extensive trade links to the American colonies. The excitement and profits that were a part of that trade appealed to Logan, and in 1697 he agreed to go to Jamaica as the agent of a British merchant.

Before setting out, Logan returned to Ireland to bid his parents farewell. To his chagrin he found his mother vehemently opposed to the idea; indeed, Logan later wrote, "my Mother was so averse to it, that she affirmed that she would much rather see me dead." Disappointed but dutiful, Logan changed his plans. He sold his precious books, bought a cargo of linens with the proceeds, and went into business as a merchant, shipping cloth from Dublin to Bristol.

Such a move seemed promising—the Irish economy was picking up. This was particularly true in Ulster where a combination of low rents and productive land stimulated prosperity. Even more a factor in the region's economic growth was its flourishing cloth trade in linen and especially wool. The rise of Ulster's woollen cloth industry, however, aroused the jealousy of English producers who complained about the competition. In response, England in 1699 imposed the Woollens Act, which barred the shipment of Irish wool or woollen cloth to foreign or colonial markets. This proved a crippling blow to the Irish cloth trade and initiated a steep decline in the region's economy.

At virtually the same time that the Woollens Act was casting a pall over Ulster's economic prospects, James Logan was approached by William Penn, who asked the young man to be his personal secretary. Penn, the most prominent Quaker in England, was a resident of Bristol and served on the supervisory board of Logan's school, which he visited occasionally. Penn was also proprietor of the colony of Pennsylvania, founded in 1681.[3] He had not visited the New World, however, since 1684, and after a fifteen year absence was eager to return. In anticipation of the complexities associated with administering a colony, Penn sought the assistance of a lively and learned mind. Logan took only a few days to consider before accepting Penn's offer; the imminent collapse of the trade in which he was engaged may well have influenced his decision.

The voyage to America took three months. En route their ship, the *Canterbury*, encountered what at first appeared to be a pirate vessel, and made ready to fight. All the Quakers, following the pacifist dictates of their religion, retired below—all, that is, except James Logan, who years later recounted the story to Benjamin Franklin. After the crisis had passed Penn chided his young secretary for helping prepare the ship for a fight, to which Logan replied, "I being thy servant, why did thee not order me to come down? But thee was willing enough that I should stay and help to fight the ship when thee thought there was danger." The incident is a revealing one, foretelling Logan's later willingness to sacrifice Quaker principles of non-resistance to the practical demands of colonial defense.

Their difference of opinion in this matter caused no breach in the relationship between Penn and his secretary. Immediately upon their arrival Logan found himself entrusted with a variety of responsibilities, ranging from mundane chores like ordering supplies for the Penn household to the important duty of administering Penn's lands. This involved selling tracts of land, securing payment for lands already sold, and collecting quitrents.[4] The lack of accurate records indicating funds collected or still owed, imprecise surveys which confused claims, and a popular reluctance to pay obligations all complicated Logan's task. Yet in view of the rather dismal state of Penn's personal finances, a great deal depended upon Logan's effectiveness at his job.

Despite the best efforts of his secretary, Penn found his colony to be more of a drain than a source of revenue. Pennsylvania presented its proprietor with political, as well as economic, problems. In fact, late in 1701 Penn found it necessary to return to England in order to ward off attempts to revoke his charter and place Pennsylvania under direct royal control. Before departing, he left his secretary instructions that emphasized his

---

[3]Proprietary colonies were the personal holdings of individuals, unlike corporate colonies like the Massachusetts Bay Colony. In addition to Pennsylvania, New York, New Jersey, Maryland, Delaware, North Carolina, South Carolina, and Georgia were all proprietary colonies.

[4]Quitrents were annual fees paid by landowners to colonial proprietors in lieu of performing certain traditional obligations (such as repairing roads or fences), which had carried over from feudal times.

need for money: "Get in quit-rents; sell lands . . .; look carefully after all fines. . . . Get in the taxes. . . ." To ease Logan's task Penn endowed the young man with as much official weight as he could, making him Clerk of the Council, Secretary of the Province, Receiver-General of Pennsylvania, and Commissioner of Property.[5]

It did little good. Letter after letter from Penn urged "hasten in my rents;" "I must renew my pressings upon thee about returns;" "hasten over rents and all thou canst;" "make returns with all speed or I am undone." In frustration, Logan could only reply: "there is no way of getting money in, but what I have industriously tried;" "it [is] exceeding difficult to get any rents;" "the rents are still behind;" "people will not pay;" "We sell but little land." Logan's relentless efforts to satisfy Penn's demands—including even an attempt to seize goods for nonpayment—contributed to a growing dislike for the secretary. Logan's decreasing popularity was due not merely to his office, however; his aloof and somewhat forbidding personality took its toll as well. In fact William Penn, troubled by reports from America, had to gently rebuke Logan in 1704 for having "grown touchy and apt to give short and rough answers, which many call haughty." Clearly Logan's duties bore heavily on the young man.

Part of his difficulty in collecting money was owing to the War of the Spanish Succession (known in America as Queen Anne's War), which broke out in 1702. Pitting England against her arch-rival, France, and involving a number of other European nations as well, the conflict disrupted the West Indies trade so vital to Pennsylvania and plunged the colony into a depression. Cash became so scarce that in those rare cases when Logan was able to collect rent or debts, he had to accept wheat. "Unless I take bread and flour, whether it will do or not, I can get nothing," he reported to Penn. But even that could be made to pay. Calling upon his brief experience in the cloth trade, Logan shipped Pennsylvania wheat to other colonies for goods, credit, or cash.

He realized that one of the surest ways for Penn to make money was the sale of more of his vast lands to settlers. This the war made extremely difficult, however, because the disruption of commerce also reduced the number of immigrants arriving in the colony. Logan worried that the conflict might affect Pennsylvania even more directly than that: he received reports of French vessels preparing to attack the colony. The consequences of such a raid would be disastrous: "The sale of thy land, upon the first insult that way, would be at an end," he warned Penn in 1702, "especially where we have it to sell, viz., in the remoter places." Their chief instrument for protecting those "remoter places" was the Iroquois Confederacy, a powerful league of five Indian nations allied with the English. The Iroquois resisted French encroachment on the Pennsylvania frontier (and that of New York) and protected the colonists from hostile tribes associated with the French. Warning Penn that "if we lose the Iro-

[5]A body charged with advising the governor, the Council performed some of the functions of an upper legislative house.

quois, we are gone," Logan made the preservation of their good will one of his highest priorities. His unswerving dedication to that aim would cause him enormous problems with the Scotch-Irish who flooded the frontier in the years to come.

No less troubling than the apparent external threat to the colony was the turbulent state of its politics. As the principal agent of the Penn family, James Logan was naturally among the leaders of the "proprietary party," which supported the proprietor's interests as well as the notion that Pennsylvania was his personal fief. This position was increasingly challenged by a "democratic party," which claimed a larger share of power for the Assembly, representative of the popular interest. Aggravated by the Assembly's independent spirit, William Penn believed that it was the result of a peculiar metamorphosis that resulted when people migrated to America:

> There is an excess of vanity that is apt to creep in upon the people in power in America, who, having got out of the crowd in which they were lost here . . . think nothing taller than themselves but the trees, . . . I have sometimes thought that if there was a law to oblige the people in power, in their respective colonies, to take turns in coming over for England, that they might lose themselves again amongst the crowds of so much more considerable people at the custom-house, exchange, and Westminster Hall, they would exceedingly amend in their conduct at their return, and be much more discreet and tractable, and fit for government.

Because William Penn remained in England, James Logan acted as the primary counterweight in his tug-of-war with the Assembly. But Logan served the proprietary cause not merely out of loyalty to Penn. His political perferences inclined him against the popular side: "This people think privileges their due, and all that can be grasped their native right," he disapprovingly sniffed. Where he could, he labored to diminish the Assembly's influence and enlarge that of the proprietor. In 1704, for example, he proposed enlarging the Council's power at the expense of the Assembly, giving the former body an active role in the legislative process. Logan's actions prompted some of his colonial adversaries to complain to London of his "very great abuses." Over the course of the next several years the political warfare ebbed and flowed. Late in 1706 the Assembly charged Logan with having given "pernicious counsel" to the governor and declared him "an enemy to the Governor and government of this province." An attempt to impeach and remove Logan a few months later came to nothing, but showed the extent to which the two sides had drifted apart.

This troubling situation was made even more complicated by the fact that in 1705 William Penn temporarily lost title to Pennsylvania. A few years earlier he had unwittingly signed a document transferring ownership to an unscrupulous associate, and from 1705 to 1708 title to the colony was a matter of intense dispute and litigation. The resultant chaos strengthened the resolve of the democratic party to resist the pretensions of the proprietor and his agent. And of course Logan found it absolutely impossible to collect any rents as long as Penn's right to them remained in question.

Despite his inability to carry out that task, Logan had to face other, equally pressing responsibilities. Foremost of these, as long as the war with France continued, was seeing to the defense of Pennsylvania. The necessity for action was brought home dramatically in 1709 when a French privateer attacked one of the province's ports. This incident, coupled with a royal directive that the colony contribute 150 men to a force being raised for an invasion of French Canada, posed a real dilemma for Quaker Pennsylvanians: how could military measures, even of a defensive nature, be reconciled with pacifist beliefs? Logan, who had confronted that problem ten years earlier, bound for America aboard the *Canterbury*, proposed an indirect solution. He suggested that the Assembly appropriate a sum of money sufficient to arm and equip 150 soldiers, convey it to the Queen "to be employed as she shall see fit" —and let her bear the moral burden of military action. When the Assembly rejected this plan and refused to make any reasonable provision for the protection of the colony, Logan became irreversibly convinced that rigid adherence to Quaker principles was incompatible with responsible government.

This particular episode did little to improve Logan's standing with the antiproprietary group, which once more launched an attack against him. New charges were levelled by the Assembly (he had denounced it as a collection of "knaves and fools"), which declared Logan incompetent to hold public office and ordered him jailed. The colony's governor angrily refused to carry out the Assembly's directive. A few days later Logan sailed for England, conveniently summoned there by Penn to help sort out the proprietor's tangled finances.

While in London Logan was given a rather painful reminder that his own financial state, long neglected in the interest of the Penns, required attention. He proposed marriage to a young woman, only to have her family reject him as unsuitable for his lack of wealth. A similar disappointment had befallen him a few years before in Philadelphia, when he had sought to marry the daughter of a substantial merchant. Logan consequently resolved to acquire a sufficient fortune to insure that he would not be rejected again. Before returning to Pennsylvania, therefore, he set about buying up at bargain prices the claims of investors who had purchased rights to land when the colony was first organized, but who had never followed up on securing their patents. In short order Logan had succeeded in gaining a claim to over 7,000 acres of land. Upon his return to Pennsylvania in 1712, he was able to insure, by virtue of his control over land sales, that his were the best lands still available in the colony.

Logan furthered his quest for wealth by embarking on an extensive trade in furs, an item much in demand in Europe. His conduct of this business revealed a side of Logan's nature that was less than admirable. He maximized his profits at the expense of his traders—frontiersmen who secured their pelts from Indian trappers—by overcharging them for the goods they needed to exchange for furs. In addition, he supplied them with liquor, in defiance of measures which made it illegal to furnish alcohol to Indians. Such questionable practices paid off, however; within a few years Logan had a virtual monopoly over the Pennsylvania fur trade. And as he had intended, his economic rise improved his social prospects: in 1714 he married Sarah Read, a Philadelphia Quaker.

As profitable as the fur trade proved to be, Logan recognized that the chief instrument of his financial success would be the land which he had bought up in England. The key to making it pay, of course, was to sell it to settlers, or rent it to tenants. That, in turn, depended upon an increase in immigrants. Just a year after his return from England in 1713, the Treaty of Utrecht ended the war. Almost immediately German peasants began to pour into Pennsylvania, a movement that was surpassed within a few years by immigrants from Logan's own homeland, Ulster.

Since Logan's departure from Ulster in 1699 the quality of life for most of the region's Protestants had diminished markedly. In 1704 England imposed the Test Act, requiring civil and military officers to take the sacrament as prescribed by the Church of England. Ulster's Scottish population, composed overwhelmingly of Presbyterian dissenters from the established church, suddenly found itself proscribed from holding public office. Ten of Londonderry's twelve aldermen were rendered ineligible for their posts; in Belfast the disqualification was complete. Dissenting ministers were evicted from their pulpits. Marriages which they performed were denied legal standing; the children which issued from such unions were, in legal terms, bastards. Even though the rigor with which these limitations were applied began to abate by 1709, it was not until 1782 that they were rescinded altogether.

As troubling as this religious discrimination may have been for the Ulster Scots, their rapidly eroding economic status gave them even greater cause for complaint. Mostly tenants who rented the land they worked, they were victimized by a system which came to be known as "rack-renting." In the early 1690s, landlords who were eager to repopulate land left vacant by the violence accompanying the Glorious Revolution had attracted Scottish tenants by offering lengthy leases at artificially low rates. By 1717 large numbers of these agreements were up for renewal— and tenants were no longer in short supply. Renters were anguished to discover that their landlords were bent on doubling or even tripling the rents. Industrious tenants who had increased the value of the land they worked by erecting fences or undertaking some other improvement were in effect penalized for their efforts by being assessed higher rents. The fact that many of the landlords were absentee owners, unacquainted with— and apparently uninterested in—their tenants, further amplified the feelings of alienation and exploitation felt by many renters.

Against this background of agrarian discontent, a number of lesser disasters befell Ulster's farmers at virtually the same time. England's mercantilist policy bore increasingly heavily on Ireland's trade, so that by 1715 it labored under more restrictions than any other British colony. In addition, for a half-dozen years (1714–19) severe drought curtailed farm production; toward the end of the decade extreme frosts took their toll on crops as well. An affliction known simply, but descriptively, as "rot" spread among the herds of sheep, while an epidemic of smallpox swept through the human population.

It is little wonder, given the cumulative weight of these various woes, that thousands of emigrants left Ireland beginning in 1717. Almost exclusively they were Ulster Scots, or Scotch-Irish as they began to be called in America. Ireland's native population remained stubbornly in place, its roots extending far deeper into her soil than those of the recent arrivals from Scotland. The conditions which drove the Scotch-Irish from Ulster were nothing out of the ordinary for the native Irish and, in fact, offered them a perverse opportunity for improving their miserable circumstances: groups of Irish Catholics pooled their resources to lease the land abandoned by their Protestant counterparts.

The first Scotch-Irish immigrants were drawn to Massachusetts, their strict Calvinism suggesting compatibility with the Puritan atmosphere of that colony. But New Englanders were no more hospitable toward newcomers then they had been in John Winthrop's time—particularly newcomers so bent on clinging to their own ways as the Scotch-Irish were. For their part, the Scotch-Irish quickly discovered that much of the best land in Massachusetts had already grown scarce, so almost immediately the mainstream of their movement was redirected elsewhere.

In Pennsylvania, founded half a century later than the Massachusetts Bay Colony, rich land was still abundantly available. No less important was the fact that William Penn, sensitive to the problem of religious intolerance by virtue of his own Quaker beliefs, had established his colony as a religious haven—freedom of worship was a reality there. Unlike the chilly reception they had met in New England, the Scotch-Irish were accorded a warm welcome in Pennsylvania. James Logan was especially gratified by the arrival of his countrymen: "They will . . . , I expect, be a leading example to others," he optimistically wrote.

Actually, even if official attitudes in Pennsylvania had been less receptive and even if economic and religious prospects had been less promising, in all probability the colony would still have drawn a substantial share of the Scotch-Irish immigrants. Philadelphia was the American port with the most direct commercial link to Ulster. Immigrant traffic tended to follow the lines of commerce. There were still no ships built especially to transport passengers; people traveled aboard vessels engaged in trade. Most ships which sailed from Londonderry, Belfast, and other ports in northern Ireland were involved in the flaxseed trade, of which Philadelphia was the American center.

Despite the fact that English colonists established permanent outposts in America a full century before the Scotch-Irish began to arrive, the edge of settlement had advanced but little since then. The frontier—untamed, seemingly impenetrable, and potentially hostile wilderness—lay at most forty miles to the west and north of Logan's Philadelphia. To attempt to dwell there was out of the question for most European immigrants; even

to risk passage through the wilderness without the acquiescence and assistance of its Indian inhabitants lay beyond their capability. English colonists like John Winthrop had demonstrated little desire to conquer the
American interior anyway; their object was less to create a separate, new
society than to establish an improved English one on America's shore.
Their orientation—cultural, commercial, and otherwise—lay to the east,
across the Atlantic, rather than westward into the American heartland.
This state of mind was reinforced by Britain's mercantilist policy, which
strengthened economic links between mother country and colony and
encouraged American dependence.

Although this situation served the needs of English officials, it satisfied neither land-hungry colonists nor land-rich entrepreneurs like the
Penns—or James Logan. Their interest lay instead in finding some way of
taming the wilderness, subduing the Indians, and expanding the area of
settlement. The sudden influx of Scotch-Irish immigrants after 1717 offered just such an instrument. Intimately familiar with the special qualities which hard experience had created in the Scotch-Irish, Logan actively
encouraged them to settle on the frontier. Years later he recalled:

> About that time considerable numbers of good, sober people
> came in from Ireland, who wanted to be settled. At the same
> time, also, it happened that we were under some apprehensions
> from the Northern Indians. . . . I therefore thought it might be
> prudent to plant a settlement of such men as those who had so
> bravely defended Londonderry and Inniskillen, as a frontier, in
> case of any disturbance. Accordingly, the township of Donegal
> was settled.

Although they disembarked in Philadelphia (or New Castle, Chester, or
some other Delaware River port), few of the Scotch-Irish immigrants who
were free to move remained in the city very long.[6] Farmers eager to work
their own land, they were instead drawn almost inexorably to the frontier.
There, fertile land could be purchased for little money—or simply taken
over by "squatters" unwilling or unable to buy it. The frontier offered
more than land—its remoteness insulated the Scotch-Irish against the
reach of government. Long victimized by authority, they were suspicious
of it, hostile toward it. The frontier attracted them in large degree because
it lacked official order.

Their experience in Ireland not only inclined the Scotch-Irish to favor
the frontier, it also prepared them well to meet its challenge. In each place
they were intruders whose presence was resented by the native people.
The resistance which they had encountered from the native Irish equipped
the Scotch-Irish to hold their own against the Indians. The pain and hardship which had been an accepted part of their lives in Scotland and Ulster
toughened them to survive in a wilderness that had held earlier European
settlers at bay.

---

[6]The only immigrants who were *not* free to move were those held as indentured servants.
See Chapter Four for a detailed look at indentured servitude.

Logan was initially convinced that his countrymen—those "good, sober people"—would unquestioningly serve Pennsylvania's purpose in much the same fashion that their ancestors had served England's. "These people," he assured a colleague, ". . . if kindly used will, I believe, be orderly, as they hitherto have been, and easily dealt with." But Logan soon discovered that the Scotch-Irish, freed by the frontier from the restraints of government, were not so pliable as he had anticipated. They settled where they chose, often without seeking permission or offering payment. By 1724 Logan was complaining to the Penn family about the "bold and indigent strangers" who offered "as their excuse when challenged for titles, that we had solicited for colonists and they had come accordingly." Nor did the immigrants even cooperate to the extent of settling exactly where Logan desired them to. Some cleverly took advantage of an intercolonial quarrel over the Maryland-Pennsylvania boundary as a means to avoid paying for land: "The Irish settle generally toward the Maryland line, where no lands can honestly be sold till the dispute with Lord Baltimore is decided," he reported with ill-concealed frustration.[7] The problem reached such proportions that in 1726 Logan gloomily informed William Penn's widow, "there are at this time near a hundred thousand acres possessed by persons, who resolutely sit down and improve, without any manner of Right or Pretence to it."[8]

His repeated complaints about Scotch-Irish squatters notwithstanding, Logan was himself in some instances the author of his own distress. He tacitly encouraged settlement on land west of the Susquehana River as a means of undermining Maryland's claim to the region, despite the fact that it was still reserved for Indians. He nonetheless authorized a local magistrate to issue temporary licenses to the land, title to which he could not confirm himself.

More often than not, however, Logan labored to protect Indian lands from encroachment by eager pioneers. In early 1718 he directed that the domain of the Conestega Indians, a tribe previously forced from its ancestral lands by the more powerful Iroquois, be fenced to safeguard it against trespassers. Usually Logan was forced to scramble to catch up with the settlers. On several different occasions the Penn family was compelled to buy from Indians territory that had already been invaded by squatters. Such action was necessary to minimize friction on the frontier: the ultimate safety of the colony still depended upon maintaining the good will of the Iroquois.

That became an increasingly difficult proposition. "The Indians themselves are alarmed at the swarms of strangers," Logan noted in 1729, "and we are afraid of a breach between them, for the Irish are very rough to them." Not so heavy-handed as his cousins on the frontier, Logan was no

---

[7]Charles Calvert, the fifth Lord Baltimore, was Penn's proprietary counterpart in Maryland. The first Lord Baltimore, Sir George Calvert, had been granted a charter for Maryland in 1632 by King Charles I.

[8]Penn died July 30, 1718, at the age of 74.

less "rough" than they, albeit in his own civilized way. In 1737, responding to complaints by the Delaware Indians that pioneers had illegally pushed onto their land, Logan hauled out a 1686 agreement between William Penn and the tribe's chiefs which conveyed to Penn a tract on the Delaware River extending "back into the woods as far as a man can go in a day and a half," and convinced the Indians it was time to arrive at a more precise definition of the claim by actually having the land paced off. First, however, he arranged for a road to be carved through the wilderness, engaged three athletic young men to conduct the "survey," and sent their supplies ahead by horse. On the morning that the ill-named "Walking Purchase" began, Indian observers were stunned to see the surveyers dash off down their prepared path. Even though two collapsed along the way, the third, Edward Marshall, managed to cover over sixty-six miles during the prescribed period—far more than the twenty or thirty miles the Indians had expected.[9] The Delawares understandably resented Logan's sharp dealing; one chief protested that the surveyors "should have walked for a few miles, and then sat down and smoked a pipe, and now and then shot a squirrel, and not have kept upon the run, run all day." Unconscious of any irony, Logan would later declare "most of the Indian wars have generally been owing to their being wronged in their lands."

The frequency with which the Indians were "wronged in their lands" increased in direct proportion to the influx of Scotch-Irish settlers. A series of failed harvests in Ulster between 1725 and 1728 compounded a bad situation and helped trigger another surge of immigrants. The Pennsylvania *Gazette* commented sympathetically upon "the unhappy circumstances of the Common People of Ireland:"

> The English papers have of late been frequent in their accounts of the unhappy circumstances of the Common People of Ireland; That Poverty, Wretchedness, Misery and Want are become almost universal among them; That . . . there is not Corn enough rais'd for their Subsistence one year with another; and at the same Time the Trade and Manufactures of the Nation being cramp'd and discouraged, the laboring People have little to do, and consequently are not able to purchase Bread at its present dear Rate: That the Taxes are nevertheless exceeding heavy, and Money very scarce; and add to all this, that their griping, avaricious Landlords exercise over them the most merciless Racking Tyranny and Oppression. Hence it is that such Swarms of them are driven over into America.

Despite his familiarity with conditions in northern Ireland, Logan was astonished by the increased volume of immigrants. Late in 1727 he observed to a Belfast correspondent, "we are very much surprised here at the vast crowds of people pouring in upon us from Ireland." Two months later he informed John Penn, "We have from the North of Ireland great numbers

---

[9]Angry Indians took a bloody revenge upon Marshall, killing his wife and son, and wounding his daughter.

yearly, 8 or 9 ships this last fall discharged at New Castle." Over the next few years the volume of arrivals increased steadily. In 1729 more than 5,600 Scotch-Irish immigrants swarmed into Pennsylvania, about double the rate of the first surge a dozen years before. Sounding a good deal more alarmed, Logan reported to John Penn, "It now looks as if Ireland or the Inhabitants of it were to be transported hither. Last week I think no less than 6 ships arrived."

Logan's uneasiness was reflected on the opposite side of the Atlantic. Hugh Boulter, Anglican Archbishop of Ireland, noted that the desire to emigrate had by late 1728 "spread like a contagious distemper, and the people will hardly hear of anybody that tries to cure them of their madness. The worst of it is, that it affects only Protestants, and reigns chiefly in the north." Boulter's comment suggests why English authorities were disturbed by the exodus—if allowed to continue unabated, it could undermine Protestant domination of Ireland. Although no official measures were implemented to stem the tide, vain attempts were undertaken to discourage emigration. One ship captain complained to Thomas Penn that British officials were deliberately delaying the departure of ships bound from Belfast to Pennsylvania for weeks at a time, a policy which left the affected passengers "in most deplorable circumstances."

Pennsylvania proved scarcely less reluctant to take official action to address the situation. Although the colony's governor opened the 1728–29 legislative session by urging the Assembly "to provide, by proper law, against those Crowds of Foreigners who are yearly pour'd in upon us," the legislature did nothing other than to place the blame vaguely upon "those in Authority over us" and enact a duty of forty shillings on Irish servants. Official concern stemmed at least in part from worry among the colony's ruling elite that its position was rapidly eroding. By 1720 Quakers were already a minority in Pennsylvania, although property qualifications for voting would insure their political dominance for another third of a century.

Similar fears haunted James Logan. "If some speedy Method be not taken," he warned John Penn in 1729, the Scotch-Irish "will soon make themselves Proprietors of the Province." It was not so much the large number of his countrymen which troubled Logan; it was the "audacious and disorderly manner" in which they behaved. In 1730 Scotch-Irish squatters invaded a choice 15,000 acre parcel he had reserved for the Penn family, and brushed aside his protests by claiming it "was against the laws of God and nature, that so much land should be idle while so many Christians wanted it to labor on and raise their bread." Sometimes Logan resorted to drastic means to discourage illegal settlement, ordering the eviction of squatters and the destruction of their cabins. But such occasional actions had no visible effect upon the stubborn Scotch-Irish, who continued to settle anywhere they chose. Completely disgusted, Logan grumbled in 1730, "the settlement of five families from Ireland gives me more trouble than fifty of any other people."

Logan's sense of frustration was fed by more than his unhappy experience with the Scotch-Irish. His career in the 1720s was marked by a protracted power struggle with an ambitious governor and new demands by the Assembly that Logan be impeached. Compounding his misery was a crippling accident which he suffered in January 1728, when the 53-year-old Logan slipped on some ice and broke his hip. For the rest of his life he would be unable to walk without the aid of crutches. The weight of his woes, plus the fact that in 1729 the Penn family was able to pay off the mortgage on their colony, clearing their title to it, led Logan to seek his release from their service. Obviously the Penns owed Logan a great deal; it was in large part due to his management of Pennsylvania that they had retained possession of it. But since many other debts left by the improvident William Penn still remained, his heirs begged Logan to continue in their employment, a request which he reluctantly granted.

If anything, Logan's burden became heavier, not lighter, over the next decade. From 1731 to 1736 he served as Chief Justice of the colony and from 1736 until 1738 acted as its governor. After he stepped down from the latter post, Logan continued to play a pivotal role in public affairs as President of the Council. His active participation in Pennsylvania government forced Logan to confront once more the dilemma that had first presented itself on his journey to America—the apparent contradiction between Quaker pacifism and the obligation for self-defense. The outbreak of war between England and Spain in 1739—the War of Jenkins' Ear—brought this problem to a head.[10] As had happened thirty years before in 1709, the crown imposed a levy upon the colony, requiring it to raise several companies of soldiers. Once more the Quaker-dominated Assembly refused to cooperate. As the war evolved into a more general conflict in 1740—the War of the Austrian Succession—the problem became more acute: the entry of France, supported by its Indian allies, created enormous danger on the Pennsylvania frontier. The apparent inability of Quaker legislators to provide effectively for the colony's defense in the face of this crisis convinced Logan that only one remedy remained. In 1741, just before the election to choose a new Assembly, he publicly proposed that Quakers not seek office. "All civil government," he noted, ". . . is founded on force." As a consequence, Logan concluded, Quakers "in the strictures of their principles ought in no manner to engage in it." His suggestion, despite its logic, was ignored. In this instance, Logan demonstrated he had less in common with his pacifistic Quaker brethren than he did with his Scotch-Irish countrymen, who exhibited few qualms about asserting their right to the Pennsylvania wilderness by force of arms.

A new surge of settlers from Ulster at just this time intensified Logan's concern about the frontier. Another famine, much more severe in its ef-

---

[10]The War of Jenkins' Ear (1739–1740) erupted after Spanish customs officials sliced off the ear of an English shipmaster, Robert Jenkins. In 1740 it evolved into a general European conflict, the War of the Austrian Succession.

fects than that of the 1720s, claimed 400,000 lives in Ireland in 1740–41. The arrival of more Scotch-Irish immigrants, in flight from hunger, intensified competition for land and led to considerable friction with German settlers. The Penns responded in 1743 by resolving to sell no more land to the Scotch-Irish in the area contested by Germans. Instead, the Ulster immigrants were to be lured further into the wilderness by the offer of generous grants to the west. Their hardship would be the colony's gain, for once more the Scotch-Irish could be counted upon to tame the frontier and provide protection for colonists to the east.

By this time the vanguard of Scotch-Irish settlement was reaching the Allegheny Mountains, a natural barricade which deflected their movement south. Proceeding down Virginia's Shenandoah Valley, they scattered along the southern piedmont, from Maryland to Georgia, over the course of the next several decades. Indeed, even though most Scotch-Irish immigrants continued to travel first to Pennsylvania, increasing numbers were drawn directly to North and South Carolina by attractive offers of cheap land on the frontier. Aware of the well-deserved reputation as Indian-fighters that the Scotch-Irish had already won in Pennsylvania, southern colonies recruited them to purge their wilderness of its native inhabitants.

Logan was dissuaded from playing too active a role in pushing the Scotch-Irish further west by a stroke which he suffered in 1740. Although his 65-year-old body was left partially paralyzed, his mind remained lucid as he compensated for the loss of physical activity by increasing his mental output. Actually Logan displayed throughout his career in Pennsylvania the same keen love of learning that he had exhibited as a 19-year-old-schoolmaster in Bristol. During the 1720s and 1730s, he had experimented with plant fertilization, publishing several essays on that subject as well as others in the *Philosophical Transactions* of the Royal Society. Despite his physical isolation thousands of miles from the center of European culture, Logan conducted an active correspondence with Carolus Linnaeus and other leading intellectuals.[11] And he collected books. "Books are my disease," Logan once confessed. His 3,000-volume library, containing books on all subjects, was one of the finest collections in colonial America. As his correspondence and publications indicate, Logan understood that such knowledge was to be shared, not hoarded. In 1745 he therefore authorized construction of a building in Philadelphia to house his collection, and founded a trust fund to insure its maintenance and expansion. His purpose was to establish a free public library, open to all in the colony who wished to use it. Although death would overtake Logan before he could implement his plans, his heirs completed the project and created the Loganian Library.

Logan's love of learning was a nearly universal trait among the Scotch-Irish, despite the crude style of life their circumstances often imposed

---

[11]A Swedish botanist, Linnaeus devised the system for classifying organisms in established categories.

upon them. Presbyterian ministers were expected to be scholars, familiar with Latin, Greek, and Hebrew. Their sermons, which were often published, tended to be protracted dissertations requiring a fairly sophisticated level of understanding. As a result, in both Scotland and Ulster, schools were frequently attached to the church. Such institutions were seen by the Scotch-Irish as being especially important in America, not merely to insure churchgoers the rudimentary knowledge their beliefs necessitated, but particularly to train ministers. Relatively few Presbyterian clergymen accompanied the 250,000 or so Scotch-Irish immigrants to the colonies between 1717 and 1776, so some means of educating a colonial ministry was urgently needed.

Perhaps the most noteworthy such institution was the "Log College," established by William Tennent at Neshaminy, near Philadelphia, in 1726. Tennent, a cousin of James Logan, had come to Pennsylvania in 1718, among the first wave of Scotch-Irish immigrants. Although a Quaker, Logan appreciated the importance of his Presbyterian cousin's mission and supported it by granting Tennent 50 acres on Neshaminy Creek "to encourage him to prosecute his views, and make his residence near us permanent." More properly an academy than a college, the institution gave its students a classical liberal education, including a dose of arts and sciences, as well as theology. A number of distinguished Presbyterian ministers were trained at the Log College, including Tennent's own sons, before it closed its doors in 1742.

No less important, the Log College gave rise to another institution, established in 1746 at Princeton, New Jersey. Known as the College of New Jersey (later Princeton University), its mission was the same as that of Tennent's school. Perhaps as a means of annexing Logan's celebrated library, the new college invited him to head its board of trustees. Put off by the strong Presbyterian flavor of the place, he declined. In 1749, however, he agreed to serve as a trustee for the newly proposed College of Philadelphia, a nondenominational institution which would become the University of Pennsylvania. Before he could embark fully on this new project, Logan in 1750 suffered a crippling stroke which paralyzed his right side and robbed him of the power of speech. In this reduced state, he lingered for another year before finally dying, late in 1751, at the age of 77.

Two years before his death, Logan had made out a will which listed among his assets nearly 18,000 acres of land in Pennsylvania and New Jersey, as well as £8,500 in cash and bonds. Clearly, the frontier, focus of his fur trading and land speculation activities, had been no less important to Logan than to his fellow Ulstermen who carved out new homes there. And just as it left its imprint upon him, in the form of a substantial personal fortune, the wilderness also affected the Scotch-Irish pioneers who ventured into it. Dispersed on the frontier and frequently on the move to greener pastures, the Scotch-Irish developed little in the way of community life or even extended families. Consequently, their sense of ethnic identity was considerably less than that of other immigrant groups—like the Germans, for example—whose members self-consciously tended to cluster together. Because they spoke English, the Scotch-Irish blended easily into the cultural mainstream of colonial society, virtually disappearing as a distinct ethnic entity. So, even though James Logan sometimes regretted having ever encouraged their settlement in America, his Scotch-Irish countrymen were, in a very real sense, the first true Americans—immigrants who shed their European identity and gave themselves over to the new land.

FURTHER READING

BRONNER, EDWIN B. *William Penn's "Holy Experiment": The Founding of Pennsylvania, 1681–1701.* Philadelphia: Temple University Publications, 1962.

CUMMINGS, HUBERTIS M. *Scots Breed and Susquehanna.* Pittsburgh: University of Pittsburgh Press, 1964.

FORD, HENRY JONES. *The Scotch-Irish in America.* New York: Arno Press, 1969.

KELLEY, JOSEPH J., JR. *Pennsylvania: The Colonial Years, 1681–1776.* Garden City, N.Y.: Doubleday and Co., 1980.

LEYBURN, JAMES G. *The Scotch-Irish: A Social History.* Chapel Hill: University of North Carolina Press, 1962.

TOLLES, FREDERICK B. *James Logan and the Culture of Provincial America.* Boston: Little, Brown and Co., 1957.

4

The Harbor at Amsterdam, c. 1800

Rijksmuseum, Amsterdam

4

Johann Buettner

DARK WAVES LOOMED like mountains above the tiny ship and then crashed across its deck. Violent winds tore through the rigging; lightning exploded overhead. As the ship shuddered and groaned under the assault of the storm, Johann Buettner joined his fellow passengers in a desperate prayer for deliverance. He later recalled: "Every one . . . even the nefarious and the God-forsaken, of which there was plenty on board the ship, folded their hands as the Lord of the worlds spoke to them through the heart-crushing voice of the elements." The immigrants' hopes for a better life in a new world fled in the face of the realization that they might not even survive the voyage to America.

The violence of the storm which threatened Buettner's life mirrored the turbulent conditions which plagued his homeland in the seventeenth and eighteenth centuries. Germany, particularly those states along the Rhine, was devastated by almost incessant warfare.[1] The most destructive conflict, the Thirty Years' War (1618–1648), claimed more than half the inhabitants of some regions. The survivors often endured such horror that they envied the dead. German, Austrian, French, Spanish and Swedish armies crisscrossed Germany, burning, looting, raping, and destroying crops. Famine was widespread; some starving peasants even resorted to cannibalism. Over the next century, these same scenes were repeated in other conflicts: the Dutch War (1672–1678), the War of the League of Augsburg (1688–1697), the War of the Spanish Succession (1701–1713), the War of the Polish Succession (1733–1735), the War of the Austrian Succes-

---

[1]There was no unified German state until the latter part of the nineteenth century. Instead, Germany was little more than a state of mind, its people united by some aspects of their culture, but fragmented politically into over two hundred kingdoms, principalities, ecclesiastical states, and imperial towns.

sion (1740–1748). Even in times of "peace" the Rhineland was regarded as fair prey by France's Louis XIV—his armies regularly plundered the Palatinate. Such invasions were so frequent that some farmers stopped planting in despair: they realized their fields would be laid waste before the crops could be harvested.

Religious intolerance and persecution compounded the misery caused by warfare. Subjects were expected to conform to the religious preferences of their rulers—those who deviated from this stand risked punishment. So Catholic kings oppressed their Protestant subjects; Protestant princes tormented Catholics under their jurisdiction. The embers of the Reformation still glowed red-hot. Religious antagonisms were complicated by the fact that many German Protestants believed that the major Protestant denominations (Lutheran and Reformed) had not carried the Reformation far enough. Consequently, numerous fundamentalist, pietistic sects arose—Schwenckfelders, Mennonites, Waldenses, Swedenborgians, and more. These sects enjoyed neither official standing nor protection; their adherents were victimized by Catholic and Protestant rulers alike.

The deleterious effects of this political and social instability were magnified by the self-indulgent and irresponsible behavior of many of the German rulers. In imitation of the lavish example set by Louis XIV, they dedicated themselves to ostentatious living. The revenue to support their extravagant ways was wrung from the impoverished masses, making their miserable condition even worse. The combination of these factors dislodged masses of Germans from their homes. Some of them sought refuge in different parts of Germany, some in other European countries. In increasing numbers, still others fled to America. During the eighteenth century only the Scotch-Irish outnumbered Germans among European immigrants to the future United States.

Johann Buettner managed to escape only some of the misfortune which cursed so many of his countrymen. Born in 1754 in Lauta, a village in Saxony, Buettner was introduced early to the horrors of war. Throughout the Seven Years' War (1756–1763), Saxony, one of the principal arenas of conflict, was occupied and plundered by the Prussians. Still, his father's situation as a Lutheran minister in the home of the German Protestant Reformation insured a steady income and secure position. As a boy Buettner attended first a local school and later an academy in a nearby town. During the course of his education, young Buettner became increasingly interested in America. He was particularly fascinated by the accounts of adventurers who had discovered wealth there. Years later he would ruefully recall, "I began to consider seriously the possibility of visiting those celebrated regions of the world, after I had completed my studies; and with these thoughts I combined the hope that perhaps I too might succeed in returning . . . a rich man. How I was deceived in my hopes!" In order to advance his youthful dream, Buettner apprenticed himself to a surgeon. Although at the time a surgeon was little more than a glorified barber whose principal occupation was trimming beards and bleeding patients, Buettner hoped his profession, in demand everywhere, would be his ticket to the New World.[2]

Upon the completion of his apprenticeship, Buettner—a restless youth of perhaps nineteen—began to wander through central Europe. His travels eventually brought him to Hamburg, a bustling seaport. There Buettner met several men who, after learning that he hailed from Saxony, claimed the same origins. In their apparent joy at discovering a countryman, Buettner's new companions invited him to dinner. Over food—and more than a little wine—the men steered the conversation to overseas adventure, a subject which Buettner enthusiastically embraced. The faces of the men seemed to Buettner "to mirror some secret joy;" they promised the young man free transportation to Amsterdam and from there employment as a ship's surgeon aboard a vessel bound either for America or the East Indies. Too excited to think clearly, Buettner failed to realize that he had fallen into the clutches of "soul-sellers."

Soul-sellers, or "newlanders" as they were also known, were recruiting agents who persuaded people—often through misrepresentation—to go to America. Frequenting seaports or travelling around the countryside, they sometimes posed as recently returned immigrants who had struck it rich in America. A newlander's fancy clothes and expensive-looking ornaments could be as persuasive as his honeyed words. Such agents commonly operated on a commission basis; ship captains paid them by the head. Consequently, many soul-sellers went beyond mere persuasion in their recruiting efforts. They were known to lure children aboard ship with the offer of candy, to roll drunks in waterfront taverns, or even to kidnap those who resisted their blandishments. They also afforded a means for fugitives and criminals to escape justice.

Such agents represented a major influence in directing immigration to the colonies in the eighteenth century. Soul-sellers were also quite active in England, where they were known as "spirits." So sizeable was the problem there, in fact, that as early as 1645 Parliament attempted—without success—to halt their activities.

Buettner grasped his situation aboard the ship which took him to Amsterdam. He discovered himself in the company of about 50 other young men and women who had been similarly duped. In Amsterdam, Buettner was locked up in a large room with perhaps 100 other victims. They were fed regularly and well and allowed outside to exercise from time to time, but they were all nonetheless quite clearly prisoners of the soul-sellers. And, indebted as they now were for their transportation to Amsterdam and the food they had already eaten, they were without legal recourse. In fact, Buettner could consider himself lucky that he had not been treated more brutally. Soul-sellers sometimes roughed up their victims and held them in miserable quarters on board ships or in brothels.

---

[2]Bleeding—the act of drawing blood from a patient—was a common medical practice until well into the nineteenth century. The prescribed treatment for a wide variety of ailments, bleeding was accomplished by opening an incision or through the application of leeches to the patient's body.

The extent of this commerce in humanity, both on the Continent and in England, reflected the enormous demand for labor in the colonies. From the very beginnings of colonization, England's American possessions—especially those in the South—had suffered from a labor shortage. The practice in some colonies of awarding headrights, free grants of land, offered only a partial solution; it attracted only those who could afford to pay their passage to the colonies. What was needed was an arrangement which would pay for the transportation to America of large numbers of laborers too poor to come on their own.

In answer to this need, the practice of indentured servitude arose. Under the indenture system, labor for a limited term—usually three to seven years—was exchanged for transportation to the colonies.[3] The relationship between servant and master was spelled out in a contract which committed the former to faithful service for a specific period and obligated the latter to provide adequate food, shelter, and clothing. Often the servant was also entitled to freedom dues upon the completion of the term of service. Freedom dues usually consisted of a new suit of clothing, some tools, seeds, or even a small amount of money or land. The purpose of freedom dues was twofold: they encouraged servants to fulfill their contracts instead of running away and they offered newly freed servants a prospect of self-sufficiency. Clearly the system answered a considerable need—as many as one half of the European immigrants who arrived in the colonies prior to the American Revolution came either as indentured servants or redemptioners.

Redemptioners were passengers who had paid most of their fares. They travelled to America without indentures, with the understanding that within a short time of their arrival (usually two weeks) they would pay the amount due. They might be able to borrow the money from friends already established in America. Or they sometimes sold one family member into service in order to relieve the obligation of the rest. Frequently, however, they were unable to make any arrangement; in such cases they would be sold into service by the ship's captain. The duration of their servitude was determined by the amount which they owed for their fare. In most cases, therefore, redemptioners served shorter terms than indentured servants.

Several other factors further distinguished these two groups from each other. Redemptioners often travelled as family units; indentured servants were usually unattached. Most colonial immigrants from Ireland or England who did not pay their own way came as indentured servants; among Germans the proportion of redemptioners was larger, a reflection of the fact that many of the German immigrants were not nearly so destitute as those from the British Isles.[4] In fact, some Germans who had the means to pay their fares in full nonetheless travelled as redemptioners, so that

[3]Children were generally held until they reached the age of twenty-one.

[4]The difference further accounts for the comparative lack of strong family ties among the Scotch-Irish. See Chapter Three.

they would not have to provide for themselves for a few years while they adjusted to an alien life and culture. Overall, more than half of the Germans who came to America during the colonial era travelled as redemptioners; in all likelihood, the proportion of indentured servants among the Scotch-Irish was even higher.

Not all of those who came to the colonies as servants did so voluntarily. In addition to the victims of kidnapping, much of the human refuse of English society was transported involuntarily to America. British authorities early conceived of the colonies as a dumping ground for criminals and other undesirables. As early as 1617, just ten years after the establishment of Jamestown, the Privy Council recommended shipment of vagrant Londoners to Virginia. Ultimately upwards of 50,000 English felons (not to mention lesser criminals) were dispatched to America during the colonial period, most of them after 1717.[5]

Understandably many colonists resented this policy. The *Pennsylvania Gazette* offered a sarcastic endorsement:

> Our Mother knows what is best for us. What is a little House-breaking, Shop-lifting, or Highway-robbing; what is a son now and then corrupted and hanged, a Daughter debauched, and Pox'd, a wife stabbed, a Husband's throat cut, or a child's brains beat out with an Axe, compared with this Improvement and Well peopling of the Colonies!

The indignation vented by the *Virginia Gazette* was no less intense: "In what can Britain show a more sovereign contempt for us than by emptying their jails into our settlements; unless they would likewise empty their jakes [privies] on our tables!" The dismay at these arrangements was mutual: many convicts understood that servant life in America was brutal and often fatally brief. It is a revealing commentary upon conditions in the colonies that murderers, given the choice between being hanged in England and 14 years servitude in America, sometimes elected to hang!

In Amsterdam, Johann Buettner faced a decision that seemed only a little less momentous. Informed that the ships bound for the East Indies had all sailed for the season—and with them his prospects for a position as a ship's surgeon—Buettner was told he could either remain in the lockup or ship out for America as an indentured servant. Had he clearly understood the perils of transatlantic travel in the early 1770s, Buettner might not have so readily chosen the latter alternative.

The hazards ran the gamut from attack by pirates to shipwreck. The ships were small, fragile, wooden sailing vessels of 300 tons displacement or less, built to haul freight and not adapted to the comfort or needs of their human cargo. Three hundred or more passengers would be crowded aboard, with each allotted a space only about two feet by six feet. Privacy was non-existent. Since the sexes were not separated, females were sometimes the victims of sexual assault by crew members or male passengers.

---

[5]The draconian English penal code defied as felonies not only serious crimes but also violations which would today be considered only minor offenses.

Aboard Buettner's ship, 60 women and girls were quartered with 300 men. "It can be easily understood how wide, under these circumstances, the doors of immorality were opened," he noted. "I would advise unmarried women who have not the means to take quarters in the Captain's cabin, not even to enter a ship. Their innocence is much more in danger than on land."

The crowded conditions affected health as well as morals. According to Gottlieb Mittelberger, another German immigrant who came to America in 1750, passengers suffered a variety of ailments: "vomiting, many kinds of sea sickness, fever, dysentery, heat, constipation, boils, scurvy, cancer, mouth-rot and the like." Cholera, typhus, and smallpox were also common. Lice were "so frightfully [abundant], especially on sick people, that they [could] be scraped off the body."

Buettner became seriously ill with fever during his voyage. His delirium and its "cure," being bled, brought him very near death. Quite a few of Buettner's fellow passengers were even less fortunate. Their corpses were unceremoniously pitched overboard. Buetter observed that "usually the bodies thrown into the water were immediately claimed as prey by the big fish. The captain found that if a number of these fish were swimming near the ship in the morning, he might conclude that corpses had been thrown overboard in the night."

The consequence of all this was, of course, an alarming mortality rate. In 1738 only two out of the fifteen ships which brought passengers to Philadelphia (the most frequently used port of entry for eighteenth century immigrants) arrived with their human cargo in relatively good health. The other ships, on the average, lost well over 100 passengers each. One ship arrived in 1745 with only about 50 of its 400 passengers left alive; on another in 1752 there were just nineteen survivors out of 200. Approximately 2,000 German immigrants died in transit in 1749. It is no wonder that one survivor of this traffic recalled, "the sighing and crying and lamenting on board ship continues night and day, so as to cause the hearts even of the most hardened to bleed when they hear it."

The misery of the immigrants reached a climax during stormy weather. Then the hatches had to be battened down and passengers confined below decks. Seasick, they pitched and stumbled around in the sweltering heat, suffocating for lack of fresh air. Just a few days west of Great Britain, Buettner's ship encountered a storm. His recollection of the results remained vivid throughout his life: "The greater part of the ship's crew became violently ill; even the captain himself vomited constantly like the rest of us, and almost threw up his intestines. This sickness, caused by the constant rolling of the ship, lasted with some for eight days." Even more violent was the hurricane which overtook the ship just as it was about to make port in America after nearly four months at sea. So furious was the storm that it drove the ship once more far out to sea. Three long weeks passed before Buettner and his fellows again sighted land.

This unexpected delay placed a considerable strain upon the ship's supplies. "The drinking water became scarce," Buettner later recalled, "and for this reason we did not receive more than half a measure of water daily. Besides, this had a very unpleasant smell and tasted like ink. . . . Not only did this portion of water that we received not suffice to quench our thirst, but it was also needed to soften the ship's biscuit, to cook the peas, the oatmeal, and the meat. The bread that we received was so hard that an axe was required to break it, and it looked green and yellow inside."

Such privation was not at all unusual. Since the progress of ships depended upon winds and currents, transatlantic voyages were very uncertain in their duration, lasting anywhere from four weeks to six months. It was, therefore, extremely difficult to plan for adequate supplies of food and water. Passengers who paid their own way frequently had to furnish and cook their own provisions, responsibilities for which few of them were suitably prepared. Servants like Buettner had their provisions furnished for them, but such rations were usually of poor quality and in short supply in order to maximize profits. Another German immigrant offered a grim, but typical, account of this aspect of life aboard ship:

> Warm food is served only three times a week, the rations being very poor and very little. Such meals can hardly be eaten, on account of being so unclean. The water which is served out on the ships is often very black, thick and full of worms, so that one cannot drink it without loathing, even with the greatest thirst. . . . Toward the end we were compelled to eat the ship's biscuit which had been spoiled long ago; though in a whole biscuit there was scarcely a piece the size of a dollar that had not been full of red worms and spiders' nests.

In some instances the consequences of extended voyages were even more horrible. The *Sea Flower,* out of Belfast in 1741, lost 46 of its 106 passengers to starvation. Some of the survivors managed to sustain themselves by cannibalizing six of the corpses. Ten years earlier, the *Love and Unity* departed Rotterdam with more than 150 German immigrants aboard. About one year later the ship limped into Philadelphia with just 34 passengers left alive. After their food supplies had run out, rats and mice had sold at a premium. These cases are perhaps extreme, but less unusual than one might imagine. The mortality rate among German immigrants tended to be higher than that of immigrants from the British Isles for the simple reason that the longer voyage left Germans that much more exposed to the hazards of transatlantic travel.

Because of all the hygienic problems associated with ocean travel, new arrivals posed a considerable threat to the health of the colonial population. Consequently some colonial governments attempted to protect their citizens through the passage of regulatory legislation. As early as 1700 Pennsylvania prohibited all "unhealthy or sickly" vessels from approaching within one mile of its shores, a measure which was far from perfect in terms of the protection it provided. When the arrival of a shipload of German immigrants in 1738 touched off a smallpox epidemic in Philadelphia, George Thomas, who had replaced James Logan as governor of Pennsylvania only a few months before, assured the colony's Assembly that everything possible was being done to meet the emergency.

> The Law to prevent sickly Vessels from coming into this Government, has been strictly put in Execution by me. A Physician has been appointed to visit those Vessels, and the Masters obliged to Land such of the Passengers as were sick at a Distance from the City, and to convey them at their own Expense to Houses in the Country, convenient for their Reception. More could not have been done, without inhumanly exposing great Numbers to perish on board the Ships that brought them.

Thomas noted that "had you been provided with a Pesthouse or Hospital . . . the Evils which have been apprehended, might, under God, have been entirely prevented." Following the governor's suggestion, Pennsylvania a few years later established a pesthouse where diseased immigrants would be quarantined. Other colonies maintained similar institutions and enacted measures requiring the inspection of ships, regulating the number of passengers to be transported, and so on.

Colonial governments were concerned not only about physical infection, they also sought to protect against moral and social contamination. Some governments prohibited the entry of paupers, criminals and other undesirables. These regulations, conflicting as they did with England's practice of dumping its social problems in America, had no real effect upon that policy, but they did at least serve to register American objections to it. Some colonies also instituted ethnic and religious restrictions, which more often than not pertained to immigrants who were Irish or Catholic.

Having fully recovered from his fever, Buettner ran afoul of no colonial regulations when his ship finally made port. In entering America at Philadelphia, he was following the route taken by most German immigrants during the pre-Revolutionary era. The earliest German arrivals in colonial America were religious sectarians (that is, members of various despised and persecuted sects) who had been drawn to Pennsylvania by William Penn's promise of religious liberty. Penn, a Quaker sensitive to the problem of religious intolerance, had received a royal charter for an American colony in 1681. Declaring it to be a religious haven, Penn had advertised that fact extensively in England and on the Continent. Almost immediately religious refugees began to trickle in from Germany. In 1683 the first German settlement in America, Germantown, was founded a few miles outside Philadelphia. Although it never grew very large—a hundred years later its population was still less than 3,000—Germantown would for some time continue to play a significant role for many newly arrived German immigrants, serving as a sort of reception center where they could get their bearings and catch their breath before striking out on their own. Nearly a century after its establishment, Buettner noted that Germantown was still "mostly inhabited by Germans."

By the early 1700s the trickle of Germans into Pennsylvania had become a flood. Increasingly it was composed of immigrants drawn to the New World by its economic, rather than its spiritual, opportunities. While some eighteenth century Germans settled in South Carolina, Virginia, and other colonies, by far the largest number of them continued to pour into Pennsylvania. As a result, by the time of the American Revolution the colony's population was one third German.

The substantial size of the German community in Pennsylvania had significant social and political ramifications. Instead of being forced to adapt themselves to a largely English society, many German immigrants were required to make relatively few adjustments: they had German neighbors, maintained German schools, attended church services conducted in German, transacted business in German. Although immigrants who resided in Germantown and other urban environments were sometimes exposed to a greater cultural variety, many German settlers in rural regions had little direct contact with the English mainstream of colonial society. The strong sense of German identity and community which grew out of this carried over into the political arena in Pennsylvania, where by 1750 Germans wielded considerable political influence. Benjamin Franklin spoke for many of his fellow Pennsylvanians when he railed against this situation: "Why should the Palatine boors be suffered to swarm into our settlements, and, by herding together, establish their language and manners, to the exclusion of ours? Why should Pennsylvania, founded by the English, become a colony of aliens, who will shortly be so numerous as to Germanize us, instead of our Anglifying them?" Franklin's complaint echoed a warning which James Logan had issued to John Penn in 1727: "At this rate, you will soon have a German colony here."[6]

On the other hand, some colonists readily acknowledged the various benefits resulting from the German influx, including the first paper mill in the colonies (established at Germantown in 1690), one of the first grist mills in Pennsylvania, and the first Bible printed in America. The settlers at Germantown produced "very fine . . . Linen such [as] no Person of Quality need be ashamed to wear," as well as other goods. Even Franklin grumpily admitted that the "Germans . . . have their virtues. Their industry and frugality are exemplary. They are excellent husbandmen, and contribute greatly to the improvement of a country." Less grudgingly, the colony's governor reported that "their Industry and Frugality have been the principal instruments of raising [Pennsylvania] to its present flourishing condition beyond any of his Majesty's Colonies in North America."

Since many colonists shared the governor's estimation of them, German servants tended to be more highly regarded than those from other ethnic backgrounds. Only the Scots, with their reputation for thrift, clev-

---

[6]Both Logan and Franklin had ulterior motives for grumbling about German immigration. Logan's displeasure arose from the fact that most Pennsylvania Germans who became politically active allied themselves with the anti-proprietary group and helped frustrate his plans for colonial defense. Franklin's pique stemmed at least in part from the refusal of German settlers to support his German-language newspaper, which failed as a result.

erness, and hard work, were more highly esteemed, while Irish servants (including the Scotch-Irish)—stereotyped as unruly, irresponsible, and stupid—rated at the bottom. The value of servants varied not only with ethnicity; it was also sometimes affected by sex. Buettner noted that some of his female shipmates were sold quickly and at high prices, a clear confirmation of the law of supply and demand. In other instances, though, women servants, less suited to the kind of back-breaking labor wrung out of their counterparts, commanded lower prices.

The sale of servants began aboard Buettner's ship shortly after it docked. He and his fellows were forced to strip naked while prospective purchasers swarmed around and examined them minutely. Often such buyers would include "soul drivers," dealers who would purchase several dozen servants at a time, chain them together and march them into the interior for sale to the highest bidder. Many of the abuses later associated with slavery, such as the separation of husbands from wives or parents from children, were also a part of the trade in indentured servants. Fortunately for Buettner, he was purchased by a Quaker farmer from New Jersey rather than a dealer. His price was £30 (about $150), which obligated him to six years service.[7]

Buettner quickly settled into a wearisome routine that occupied him from daybreak until past sundown. His chores included chopping and hauling firewood, clearing and cultivating land, as well as caring for and butchering livestock. Most indentured servants were similarly engaged, although a few were employed as artisans or teachers. Servants on southern plantations faced prospects that were particularly unpleasant. The debilitating effect of their hard work was amplified by the hot, humid climate of the region—a combination that proved fatal for many. The position of southern servants was further eroded by the high proportion of convicts among them. They were, in fact, treated worse than the African slaves who sometimes worked alongside them, according to one witness. Since masters had a lifetime investment in their slave property, it behooved them to exercise a certain degree of care in their treatment; in contrast, the limited term of the indentured servant encouraged masters to attempt to extract as much labor as possible within a few years. The results were grim. Anywhere from one half to three quarters of the servants died during their first years in America.

Indentured servants did enjoy some legal protection against abuse by their masters. One morning Buettner broke a new plow on a large tree root. The anguished gestures and curses of his master appeared so comical that Buettner was unable to conceal his amusement. This of course even further enraged his master, who attacked Buettner, bloodying the servant's nose. Buettner fled to the home of a local judge, related what had happened and demanded protection. The judge then drafted a letter of

---

[7]Profits in the servant trade were considerable; merchants' costs for transporting servants to the colonies averaged under £5. Likewise, servant labor was enormously profitable: annual maintenance expenses ran about £14, while the yearly return was figured at about £50.

harsh rebuke to Buettner's master, instructed the servant to deliver it, and assured him that he would not be abused again.

Despite such safeguards, masters exercised considerable power over their servants. A servant could not marry without his master's consent; he could not engage in trade, although he could own property; he could not travel about unless permitted by his master; he could neither vote nor hold public office. Servants could be whipped for disobedience; other prescribed punishments included imprisonment, fines, and extension of the term of service. Clearly such a relationship, in which one party exercised enormous power over another, was open to abuse. Not surprisingly women and children were particularly vulnerable in this regard. Women servants who became pregnant, for example, routinely had their terms of service extended. Some masters took advantage of this situation by themselves impregnating their female servants.

His lack of freedom grated on Johann Buettner's youthful spirit. His discontent was increased by the behavior of his master who, according to Buettner, "was a very violent man . . . especially when he was drunk." What's more, Buettner found himself increasingly homesick. After about a year in America his unhappiness was given focus by several other German servants who had fared badly at their masters' hands. They hatched a vague plan of escape which they hoped would lead ultimately to their return to Europe. At first Buettner refused to share in their scheme, but at last he agreed. Travelling by night and hiding during the day, the runaways managed to reach Virginia before bloodhounds tracked them down and they were captured.

Running away was fairly common among servants. Colonial newspapers abounded with advertisements seeking their return. In Buettner's case, as in many others, a reward (£5) encouraged the cooperation of authorities and the general public in securing his capture. Because colonists were required to carry passes or identification papers, runaways were relatively easy to detect. German servants, faced with the additional obstacle of a language barrier, were far less likely to bolt than were those from England or Ireland. Captured servants faced a variety of punishments ranging from fines and whippings to the extension of their servitude. Unclaimed runaways were disposed of at public auction.

Sobered by what he had seen of servant life in the South, Buettner was relieved to be returned to New Jersey from Virginia. To his surprise, his master, convinced that a gullible Buettner had been goaded into escaping by unsavory companions, accepted him back without recrimination. A repentant Buettner then promised "that I would never run away again, and would serve him sincerely in the future." In turn his master pledged that upon completion of his contract Buettner would receive "a certificate of freedom which would . . . [open] for me the doors of all America."

The prospect extended was illusory; the doors of America would not be opened very wide. Even though there was no real stigma attached to having been a servant (some former servants even rose to considerable heights in American society), the possibilities for most were severely limited.[8] Only about one servant in ten could expect to succeed in acquiring land and becoming prosperous. Another 10 percent, although remaining landless, could look forward to enjoying lives of reasonable comfort as artisans, tutors or overseers. The other 80 percent either died during servitude, returned to their homelands, or settled into lives of perpetual poverty at the bottom of colonial society. Naturally these prospects varied over time and from place to place, but overall the outlook for the indentured servant was not particularly bright.

The truce between Buettner and his master lasted about two years before it was shattered by Buettner's inadvertent destruction of the plow and the unfortunate complications which arose from it. Incapable of a reconciliation, his master traded the young German—then in his early twenties—for a pair of oxen. Buettner's sense of indignation at this treatment was evident even half a century later, but as he noted, he "could not remonstrate against the trading of the two gentlemen"—they were perfectly within their rights.

Buettner's new master was an innkeeper who maintained an establishment on the highway to Philadelphia. Buettner was employed as a porter at the inn, a marked improvement over the heavy farm labor he'd performed for the previous three years. By this time the American Revolution had broken out, resulting in a considerable traffic of American soldiers along the highway. The officers customarily tipped Buettner to care for their horses, enabling him to save what he termed "a rather respectable amount of money" in a relatively short time. While he of course appreciated his earnings, Buettner hoped that the conflict might bring him something more—a chance to return to his homeland.

The American Revolution, which erupted in 1775, was more than an upheaval within the British Empire. It was, in fact, an international conflict, involving many more participants than just the English and their American colonists. England's principal European rivals, France and Spain, became active supporters of the rebellion in 1778, resulting in the involvement of thousands of foreign soldiers on American soil.[9] The English purchased foreign support in the form of about 30,000 German mercenaries. Called Hessians because more than half of them came from Hesse-Cassel, their services were sold to the English by their avaricious rulers. Although the Revolution brought a temporary halt to conventional immigration—a war-torn America, after all, offered few attractions—it nevertheless did promote the settlement of some foreigners. A small num-

---

[8]Among the most notable were Daniel Dulany, a prominent Maryland lawyer, Mathew Thornton and George Taylor, signers of the Declaration of Independence, Charles Thomson, Secretary of the Continental Congress and Matthew Lyon, Republican congressman from Vermont.

[9]Their importance to the success of the rebellion is illustrated by the fact that when Lord Cornwallis surrendered the British forces at Yorktown, the last battle of the war, about one half of the soldiers and the entire fleet which surrounded him were French.

ber of French soldiers and many more Hessians remained in the newly formed United States at the war's end.

Within a month of the Declaration of Independence in July 1776, the Continental Congress began to encourage the desertion of Hessians by offering them citizenship and grants of land. Christopher Ludwig, the chief baker for George Washington's army and himself a German immigrant, proposed another approach: "Bring the [Hessian] captives to Philadelphia, show them our beautiful German churches, let them taste our roast beef and homes, then send them away to their people and you will see how many will come over to us." These policies succeeded: upwards of 5,000 Hessians remained in America after the war, many of them having deserted during the conflict. Johann Buettner encountered a number of these deserters at the inn and extracted from them information on the location and strength of their units. His motives, he later acknowledged, were completely selfish. "I learned this with the end in view, if the occasion arose, to join the [Hessian] army and to return with it, after the war was over, to my fatherland, for which I constantly grew more homesick." But the twenty-two-year-old Buettner's resolution wavered: "When I considered the danger which threatened me should I be captured by the Americans after I had gone over to the English and the Hessians, I gave up each time my secretly cherished plans, and decided at least to wait a little longer before trying to realize my desires."

Many other German immigrants, unlike Buettner, sought to protect their new homes rather than return to their old ones. Several German regiments were formed and rendered noteworthy service throughout the Revolution. In December of 1776 Congress authorized a Baron von Ottendorff to form a company of German volunteers in Pennsylvania. German servants were permitted to enlist, on condition that a portion of their pay go to their masters. At the end of the war the veterans would each be awarded 13 acres of land. Buettner found himself caught up in the excitement of the moment: "I was persuaded to enter this volunteer corps, and although I was less concerned about the freedom of North America than about my own, and though I longed for my fatherland, still when I saw the great enthusiasm for the cause of freedom manifested in Philadelphia, I straightaway forgot Germany and the plans for my own freedom, [and] took service in Major Ottendorff's corps." Buettner's master, himself a lieutenant in the militia, readily agreed to his enlistment.

Buettner found the life of a soldier no improvement over that of a servant. Supplies were so scarce that his unit wintered in huts made of tree boughs and foraged for food throughout the countryside. Six months of this was enough to rekindle Buettner's homesickness. With a half dozen of his fellows he devised a plan to desert to a nearby Hessian encampment. The conspirators attempted to sneak out of camp one night, but before proceeding more than 50 yards they were challenged and shot at by a sentry. The deserters fled in all directions, with Buettner scrambling hastily back to camp, undetected. However, a few days later a battle enabled

Buettner to accomplish his immediate object. After a brief fight, the American position was overrun by a combined force of English and Hessian soldiers. As his comrades fled into the forest, Buettner hid in some underbrush until the shooting stopped. He then emerged, entered the Hessian camp, and explained his situation, making a favorable impression on the German commander. After providing his new allies with information about American strength and defenses, Buettner took a loyalty oath to the British king and was enrolled in a Hessian regiment.

Buettner's obvious ambivalence about the Revolution reflected divisions within the American nation itself. The conflict not only pitted colonists and their foreign allies against the British; it was also a civil war within American society. Although many colonists supported the cause of independence, others remained loyal to the crown, while substantial numbers—to the extent that it was possible—stayed prudently aloof from the struggle. This was true not only of those born in America, but of immigrants as well. A variety of factors other than ethnicity—local issues, geography, religious beliefs, social class, expediency—determined their posture and behavior during the Revolution.

For the next several years Buettner remained with the regiment, seeing action in a number of battles and campaigns, from Brandywine to Charleston. During one engagement he was wounded and captured by rebel forces. While his injuries were attended to, he was recognized by one of his former comrades, who suspiciously inquired how he happened to be with the Hessians. Buettner protested his innocence: "I answered, being afraid of the consequences did I confess my desertion, that I had been captured during the skirmish at the mountain in Pennsylvania when the volunteer corps had been overwhelmed, and that I had been kept a prisoner since that day." After winning the confidence of the Americans, Buettner was able to escape once more and rejoin his Hessian regiment. There he remained until the war finally ended in 1783. Then, realizing his dream at last, Buettner boarded a transport with the rest of the German mercenaries and sailed for Germany.

Buettner's sojourn in America, eventful though it was, was rather short—only about ten years. But the temporary nature of his stay did not mark Buettner as especially unusual. From the very beginning of European settlement in the New World there had been a steady stream of people returning to their homelands. Their motives varied: some were failures who quit America in disappointment; others were successes planning to live lives of ease supported by their New World gains. And there were those, like Buettner, unable to sink their roots into America's soil because of their undiminished love for home.[10]

---

[10]After the steamship replaced sailing vessels as the principal mode of transportation in the late nineteenth century, the volume of returnees increased markedly. In fact, in some years during the twentieth century the number of emigrants from the United States exceeded immigration into the United States. See Chapter Eleven.

Even though Buettner later wrote that he "did not find happiness" in America, it nevertheless made a favorable and lasting impression upon him. When he published his autobiography nearly half a century after his return to Germany, he titled it *Buettner, der Amerikaner*—Buettner the American. Having lived, if only briefly, in the New World, he could never again belong entirely to the Old. Even though he resettled in his beloved native Saxony, Buettner thought of himself as American. Fearing that this might be perceived as "uncalled for and arrogant," he attempted to explain the grip which America maintained upon his imagination: "Although I no longer live in America, I spent, however, my best years in that part of the world, fought in the significant, decisive North American struggle for independence, and moistened with my blood the soil of the great North American republic." He was, indeed, Buettner the American.

FURTHER READING

FAUST, ALBERT B. *The German Element in the United States.* 2 vols. New York: Arno Press, 1969.

MORRIS, RICHARD B. *Government and Labor in Early America.* New York: Columbia University Press, 1946.

PARSONS, WILLIAM T. *The Pennsylvania Dutch: A Persistent Minority.* Boston: Twayne Publishers, 1976.

SMITH, ABBOT E. *Colonists in Bondage: White Servitude and Convict Labor in America, 1607–1776.* Chapel Hill: University of North Carolina Press, 1947.

VAN DER ZEE, JOHN. *Bound Over: Indentured Servitude and American Conscience.* New York: Simon and Schuster, 1985.

WOLF, STEPHANIE GRAUMAN. *Urban Village: Population, Community, and Family Structure in Germantown, Pennsylvania, 1683–1800.* Princeton: Princeton University Press, 1976.

TO BE SOLD, on board the Ship *Bance-Island*, on tuesday the 6th of *May* next, at *Ashley-Ferry*; a choice cargo of about 250 fine healthy

NEGROES,

just arrived from the Windward & Rice Coast. —The utmost care has already been taken, and shall be continued, to keep them free from the least danger of being infected with the SMALL-POX, no boat having been on board, and all other communication with people from *Charles-Town* prevented.

Austin, Laurens, & Appleby.

N. B. Full one Half of the above Negroes have had the SMALL-POX in their own Country.

*Newspaper Advertisement,
Charleston, S.C., 1766*

5

Venture Smith

HIS HEAD ACHED from the blow struck by a gun butt; his neck had been rubbed raw by the rope which was looped around it. But these discomforts were drowned by the far greater pain of watching his father die. In horrified fascination, the young boy stared as his captors repeatedly slashed and beat the bound figure of his father. Finally the agony was over; his father's once-proud body lay broken and lifeless. But the boy's torment had only begun—he had just become a slave.

From the time that the first Africans were brought to America until the Civil War put an end to slavery, nearly ten million Africans were transported to the New World. While only about 5 percent of that total ended up in the area that would become the United States, their numbers were substantial enough to establish the Africans as the largest immigrant group in American society prior to the Revolution. The slave trade which caused their migration was one of the principal underpinnings of colonial commerce, while slavery itself formed the basis for American agriculture and prosperity.

The same quest that sent Columbus and other intrepid navigators west across the Atlantic dispatched Portuguese explorers down the western coast of Africa in the mid-1400s. Europeans were eager to discover a new route to the riches of the Orient. The Portuguese started out in the direction of a south-east passage, attempting to find a way around the barrier of the African continent. In the process, they transported back to Portugal the valuable products of the regions they explored—including ivory, gold, and slaves.

The Portuguese traffic in African slaves developed without any resistance in Portugal; the institution of slavery had existed in that land since ancient times. Nor was there opposition in Africa, where slavery was even more firmly rooted. But it was not for several decades—until the establishment of colonies in the New World created an enormous demand for labor—that slaves became the principal focus of European interest in Africa.[1] At that point, the Spanish, Dutch, English, Danes and French began to compete with Portugal for control of the traffic. As the slave trade developed, Europeans and coastal tribes formed an unholy partnership: African traders, preying upon their neighbors in the interior, supplied the increasingly insistent demands of European merchants for human cargo to deliver to America. Only rarely was it necessary for whites to penetrate the African interior in search of slaves—black dealers peddled them along the western coast. It was an arrangement which benefited nearly all parties, with the principal exception of its victims.

The young boy, who would later be called Venture Smith, was one of those victims. He was born around 1729 and brought up in Dukandarra, a rich agricultural region several hundred miles inland from the Gulf of Guinea. His people were farmers who tended flocks of sheep and cultivated a variety of crops. The tranquility of their existence was abruptly shattered one day with the arrival of refugees from a neighboring village. The fugitives reported that their land had been invaded by well-armed warriors from the coast. The attack had been instigated by whites who had supplied the raiders with firearms.

Hard on the heels of this disturbing news came the invaders themselves. Initially they merely demanded the payment of valuables and livestock. But after collecting their tribute, the raiders refused to depart—clearly they desired something more. Perceiving that their lives (or at least their freedom) were in peril, the villagers fled, but they were easily overtaken and subdued. Because the boy's father fought so desperately against capture, he was killed. The survivors had rope halters placed around their necks and then the entire party of warriors and captives began the long march toward the sea. En route more villages were attacked, more prisoners added to the caravan. Although he was only about six years old, the boy was pressed into service as a porter. Burdened with a huge grinding stone and a heavier weight of his fear and grief, he stumbled along in a daze.

As they neared the coast the raiders were themselves attacked and defeated by another tribe. This turn of events had no effect upon the status of the captives; it only afforded them the small satisfaction of seeing their conquerors become slaves as well. The prisoners were then taken to the fort at Anamabo, one of the principal English trading posts on the Gold Coast.

---

[1] Early in their colonization of the New World the Spanish found that Indians made poor slaves—the Arawaks, for example, died out from the hard labor expected of them. Catholic monks like Bartolomé de las Casas, in order to spare other Indians the same end, proposed importing slaves from Africa, an idea which caught on very quickly. English efforts to enslave the Indians proved no more satisfactory than those of the Spanish, and led ultimately to the same solution.

The Gold Coast had acquired its name from the precious metal mined in the nearby hills and extracted from the beds of streams flowing into the sea. But by the seventeenth century, slaves had replaced gold as the principal attraction for white traders.[2] Within a relatively short stretch of shoreline there were several dozen forts or trading depots, manned by the different European competitors in the slave traffic. Initially that trade had been conducted by royally chartered companies which enjoyed monopoly privileges. In the case of the British Company of Royal Adventurers (established in 1663), a favored status was not enough; it soon lost nearly the entire amount invested in it. A more successful operation, the Royal African Company, superseded the Royal Adventurers in 1672. For the next quarter century the Royal African Company dominated the British portion of the African slave trade. In 1698, however, yielding to the complaints of English and American merchants and planters, royal authorities opened the traffic to all British subjects. One result of that action was an immediate surge in the number of slaves imported into England's American colonies. Consequently the great majority of Africans imported into North America was transported there between 1698 and 1808, when the United States and Great Britain agreed to abolish the slave trade.

Because the supply of slaves along the Gold Coast was uncertain, traders sometimes spent several months cruising the shoreline, picking up human cargo wherever they could. Security considerations also figured in this practice. According to one eighteenth-century slave trader "the safest way is to trade with the different Nations, . . . and having some of every sort on board, there will be no more likelihood of their succeeding in a Plot, than of finishing the tower of Babel." It was, therefore, necessary to carry a large stock of goods to exchange for slaves, including rum, iron bars, guns, bells, cloth, as well as dozens of other items. When the small boy was taken out of the fort at Anamabo and sold, he was exchanged for four barrels of rum and a piece of calico cloth. His purchaser, ship's steward Robertson Mumford, named him Venture to signify the fact that the child represented Mumford's private investment, separate from the general cargo.

Although Venture's initiation into the slave trade had been terrible, the worst part still lay ahead—the murderous "middle passage" from Africa to the New World. As grotesque as Johann Buettner found his journey to America, his experience paled in comparison to that of the typical slave. Venture and about 260 of his countrymen were herded aboard a ship and packed into an airless hold beneath the deck. There they would remain for the duration of the journey, which ordinarily lasted six to eight weeks. In one sense, Venture was fortunate; the ship which transported him

---

[2]The focus of the slave trade moved with the passage of time. In its initial stages in the sixteenth century, it was concentrated in Senegal and Gambia. By the nineteenth century it had shifted far south to Angola. The area in between—especially the Gold Coast—was the center of slave trading during the seventeenth and eighteenth centuries.

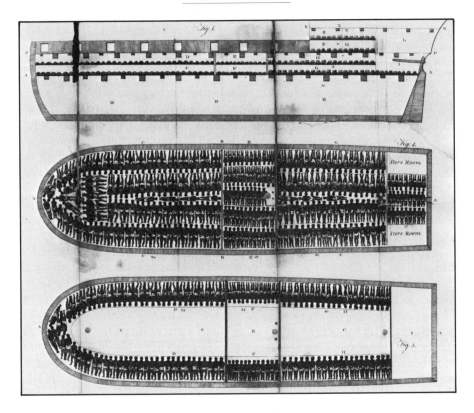

Cutaway View of a Slave Ship

Courtesy of Library of Congress.

sailed out of Rhode Island, the American center of the colonial slave trade. The typical Rhode Island slaver allowed for each slave a space about five and a half feet long by sixteen inches wide by three feet ten inches high; ships from Liverpool and other English ports were often even more restrictive! Except for rare occasions when they were exercised on deck, slaves were manacled in place, forcing them to lie in their own excrement and vomit. Women were, in addition, subject to sexual attack by members of the crew.

The crowded, unsanitary conditions bred disease. Deadly epidemics were a constant threat in such close quarters, so any African who exhibited symptoms of contagious illness was thrown overboard. Such precautions were, however, insufficient. The mortality rate among slaves approximated 16 percent during the middle passage, a figure exceeded in Venture's experience: due to an outbreak of smallpox, fewer than 200 of the 260 Africans he had set sail with survived the trip to Barbados. Despite losses of such a magnitude, the slave trade was an enormously profitable business—returns from 33 to 50 percent on the original investment were not uncommon for a single voyage.[3]

In Barbados all but four of the Africans were sold to local planters. Venture and three others remained aboard the ship for its return to Rhode Island. The rich, sugar-producing islands like Barbados and Jamaica were the usual destinations of American and English slavers; only a small proportion of Africans was carried on to North America. Among those who were, the great majority ended up in the southern colonies, from Maryland to Georgia. By the middle of the eighteenth century about 90 percent of colonial slaves would be concentrated in that area, where they comprised more than one third of the total population. In contrast, the New England colonies had a substantially smaller number of African inhabitants; after 1700, blacks—free as well as slave—never exceeded 5 percent of the total population.

The first twenty Africans in British North America had been brought to Jamestown in 1619, just a dozen years after its establishment. Although records are not conclusive as to their fate, it is probable that they were treated as indentured servants—held in bondage for a limited period and then granted freedom. But over the next 40 years the status of blacks in America rapidly eroded, until most of them were reduced to the status of slaves. By the 1630s, discriminatory laws prevented blacks in Virginia from bearing arms, serving in the militia, or having sexual relations with whites. Court records, wills, and sales receipts further document the declining status—and rising price—of black servants. By the 1660s, the concept of slavery as an inherited, life-long condition was embedded in the Virginia statutes and spreading to other colonies.[4]

Within a generation a harsh slave code evolved in the southern colonies, governing every aspect of its victims' lives. Among other things, slaves were barred from owning property and denied the protection of the courts. Their masters exercised virtually complete power over them, punishing recalcitrant slaves by whipping, maiming, or even—on occasion—killing them. In contrast, New England codes generally offered some measure of protection to slaves, allowing them to own and transfer property, entitling them to jury trials, even enabling them to testify in court against whites. In addition, slaveowners in New England were restricted in terms of the punishment which they could mete out; whipping was permitted, but branding, maiming, and execution were not. The explanation for the differences between northern and southern slave codes lies in the population

---

[3]The slave trade proved even more deadly for Europeans and Americans than for their African victims. The mortality rate among crew members of slave ships was slightly higher than that of the slaves themselves; among the European agents and soldiers who manned the trading posts and forts in Africa, about half died during their first year there.

[4]Because of their substantial trade with the West Indies, New Englanders were exposed to slavery earlier than Virginians were. By the late 1630s the institution was already transplanted into Massachusetts directly from the Caribbean and in 1641 it was officially sanctioned.

statistics; because blacks made up a large (and potentially hostile) proportion of the southern population, fearful whites resorted to extreme measures to insure their control over the slaves.

Even though the black population in the northern colonies was substantially smaller, slaves there were employed at a wider variety of tasks. Reflecting the plantation economy of the region, slaves in the South were, for the most part, used as field hands, although some were retained as domestics. Northern slaves, mirroring the more complex economy of their section, were employed not only as household servants and farm laborers, but as fishermen, miners, wood cutters, artisans, and in a variety of other ways as well.

Venture was initially employed within the Mumford home, carding wool and doing other domestic chores. As he reached adolescence, increasingly demanding jobs were given him. Years later he would recall that failure to complete any of the tasks assigned him would result in his being "rigorously punished." Venture's life was complicated by the fact that in essence he had two masters—Robertson Mumford and his son, James. Sometimes their orders conflicted. On one such occasion, when Venture refused to follow the son's instructions, James attacked him with a pitchfork. Seizing a pitchfork himself, Venture fended off the attack. While northern slave codes acknowledged that slaves had *some* rights, self-defense was not among them. Venture was suspended from a wooden frame used for hanging up the carcasses of cattle. Three dozen branches to serve as whips were brought from a nearby peach orchard. Although Venture was threatened with a whipping, the threat was not carried out and he was cut down after an hour.

In addition to a few slaves, Mumford owned several indentured servants. One of these, an Irishman named Heddy, concocted a plan for running away, which he invited Venture to share in. Although Venture initially resisted the suggestion, he finally allowed himself to be persuaded, as did two other white servants. After secretly stealing and storing supplies for their journey, the conspirators stole a small boat of Mumford's and sailed it to Long Island. Then, while the others rested, Heddy stole their supplies and made off on his own. Venture and the two servants chased the treacherous Heddy, captured him, and returned to Mumford's home. There they placed the entire blame for their escapade upon Heddy, who was sent to jail. The other three escapees were accepted back by their master without punishment. Frequent advertisements in colonial newspapers indicate that similar attempts were not at all rare among slaves and servants.

This episode evidently soured Mumford upon Venture, now in his early twenties. Within a few months his master sold Venture to Thomas Stanton, of Stonington, Connecticut. Although Venture was relieved to get away from the Mumfords, the transaction also caused him considerable distress. Perhaps a year before—around 1751—Venture had married Meg, another slave belonging to Mumford. But slave marriages had no legal standing and Mumford was neither obliged nor inclined to take the feelings of his human property into account. Venture's sale meant that he was now separated from his wife and their month-old daughter.

The disruption of his family was an experience Venture shared with all too many of his fellow slaves. One recent study indicates that about a third of all slave marriages were similarly dissolved. This grim fact makes all the more remarkable the tenacity with which slave couples strove to remain together and develop a stable family life. Despite the twin facts that the influence of male slaves was undermined by their masters and that female slaves were subject to the sexual demands of their owners, slave parents attempted to minimize the abuse of their offspring and impart to them the emotional and physical skills necessary for survival. The slave family, despite its inherent weakness and ever-present possibility of fragmentation, constituted a refuge which served to cushion its members from some of the harsher aspects of their condition.

While working for Mumford, Venture had managed to save £21 by cleaning the boots of gentlemen in his spare time, selling produce from a little vegetable patch which he cultivated, fishing at night, and trapping muskrats. Although the practice was more frequent in the North, even in the South some masters permitted their slaves to earn a little spending money in this fashion. An even better way for slaves to make money was by hiring out. Some masters allowed their slaves to hire themselves to someone else. The master would receive either a flat fee for the slave's services, or a percentage of his earnings. The slave, in turn, was responsible for providing his own food, shelter, and clothing from his wages, thus relieving the master of any maintenance expenses. Any money which the slave earned in excess of that which he owed his master, or needed to support himself, was his to save or spend as he chose.

Shortly after he was sold by Mumford, Venture lent his accumulated savings to his new master's brother, Robert Stanton. In return, Venture received Stanton's note, which he carefully locked in a small chest. As a further indication of the good relationship which initially existed between Venture and his new owner, Stanton purchased Venture's wife, Meg, and their child about a year and a half later. The relative harmony of their arrangement was, however, eventually disrupted by an argument which arose between Meg and Stanton's wife. When Mrs. Stanton began to beat Meg, Venture interceded and accepted the blows himself. The enraged woman then seized a horsewhip and began to lash him with it. Angrily Venture tore the whip out of her grasp and threw it into the fire. When Stanton returned home later in the day, his wife reported the incident, but he seemed indifferent to her complaint. Several days later, however, while Venture was busy putting logs into the fireplace, Stanton crept up behind him and smashed him on the head with a huge club, a blow which scarred Venture for life.

Although dazed, Venture grappled with Stanton and succeeded in dragging him outside the house. There he wrenched the club away from

Stanton and took it to a nearby justice of the peace as evidence to support a formal complaint against his master. Most slaves, governed as they were by the harsher codes of the South, had no such opportunity to seek legal protection. But even where it did exist in the North, that protection was often hollow and meaningless. After listening to his account of the incident, the judge simply advised Venture to return to the Stanton home and remain there until he was abused again. At that moment, Stanton and his brother Robert appeared, so the judge took the opportunity to admonish Venture's owner.

In a sullen procession, Venture and the two brothers started for home. Suddenly and without warning, both Stantons attacked Venture and began beating him violently. A large and powerful man, Venture, as he later reported, "became enraged at this and immediately turned them both under me, laid one of them across the other, and stamped them both with my feet." Even northern slaves were not permitted to strike whites for any reason—let alone trample on them—so, despite the fact that Venture had not started the fight, he was arrested by the local constable and two deputies. They took him to a nearby blacksmith shop where he was handcuffed and had an ox chain padlocked to his legs.

For the next several days Venture remained in irons, while his master periodically baited him by contemptuously and abusively asking whether Venture preferred to be released and go to work. When he stubbornly answered "No," Venture was then threatened with sale to a West Indies sugar plantation. If carried out, that threat would mean much more than merely separation from Meg and their children (for now they had several)—in fact, it would amount to a death sentence. Conditions on the Caribbean sugar plantations were so harsh that slaves were often literally worked to death. In fact, the North American colonies (and later the United States) were the only society in the New World in which the slave population increased through natural means; in other societies large-scale importations were required to achieve population growth.[5]

While Venture was shackled he was approached by Hempsted Miner, a neighbor of Stanton's. Miner asked Venture whether the slave would like to come live with him. Understandably Venture replied in the affirmative. Miner then instructed him to appear as recalcitrant as possible, in order to incline Stanton toward a quick sale at a bargain price. In return for his cooperation, Miner promised Venture that the slave would eventually be given the opportunity to gain his freedom. The plan succeeded; a discouraged Stanton sold Miner his slave for a reduced price.

---

[5]About eighty percent of the slaves imported into Brazil were males. A similar ratio was reported on the typical Cuban sugar plantation. This sexual imbalance reflected the result of a calculation that it was more profitable to continually import adult males—and work them to death—than it was to allow the slave population to reproduce itself. In contrast, the numbers of male and female slaves were nearly equal in the United States: in 1850 for every 100 male slaves in the South there were 99.9 females.

There were several ways in which a few lucky slaves acquired their freedom. One of these was through manumission—simply a release from bondage by the master. Acts of manumission were sometimes written into wills of masters, representing a sort of deathbed attempt to secure divine forgiveness for supporting an institution about which many slave-owners harbored private misgivings. Slaves were also occasionally able to emancipate themselves by paying their owners an amount of money equivalent to their value. This was the method which Venture hoped to employ with Miner, but the horrified slave discovered that during his altercation with the Stantons, one of them had broken into his chest and destroyed Robert Stanton's note. Venture was, therefore, left with no means for collecting the debt which was owed him, a situation which represented a staggering blow both financially and in terms of his aspirations for freedom.

Venture's distress was soon compounded by his discovery that his new owner had no intention of fulfilling his part of their bargain. Instead, Miner hoped to turn a quick profit by transporting Venture to Hartford and reselling him at a normal price. Before they set out for Hartford, Venture took some money which he had managed to save while in service to Stanton and buried it. As it turned out, Miner proved unable to get a reasonable price for his slave at Hartford, but because he was in need of money, Miner pawned Venture to a Daniel Edwards. Edwards employed the slave within his household, as a cup-bearer and waiter. He was so pleased by Venture's behavior and service that Edwards soon placed considerable trust in him, lending the slave a horse so that he could visit his wife and children in Stonington, where they were still owned by Thomas Stanton.

Venture's stay with Edwards was short; around 1760 Miner sold him to a Colonel Oliver Smith. Little more than thirty years old, Venture had already been sold four times and pawned once. Eager to become his own master, Venture asked Colonel Smith whether he would permit the slave eventually to purchase his freedom. When Smith agreed to the idea, Venture dug up his savings—enough for a down payment—and gave the money to a free black friend "to take [Smith's] security for it, as I was the property of my master, and therefore could not safely take his obligation myself." With some money which he made by fishing in his spare time, Venture was soon able to purchase a small plot of land. This he put into cultivation and made even more money from selling his crops. After several years of working for Colonel Smith, Venture asked his master for permission to hire himself out. Smith agreed, on the condition that Venture pay him a quarter of his wages. This arrangement proved so lucrative for the slave that, after about six months, Smith negotiated for himself a larger share of Venture's earnings.

Saving money any way he could, Venture cut wood, threshed grain, and did without everything but the barest necessities. By the time he was thirty-six years old, Venture had paid his master £95, including the down payment. He still owed nearly £14, but Colonel Smith emancipated him anyway, saying that he could pay the rest if and when it ever became convenient. Even with that concession from Smith, Venture regarded the price as "unreasonable" and "an enormous sum," but Colonel Smith claimed that he wanted to have insurance against Venture becoming a burden upon him in old age. And so, thirty years and thousands of miles removed from where he had first been enslaved, Venture became a free man. For his surname he chose Smith, the name of the last man to own him.[6]

Venture's newly won freedom was not, however, absolute. Nor could it ever be, given his color. The Virginia legislature, when it had a century before accorded official recognition of slavery, at the same time declared that free blacks "ought not in all respects . . . be admitted to a full fruition of the exemptions and impunities of the English." Other colonies, while not making official pronouncements of policy, nonetheless followed a similar standard in practice. Even the treatment of free blacks was frequently defined to a considerable degree by the harsh slave codes. None of the southern colonies, for example, permitted free blacks to testify in court against whites. On the other hand, several colonial governments conceded some rights to free blacks which could not even be dreamed about by slaves, including intermarriage with whites, voting, and even the right to hold public office. But the chief circumstance which set the free black apart from the slave—the one distinction which applied uniformly throughout all the colonies—was that the free black was no longer property. He could not be bought or sold.

The mere fact that some rights existed in an abstract sense did not in any way insure that free blacks were allowed to exercise them. America was, after all, a society in which few people questioned the belief that blacks were inferior to whites. Not simply the objects of scorn by whites, free blacks were sometimes regarded with hatred and fear by them as well. Lower-class whites felt threatened economically by free blacks, who were often willing to work for wages unacceptable to whites. And in the southern colonies, where whites were haunted by fears of slave rebellion, free blacks were looked upon as the natural leaders of such uprisings. In view of these attitudes, few objections were raised—in either the northern or southern colonies—when free blacks were mistreated or had their rights infringed upon. On several occasions after his emancipation, Venture was cheated by whites in his financial dealings but discovered he was essen-

---

[6]No accurate figures exist to suggest the number of free blacks in the colonies in 1765, when Venture was liberated, but only a small percentage of American blacks was free at that time. The first United States census, taken twenty-five years later, indicates that less than 8 percent of the black population was free in 1790. Unquestionably the proportion in 1765 was even lower, because in that quarter-century interval thousands of slaves were emancipated as a result of the American Revolution, while even more were set free by the abolition of slavery in several Northern states. Rough estimates for 1765 would indicate a total population of approximately 2,150,000, including 425,000 blacks. The number of free blacks would not have exceeded 25,000.

tially without recourse. Recalling one such incident, he bitterly observed, "Such a proceeding as this, . . . whatever it may be called in a Christian land, would in my native country have been branded as a crime equal to highway robbery. But Captain Hart was a *white gentleman*, and I a *poor African*, therefore it was *all right*, and good enough for the black dog."

White antagonism toward free blacks was reflected not only in the economic intercourse between the races, but in their social dealings as well. Most whites were put off by the notion of having anything more to do with free blacks than was necessary; as a consequence, the two groups existed as distinct and separate communities. Although in most cases this separation was informal, on occasion it was achieved through official action. Some years after Venture's emancipation, the selectmen of the township in which he then lived passed an ordinance which declared "that all negroes residing there should be expelled." However, an exception was made for Venture because by that time, as he later explained, "my temporal affairs were in a pretty prosperous condition. This and my industry was what alone saved me from being expelled."

An even wider gulf existed between white society and that of slaves. A former slave named Robert Smalls explained in 1863 that the master class knew little of the "secret life" of slaves because "one life they show their masters and another they don't show." Despite the intrusive and oppressive nature of slavery, involving as it did conscious attempts to eradicate the African roots of its victims, slaves managed to transplant in America much of their native culture. In the process the languages, customs, and superstitions of a number of tribal groups mingled together and combined with various aspects of American culture to produce practices, beliefs, and a social structure that were both unique and distinct from those of white society. The folk tales with which they amused themselves frequently concealed the slaves' continuing resistance to their condition. Their intensely emotional version of Christianity, and particularly the spirtuals which they sang, often masked a refusal to abandon hopes of freedom.

The rare slave who became free, like Venture Smith, often found that emancipation meant little change from the life he had previously known. For the first time free to choose his own dwelling place, Venture sold his property in Stonington and moved to Long Island. There he remained for the next four years, hiring himself out to do low-paying and back-breaking tasks, just as he had before his emancipation. And, just as he had saved nearly all his earnings in order to purchase his own freedom, Venture continued to live frugally so that he could liberate his family by the same means. He later recalled, "I bought nothing which I did not absolutely want. . . . Expensive gatherings of my mates I commonly shunned; and all kinds of luxuries I was perfectly a stranger to."

Around 1769, when he was about forty years old, Venture was able to purchase the freedom of his two sons, Solomon and Cuff. Four years later, when Solomon was seventeen, he shipped out on a whaling expedition, despite his father's objections. Venture's worst fears were realized;

Solomon died of scurvy during the voyage, a fate which prompted his father to note, "In my son, besides the loss of his life, I lost equal to seventy-five pounds."

Venture's attitude toward his son's death might seem mercenary, but is, at the same time, perfectly understandable. For most of his life Venture had been treated as an object rather than a person. He had been traded, sold, and pawned. He had learned to measure his own value—as well as that of others—in concrete rather than in abstract terms. In a slave society people wore price tags. It is not really surprising, therefore, that Venture's thinking, although curious or even warped by today's standards, reflected prevailing attitudes in an eminently practical way. Given Venture's situation, what might ordinarily seem materialistic and calculating was in fact unquestionably sensible, as his liberation of Meg reveals: "In my forty-fourth year, I purchased my wife Meg, and thereby prevented having another child to buy, as she was then pregnant. I gave forty pounds for her."[7]

In addition to buying members of his own family, Venture also purchased a slave who was unrelated to him. The purpose of this latter transaction was by no means altruistic; like other masters, Venture regarded his slave as a money-making machine. And, like other slave owners, Venture discovered that his property sometimes objected to this view. The slave ran away only a short time after Venture had purchased him, leading a disgusted Venture to sourly observe, "I thereby lost all that I gave for him, except for twenty pounds which he gave me before absconding." As a black man who owned a slave, Venture was unusual but not unique. As early as the mid-seventeenth century, when the institution of slavery was just beginning to take root in the colonies, Virginia courts had established the right of blacks to hold slaves. But the number of slave-owning blacks was always only a tiny percentage of the already small free black population. Moreover, in most such cases, the master-slave relationship masked a closer familial connection.

Shortly before he purchased the freedom of his wife, Venture went into business for himself. He chartered a 30-ton sloop, engaged the sailors necessary for operating it, and began hauling wood from Long Island to Rhode Island. In addition, he raised and sold watermelons, fished for eels and lobsters, and on one occasion shipped out on a seven-month whaling voyage with Colonel Smith, his one-time owner. His various enterprises proved profitable enough for Venture to be able to buy a house, as well as secure the freedom of his oldest child, Hannah—an act which completed the liberation of his family. Despite his earlier unfortunate experience as a master, Venture also purchased two more slaves. They proved only a little more tractable than his first slave had, so after a short time Venture sold them both.

---

[7]Purchasing his sons before buying freedom for his wife and daughter offers further evidence of Smith's calculation: as males, Solomon and Cuff had greater earning power than females did.

In 1776, just as the American Revolution was erupting, Venture sold his property on Long Island and moved with his family back to Connecticut. Apparently their move was unrelated to the conflict. In fact, throughout the war Venture would remain aloof from the struggle, so that it had virtually no direct impact upon him. But while Venture was largely unaffected by the Revolution, the position of many blacks in American society was fundamentally altered as a direct result of the conflict. The libertarian rhetoric which fueled the Revolution and the dislocation which inevitably accompanied the war combined to initiate the process which would eventually culminate in the abolition of slavery.

The first blow was struck late in 1775 by Lord Dunmore, the royal governor of Virginia. In an attempt to bring the refractory colonials back under control, Dunmore declared martial law, adding that any slaves willing to fight for the crown would be rewarded with their freedom. As the Revolution spread and intensified, other British commanders issued similar orders until finally, in 1779, it became the official policy of royal forces in America. In addition to the several thousand slaves who availed themselves of this arrangement, thousands more secured their freedom simply by abandoning their masters and seeking sanctuary behind British lines.[8]

Colonial military leaders were more wary in approaching the delicate issue of emancipating slaves to fight for American independence. Many of them—like George Washington, for example—were themselves slaveowners and were therefore rather uncomfortable with the idea. Despite the fact that free blacks served in the militias of several colonies and had even participated in some of the earliest skirmishes of the Revolution, the Continental Congress initially prohibited them from enlisting in the American army. But as the war dragged on, the northern states—and even some southern ones—bowed to necessity and began actively recruiting blacks. Several northern states, in imitation of the British, rewarded slave volunteers with their freedom.

Even before the first shots of the struggle were fired, the institution of slavery was dealt an indirect blow. As the delegates to the Continental Congress gathered in Philadelphia in September 1774, many were acutely aware of the contradiction between their protests, couched in terms of inalienable natural rights and liberty, and the fact that they represented a society in which human beings were bought and sold. As a consequence, one of the first actions of the Congress was the suspension of the American trade in African slaves. Although it was only a temporary measure rather than an absolute prohibition, it was nonetheless a significant first step—one which made subsequent steps a little less difficult.

The same libertarian impulse led in 1775 to the establishment of the first American antislavery society; it also inspired Tom Paine, pamphleteer of the Revolution, to author in the same year an abolitionist tract

---

[8]Not all of these remained free: in some cases they were sent—as slaves—to Jamaica or some other British colony.

entitled "African Slavery in America." The greatest statement of Revolutionary ideals was, of course, the Declaration of Independence. It too, at least in its initial form, attacked the institution of slavery. The author of the Declaration, Thomas Jefferson—himself the owner of more than 200 slaves—attempted to ease America's moral burden by unfairly shifting responsibility to the king of England, but even this disguised assault proved too much for some members of the Congress. At the insistence of delegates from South Carolina and Georgia, where slavery was of the utmost social and economic importance—as well as delegates from Rhode Island and Massachusetts, where the slave trade was vital—the clause was deleted from the final draft of the Declaration.[9]

The impact of the Revolution upon slavery was even more dramatic at the state level. Vermont adopted a constitution in 1777 which abolished slavery. In 1780 the Pennsylvania legislature passed a law which would gradually emancipate all the slaves in that state. Three years later, a Massachusetts slave named Quok Walker brought about the immediate abolition of slavery there. Walker sued for his freedom on the grounds that the Massachusetts constitution of 1780 declared that all men were born free and equal. His contention was upheld by the Massachusetts Supreme Court, which ruled that slavery was, therefore, unconstitutional. Rhode Island and Connecticut followed Pennsylvania's lead in 1784, enacting measures which gradually abolished slavery. New York and New Jersey followed suit in the next two years, although it was not until 1799 and 1804, respectively, that effective enabling measures were passed.

The Revolutionary era also saw an improvement in Venture's situation. During the late 1770s he acquired over 80 acres of productive farm land near East Haddam, Connecticut and erected a comfortable house on the property. Over the next several years he bought even more land and two additional houses, as well as a fleet of more than 20 canoes, boats, and sailing vessels used for fishing and trade. But Venture's climb to a prosper-

[9]Here is the full text of the deleted clause:

> He [George III] has waged cruel war against human nature itself, violating its most sacred rights of life and liberty in the persons of a distant people who never offended him, captivating and carrying them into slavery in another hemisphere, or to incur miserable death in their transportation hither. This piratical warfare, the opprobrium of infidel powers, is the warfare of the Christian king of Great Britain. Determined to keep open a market where men should be bought and sold, he has prostituted his negative for suppressing every legislative attempt to prohibit or to restrain this execrable commerce. And that this assemblage of horrors might want no fact of distinguished die, he is now exciting those very people to rise in arms among us, and to purchase that liberty of which he has deprived them: thus paying off former crimes committed against the liberties of one people, with crimes which he urges them to commit against the lives of another.

ous position was not easy. He continued to work hard, as he had all his life, but it was not always possible to overcome the prejudice which his color inspired. Less troublesome, but still a problem, was Venture's lack of an education: he angrily noted, "I have been cheated out of considerable money by people whom I traded with taking advantage of my ignorance of numbers."

In 1798 Venture recognized that the end of his life was rapidly approaching. His once tall frame was bent by the weight of its 69 years; his eyesight had nearly deserted him. "But amidst all my griefs and pains," he wrote, "I have many consolations; Meg, the wife of my youth, whom I married for love, and bought with my money, is still alive." And, with a perception sharpened by thirty years of bondage, the former slave declared "My freedom is a privilege which nothing else can equal."

FURTHER READING

BLASSINGAME, JOHN. *The Slave Community: Plantation Life in the Antebellum South.* New York: Oxford University Press, 1972.

COUGHTRY, JAY. *The Notorious Triangle: Rhode Island and the African Slave Trade, 1700–1807.* Philadelphia: Temple University Press, 1981.

CURTIN, PHILIP. *The Atlantic Slave Trade: A Census.* Madison: University of Wisconsin Press, 1969.

FONER, PHILIP S. *A History of Black Americans: From Africa to the Emergence of the Cotton Kingdom.* Westport, Conn.: Greenwood Press, 1975.

FRANKLIN, JOHN HOPE. *From Slavery to Freedom: A History of Negro Americans.* New York: Alfred A. Knopf, 1979.

JORDAN, WINTHROP. *White Over Black: American Attitudes Toward the Negro, 1550–1812.* Chapel Hill: University of North Carolina Press, 1968.

RAWLEY, JAMES A. *The Transatlantic Slave Trade: A History.* New York: W.W. Norton and Co., 1981.

6

Alexander Hamilton

Portrait by John Trumbull. Courtesy of the Mellon
Collection, the National Gallery of Art, Washington, D.C.

6

Alexander Hamilton

TO THE ACCOMPANIMENT of a mournful tune titled "The World Turned Upside Down," the red-coated British soldiers stacked their arms in a field outside Yorktown, then marched dispiritedly back to camp. The army of Lord Cornwallis had surrendered! A surge of emotion swept over the young lieutenant colonel who watched attentively. Alexander Hamilton took considerable pride in the knowledge that the daring assault which he had led only a few nights before had rendered the British position indefensible, forcing Cornwallis to give up. Even more, he recognized that the surrender of the British army spelled a successful end to America's revolution and confirmed the birth of the United States.

Hamilton's newly independent nation was like no other place. It was, as Hector St. John de Crevecoeur remarked enthusiastically one year after Yorktown, "the most perfect society now existing in the world."[1] Its perfection, Crevecoeur observed, arose from the fact that "here individuals of all nations are melted into a new race of men"—a new society composed of new people. "What then, is the American, this new man?" Crevecoeur rhetorically asked, then quickly answered his own question: "*He* is an American, who, leaving behind him all his ancient prejudices and manners, receives new ones from the new mode of life he has embraced, the new government it obeys, and the new rank he holds."

Had Crevecoeur set out to paint a portrait of Alexander Hamilton instead of merely offering a generalized commentary, his image of the new American could not have been more fitting. Hamilton was the son of a

[1]Born in France in 1735, Crevecoeur came to America around 1760. Settling in New York, he married an American and became a naturalized citizen. Following the Revolution he served as France's consul in New York. In 1782 Crevecoeur authored *Letters From an American Farmer*, a penetrating inquiry into the nature of the new nation and its people. He returned to France in 1790, where he died in 1813.

Scottish father and French Huguenot mother, born in the British West Indies and brought up in the Danish Virgin Islands—a background so fragmented that he properly belonged to no particular ethnic group. Because he was, in a cultural sense, something of a blank slate when he arrived in America as a teenager, Hamilton embraced its "new mode of life" with enthusiasm and made himself a part of it. He went on not merely to obey its new government but to serve it ably, and to rise to a "new rank" which his humble origins would have precluded anywhere else.

Alexander Hamilton was born on the tiny Caribbean island of Nevis in 1755, "the bastard brat of a Scotch peddler" according to one later critic. Over the next few years his family moved from one island to another as James Hamilton, Alexander's father, tried unsuccessfully to establish himself as a merchant. Despite the hardship caused by repeated business failures, the illegitimate union of his parents endured for ten years after Alexander's birth. At last in 1765, shortly after he had brought his family to St. Croix, James Hamilton abandoned his two children and their mother, leaving them in a state of near-destitution. Other than his name, Alexander Hamilton's father gave him little else.

When Alexander was thirteen years old his mother died, forcing him to go to work. He became a clerk in the counting-house of a local merchant named Nicholas Cruger, but chafed under the limitations of his position, his early poverty having bred in Hamilton a determination to improve himself. At fourteen he confided to a friend his disdain for "the grovelling condition of a Clerk or the like, to which my Fortune, etc., condemns me." Realistically, however, Hamilton recognized "that my Youth excludes me from any hopes of immediate Preferment . . . , but I mean to prepare the way for futurity." Although he had little opportunity to acquire any formal education, Hamilton read voraciously from classical and contemporary authors, studied chemistry and mathematics, and reflected upon ethical and political issues. He also applied himself diligently to his bookkeeping duties, so impressing his employer that in 1771 Cruger appointed the sixteen-year-old acting manager during a temporary absence from St. Croix.

The key to the realization of Alexander's aspiration was his escape from St. Croix—the avenues for advancement available on the island were too few and too short to be appealing. The focus of his hopes was England's American colonies, where his boyhood friend, Edward Stevens, had recently been sent to complete his education. Sooner than he could have expected, Hamilton was able to realize his dream through a fortuitous combination of natural disaster, his own abilities, and the generosity of some fellow islanders.

In August of 1772, a destructive hurricane punished St. Croix. Awed by the violence of the storm, young Hamilton attempted to capture its fury on paper, describing it in a letter. Before mailing it he showed the letter to a Presbyterian minister, Hugh Knox, who had taken an interest in the boy's development. Knox saw in the letter confirmation of Hamilton's potential and published it. The minister used the letter to secure contributions from Cruger and a few other islanders, enabling Alexander to further his education in America. In October of 1772, Alexander Hamilton, spirits soaring, set sail for Boston, proceeding from there to New York.

Upon arriving in New York, Hamilton found a bustling commercial center of approximately 25,000 inhabitants. Already the city possessed the cosmopolitan character that would distinguish it in later years. Well over a dozen languages were spoken on its streets and in its shops. And each week more arrivals from abroad landed at its waterfront with dreams of starting a new life in a new world. Their adopted society was, in the early 1770s, permeated by an air of excitement and tension, stemming from the colonies' confrontation with England over the degree of control which the mother country might exert in America. Economic burdens which had resulted from the recently concluded Seven Years War, piled on top of the debts from previous conflicts, had led Parliament to impose a series of taxes upon the American colonists: the Sugar Act of 1764, the Stamp Act of 1765, the Townshend Duties of 1767. Not only did many Americans resent the tax increases, they were deeply disturbed by the political implications of some of the measures. The Sugar Act, for example, did away with the traditional right to a jury trial in smuggling cases. The Stamp Act, a "direct," "internal" tax, represented an unprecedented Parliamentary intrusion into the prerogatives of the colonial legislatures. Moreover, some Americans were convinced that England deliberately wished to retard the growth of the colonies and keep them dependent through such means as the Proclamation Line of 1763, by which settlement west of the Appalachian Mountains was prohibited. Equally offensive was the crown's refusal in 1773 to permit the naturalization of non-English immigrants to America. The colonies, most of which equated growth with prosperity, viewed the attraction of immigrants as a certain means for economic improvement. Fearing that England's prohibition on naturalizing foreigners might discourage them from coming to America, the colonists protested bitterly against this measure.[2] England's apparent insensitivity to America's complaints led to recalcitrance in the colonies, manifested occasionally by demonstrations, boycotts, and even riots.

Coming from the Virgin Islands, a Danish possession, Hamilton was completely ignorant of these issues. His opinions were, therefore, shaped largely by the company in which he first found himself in America. His letters of introduction from Reverend Knox were addressed to the minister's fellow Presbyterians who, in part because of their opposition to the Church of England, identified with the colonial cause. The impact of these early acquaintances was demonstrated a year later when Hamilton deliv-

---

[2]Three years later, when the Declaration of Independence was drafted, this measure was cited in the list of grievances against King George which justified revolution: "He has endeavoured to prevent the Population of these States; for that purpose obstructing the Laws for Naturalization of Foreigners; refusing to pass others to encourage their migration hither. . . ."

ered a speech vindicating the Boston Tea Party as a legitimate protest against an unjust act. By that time—December of 1773—Hamilton was attending King's College, but his attention was increasingly absorbed by political events.[3] In mid-1774 he began to publish articles in the *New York Journal, or General Advertiser*. More important, he ably (but anonymously) refuted the pro-British arguments of "A Westchester Farmer" in two lengthy pamphlets.

"A Westchester Farmer" was, in fact, the Reverend Samuel Seabury, an articulate Loyalist spokesman. Seabury warned that resistance to England and insistence upon colonial union would bring economic ruin to America. He noted that unless the colonists preferred to go naked they would continue to be dependent upon the importation of woolen and cotton cloth from England. Hamilton responded by insisting that Americans could be selfsufficient, raising their own wool and cotton. What's more, he added, from immigrants America would gain sufficient technical expertise to construct and operate factories. This idea would recur frequently, over many years, in Hamilton's thinking on the subject of economic independence.

The outbreak of fighting at Lexington and Concord in April of 1775 signalled that the time for argument had passed. Hamilton reacted by forming a volunteer company; the next year he was awarded a commission as an officer of artillery. His obvious intelligence and organizational abilities led to Hamilton's rapid promotion: in March of 1777 he was appointed aide-de-camp to George Washington with the rank of lieutenant colonel. Serving in that capacity until 1781, Hamilton made himself invaluable to Washington—offering advice, drafting reports, making decisions, composing regulations. The relationship which developed between the two men was close and enduring. Washington's attitude toward the younger man was paternal. Hamilton's feelings were more complicated, involving elements of devotion, resentment, and calculation. Certainly he viewed the general as a means for advancing his own extensive ambitions—years later Hamilton would describe Washington as "an Aegis very essential to me." A quarrel with Washington in February of 1781 led to Hamilton's return to a field command. Several months later he distinguished himself at the Battle of Yorktown, the last major action of the war.

Few immigrants had Hamilton's opportunities to aid the Revolutionary cause, although Thomas Paine, who arrived from England on the eve of the conflict, played an even more significant role.[4] Still, in less spectacular ways, immigrants made their presence felt in the war. No universal rule of conduct can be discerned in their political affiliations, however. Like

[3]Now Columbia University.

[4]Thomas Paine immigrated from England in 1774. His pamphlet, *Common Sense,* which appeared in January of 1776, considerably influenced American opinion. In it Paine argued persuasively for independence from England. During the Revolution Paine penned *The Crisis,* a series of essays which boosted morale during the most discouraging periods of the struggle.

native-born Americans, immigrants were divided in their views of the Revolution. Factors other than their ethnic background governed identification with one side or the other. The Scotch-Irish in the Carolina Piedmont, for example, remained largely loyal to England, while their counterparts in Virginia and Pennsylvania fought for independence. Johann Buettner, who switched from one side to the other during the conflict, illustrates this point even more clearly.

At the same time that he helped advance America's fortunes, Hamilton promoted his own. Late in 1780 he married Elizabeth Schuyler. Her father was the well-to-do General Philip Schuyler, who represented New York in the Continental Congress. Throughout the war Hamilton had corresponded extensively with Schuyler and other members of Congress on a variety of subjects. His letters indicated Hamilton's misgivings about the loosely structured Articles of Confederation and early established him as an advocate of a stronger, more centralized system of government. Hamilton's correspondence also dealt with the new nation's financial problems, recommending the establishment of a national bank and the devaluation of America's inflated currency. Hamilton's attention to these problems intensified after the victory at Yorktown sealed America's independence. He returned to New York and immersed himself in studying law. In July of 1782, shortly after his admission to the bar, Hamilton was selected by the New York legislature to serve in Congress. The appointment provided Hamilton with the perfect forum to promote the nationalistic views his earlier letters had revealed.

In addition to the complicated matters of concluding a peace treaty, stabilizing the nation's finances, and certifying the structure of its government, America's leaders also had to contend with an upsurge in immigration. During the Revolution the flow of immigrants had been reduced to a trickle, but with the cessation of fighting it had resumed once again, conforming largely to prewar patterns.[5] This development disturbed many Americans, who wondered what impact it might have upon the new nation. Thomas Jefferson in 1782 expressed those misgivings in his volume *Notes on Virginia:*

> They will bring with them the principles of the governments they leave, or if able to throw them off, it will be in exchange for an unbounded licentiousness, passing, as usual, from one extreme to the other. It would be a miracle were they to stop precisely at the point of temperate liberty. These principles, with their language, they will transmit to their children. In proportion to their numbers they will share legislation with us. They will infuse into it their spirit, warp or bias its direction, and render it a heterogeneous, incoherent, distracted mass.

---

[5]The most numerous groups continued to be the Scotch-Irish and the Germans, although German immigration tailed off considerably by the late 1780s. Another source of immigrants was the large number of foreigners involved in the Revolutionary War. See Chapter Four.

Some Americans objected less to the immigrants themselves than to the means which many of them utilized to travel to the United States. In 1784 a public meeting in New York condemned the practice of indentured servitude as "contrary to the idea of liberty this country has so happily established." Still others warmly received the immigrants, viewing them as potentially valuable additions to a sparsely-populated nation. George Washington in 1783 assured some recent arrivals from Ireland that all people, no matter what their condition, were welcome in America: "The bosom of America is open to receive not only the Opulent and respectable Stranger, but the oppressed and persecuted of all Nations and Religions. . . ."[6]

Under the Articles of Confederation the government could take no substantive action on the issue of immigration, except to recommend that the various states prohibit foreign nations from transporting convicted criminals to the United States. On this subject—as with most other matters—the Articles government was essentially powerless.[7] In domestic affairs it could do little more than furnish advice to the states. In foreign relations, where it did exercise authority, the government frequently found its prerogatives imposed upon by the states. It was in the states, rather than at the national level, where the real political powers resided—levying taxes, issuing currency, collecting tariffs. As a consequence, the Articles government was incapable of commanding respect at home or abroad. Foreign trade languished, internal commerce was chaotic, disorder erupted, public debts mounted and went unpaid. These developments convinced numerous Americans of the necessity to restructure and strengthen the government. But many others were deeply suspicious of any such effort, equating centralization with tyranny. After all, they reasoned, hadn't England's recent efforts to centralize her empire led to oppression, forcing the Americans to rebel? It was far better to make do with the existing Articles system, despite its shortcomings, because it diffused power among the states.

From the first Hamilton rejected this notion. "The Confederation gives the States, individually, too much influence," he wrote. As for the possible dangers which restructuring the government might bring, "nothing appears more evident to me than that we run much greater risk of having a weak and disunited federal government, than one which will be able to usurp upon the rights of the people." Because he was an immigrant, Hamilton had no attachment to any particular state, as most native-born Americans did. He did not consider himself a New Yorker. Instead, he

---

[6]Despite the note of invitation in Washington's remarks, he too harbored some doubts about foreigners. During the war he had issued instructions that only native-born Americans should serve in his personal guard, perform sentry duty, or command artillery.

[7]Article IV established that the citizens of each state were the citizens of all other states. Laws governing immigration and naturalization of foreigners, however, remained the responsibility of the individual states. Understandably, there was considerable confusion on the subject of immigration.

identified with the entire American nation, whose birth had so nearly coincided with his own arrival in America. He therefore saw nothing wrong with constructing a political system which would subordinate the states to a higher authority. His brief but revealing experience in the Confederation Congress only reinforced this conviction. Even after he resigned in 1783 to return to private practice, Hamilton continued actively to promote the establishment of a stronger, more centralized system of government.

Hamilton's concerns were shared by a number of prominent men. George Washington, easily the most influential man in America, in 1783 circulated a letter to the state governors. In it he warned of further serious problems for the new nation unless a government powerful enough to "regulate and govern the general concerns of the confederate government" were established. Washington's fellow Virginian, James Madison, shortly thereafter condemned the Articles of Confederation as "nothing more than a treaty of amity and of alliance between independent and sovereign states." Others with similar sentiments included John Jay, Benjamin Franklin, Robert Morris, and John Adams. Initially critics of the Articles aimed at enlarging the responsibilities and powers of the existing government. But successive attempts to do so all ended in failure. In 1781 a measure permitting Congress to collect a 5 percent tax on imports fell one state short of the unanimity required for approval. Two years later a more limited proposal was also defeated. A 1784 amendment granting Congress limited authority to regulate commerce met a similar fate. A different approach was therefore attempted in 1786. The Virginia legislature issued a call to all the states to have a convention "to take into consideration the trade of the United States." The meeting was scheduled for September of 1786 in Annapolis, Maryland.

The idea of a convention to review the Articles of Confederation was not a new one. As early as 1780, Hamilton—barely 25 years old—had asserted that "by calling immediately a Convention, with full authority to conclude finally upon a General Confederation," steps could be taken "to give Congress powers competent to the public exigencies." Although his suggestion had been ignored at the time, Hamilton had not abandoned the idea, even half a dozen years later. The Annapolis convention was rather different from what he had proposed—its focus was much more narrow. Hamilton nevertheless saw it as an opportunity to advance his nationalist views. He therefore engineered his selection as one of New York's delegates to the meeting. The convention proved to be a considerable disappointment. Although nine states had named delegations, representatives from only five of them attended. In large part, this discouraging turnout reflected the suspicions of Articles supporters who feared that the convention would result in an extensive restructuring of the government. Such a poorly attended meeting could clearly accomplish very little, but Hamilton was able to secure the adoption of a report he drafted for the convention. In it he detailed the now-familiar problems of the Confederation government and recommended that the thirteen states send delegates to yet another convention "to devise such further provisions as shall appear to them necessary to render the constitution of the federal government adequate to the exigencies of the Union." Several months later, Congress cautiously added its endorsement, directing delegates to assemble in Philadelphia in May of 1787.

According to the Congressional announcement, "the sole and express purpose" of the meeting was "revising the Articles of Confederation." But the delegates who assembled at Philadelphia clearly intended to accomplish something else. Their sessions were conducted in utmost secrecy, behind doors that were locked and guarded by armed sentries. No reports on the proceedings were released to the public; the delegates themselves were sworn to silence. Such extraordinary precautions indicated their intention to defy their instructions—from the beginning, discussion at the convention was aimed not at the revision of the Articles of Confederation but at their replacement.

Despite the fact that he had secured appointment to the New York delegation, Hamilton felt somewhat frustrated. While the overwhelming majority in the convention shared his "federalist" views regarding the overthrow of the Articles, his fellow New Yorkers did not. Indeed, New York was the only state to send an antifederalist delegation to Philadelphia, submerging Hamilton beneath the combined weight of William Yates and John Lansing. As a consequence, Hamilton remained, for the most part, inactive during the first month of the meeting. Finally, though, he unburdened himself in a lengthy address which one delegate described as "the most able and impressive" speech he had ever heard. Rejecting the terms of debate thus far as too limited, Hamilton outlined a plan which would curtail "the excess of democracy" which he felt plagued the existing government.[8]

Citing the British government as "the best model the world ever produced," he urged election for life of a President and Senate. Hamilton noted that "the people are turbulent and changing; they seldom judge or determine right," and argued that "nothing but a permanent body can check the imprudence of democracy." As for the matter of centralization, he declared "we must establish a general and national government, completely sovereign, and annihilate the state distinctions and state operations," warning "unless we do this, no good purpose can be answered."

Hamilton came to regret the bluntness of his remarks. He would later be accused of advocating "an elective monarchy" and of being an enemy of democracy. But what he apparently intended was to open up discussion to the entire political spectrum, to insure the creation of the best governmental system through the consideration of all alternatives. Not only were his suggestions speculative in nature, Hamilton also made the mis-

---

[8]To this point in the convention debate had largely revolved around the relative merits of the "Virginia Plan," which based representation in Congress upon population (thus favoring the larger states) and the "New Jersey Plan," which would grant each state equal weight regardless of size (obviously an arrangement appealing to the smaller states).

take of assuming that they would not be widely circulated, due to the secrecy cloaking the convention.

The issue of immigration, while not directly considered, nevertheless figured prominently in debate as the delegates wrestled with the question of eligibility for public office. Considering the feelings of nationalism evident in the convention, it is not surprising that a number of delegates spoke against permitting naturalized citizens to serve in Congress. George Mason, proclaiming his distrust of "foreigners and adventurers," pronounced himself in favor of absolutely restricting membership to those born in America. A more moderate position was adopted by Gouverneur Morris, who proposed permitting naturalized citizens to serve in Congress, but only after a lengthy qualifying period had cleansed them of any foreign influence. "Otherwise," he warned, "Americans would find themselves at the mercy of "philosophical gentlemen , . . . citizens of the world as they call themselves." Hamilton countered that such restrictions would deprive the United States of the "obvious and admitted" benefits which immigration provided. Foreigners of standing and fortune, he noted, "will be fond of coming [only] where they will be on a level with the first Citizens." He therefore proposed that while the Presidency be restricted to natives, the Congress be open to all otherwise-qualified citizens. His suggestion was endorsed by James Madison, who pointed out that the states which were growing the fastest in terms of population and wealth were those where immigrants were most welcome.

As was the case with other disputes at the convention, the immigration issue was resolved by a compromise. The Constitution ultimately provided for relatively moderate waiting periods for foreigners to become eligible for Congress. Representatives were required to have been citizens for seven years; nine years' citizenship were needed to qualify for the Senate. The Presidency and Vice Presidency, however, were reserved for natives of the United States.

The Constitution that emerged from the Philadelphia convention bore virtually no trace of Hamilton's influence. He nevertheless committed himself to its adoption, certain that it represented the only realistic alternative to political and social chaos. Hamilton's initial efforts on behalf of the Constitution came in a bitter but inconclusive clash with New York's governor George Clinton in the fall of 1787. Adopting the pseudonym "Cato," Clinton used the vehicle of New York newspapers to attack the newly drafted Constitution. Hamilton responded through the same agency, under the ill-chosen name "Caesar." By the end of October, however, he had discarded his imperial pseudonym for the more reassuring "Publius" and elevated his tone from that of a political brawler to one of lofty persuasion. The occasion for these alterations was Hamilton's launching of a project that would later be labelled "the one product of the American mind that is rightly counted among the classics of political theory." In the first of *The Federalist* papers he announced his intention to publish a series of essays which would contrast conclusively the merits of the Constitution with the shortcomings of the Articles. Eventually *The*

Federalist extended to 85 essays and involved the collaboration of James Madison and John Jay, although all three men wrote anonymously as "Publius." Hamilton played the major role in the project; not only did he initiate *The Federalist*, he authored more than 50 of the papers.

The arguments made by "Publius" on its behalf fueled the federalist movement for the adoption of the Constitution. Success, however, was hardly assured: the antifederalists were firmly entrenched in several critical states, including Hamilton's New York. As a consequence, trickery, bribery, and force had their place beside persuasion in securing the Constitution's ratification. Hamilton had a hand in these activities as well, threatening the New York ratifying convention with the secession of New York City from the state if the Constitution were rejected. His efforts secured, by a narrow margin, New York's adherence to the union.

The adoption of the Constitution did not end the federalists' quest. Their objective was a strong, centralized government—the Constitution merely represented an instrument for the achievement of that end. Hamilton acknowledged as much to George Washington: "It is of little purpose to have *introduced* a system, if the weightiest influence is not given to its *establishment* in the outset." Clearly a great deal depended on the selection of officers to man the new government. Washington's election as President was a foregone conclusion, although his reluctance to serve first had to be overcome by the pleadings of Hamilton and others. John Adams of Massachusetts was elected to the Vice Presidency. As Secretary of State, Washington tapped his fellow Virginian, Thomas Jefferson.

Washington, Adams, Jefferson—a brilliant company. Three men who would monopolize the Presidency for the first twenty years under the Constitution. And yet they were all in some ways overshadowed by the man whom Washington chose to be Secretary of the Treasury, Alexander Hamilton. The policies of the Washington administration would bear his unmistakable stamp; he would be its dominant personality, the apparent focal point of all controversies.

Despite the facts that his law practice was more remunerative than government service and that he had a growing family to support, the thirty-four year old Hamilton experienced no difficulty in deciding to accept the appointment. Upon assuming office in the spring of 1789 he immediately set to work, attempting to bring order out of the fiscal chaos of America. His *Report on Public Credit*, presented to Congress early the next year, outlined a program for paying off the burdensome debts of the national government. Hamilton firmly resisted suggestions that the debt be repudiated, or at least scaled down, arguing that only payment in full could establish the credit of the United States. In addition, he secured the passage of a measure authorizing the federal government to assume the debts of the states, a policy which provided an obvious contrast to the financial dependence of the earlier Articles government. The funding and assumption measures had a political purpose, too: their passage insured for the new government the support of the moneyed classes which held the debts. Hamilton also established the Bank of the United States, capitalized at $10 million, to serve as the government's fiscal agent, stabilize the currency, and promote commercial expansion. Concern over the constitutionality of the Bank, voiced by Madison and Jefferson, was waved aside by the Treasury Secretary.

Obviously these programs would cost a great deal of money. To help furnish the necessary revenue, Hamilton initiated taxes on a number of articles, including whiskey. The weight of the whiskey tax fell squarely on the shoulders of western farmers who frequently distilled their grain crops into alcohol to facilitate transporting their produce to market by reducing its bulk. But western farmers were not particularly important in the Hamiltonian scheme of things. America's future lay, he felt, in the promotion of trade and the establishment of an industrial sector. His *Report on Manufactures*, submitted to Congress in 1791, underscored this point. In it Hamilton proposed the means by which "national independence and safety" could be secured from countries which dominated America economically. Central to such an effort was a tariff that would protect American manufacturers from foreign competition. No less important was "the promoting of emigration from foreign countries."

Returning to the argument he had offered in 1774 in response to "A Westchester Farmer," the Treasury Secretary urged "the attraction of foreign emigrants" as a means to "render the United States independent [of] foreign nations" in an economic sense. Immigrants, Hamilton noted, were "an important resource" because they provided "useful and productive labor . . . for the prosecution of manufactures, without deducting from the number of hands, which might otherwise be drawn to tillage." He argued that the encouragement of immigration would bring to America "ingenious and valuable workmen, in different arts and trade," men who offered not merely labor but much-needed technical expertise as well. To achieve that objective, Hamilton recommended the establishment of a fund "for promoting arts, agriculture, manufactures, and commerce." The resources of the fund would be utilized, in part, "to defray the expense of the emigration of artists, and manufacturers in particular branches of extraordinary importance."

Hamilton regarded the promotion of immigration as particularly important in view of recent English measures aimed at obstructing the departure of artisans. But those British restrictions led President Washington to reject his Secretary's recommendations, explaining that he could hardly urge the subjects of another nation to violate the laws of their government. Undaunted, Hamilton decided to apply his plan unofficially, through the organization of the Society for Establishing Useful Manufactures. In addition to attempting to create a model manufacturing center, he declared that the Society would also try "to procure from Europe skilful workmen. It will not be necessary," Hamilton noted, "that all the requisite workmen should be brought from thence." But, he asserted, immigration would be needed to provide supervisory personnel. The Society did actually dispatch agents abroad to recruit workmen and managers for its factory, but the results proved disappointing. A number of the workmen who immigrated under the Society's auspices had pretended to skills they did not possess. Others failed to serve out the terms of their contracts and deserted the Society's factory.

Still, some progress of the sort which Hamilton desired was made. Other organizations, similar to his Society for Establishing Useful Manufactures, struggled toward the same objective. They offered prizes to inventors, staged conventions, circulated useful information—and tried to lure immigrants. One of the products of this effort was the arrival in 1789 of Samuel Slater, a twenty-two year old English immigrant. Slater came to the United States to claim a prize offered by the Pennsylvania Society for the Encouragement of Manufactures and the Useful Arts for advancement in textile technology. In order to evade English laws which prevented the emigration of artisans, Slater had committed to memory plans for complex machinery, disguised himself, and slipped out of England. He supplied the plans for the spinning jenny, the water frame, and other devices to Moses Brown, a Rhode Island merchant. Together in 1790 they established a cotton factory as sophisticated as any in England and revolutionized industrial production. Samuel Slater was, of course, an exception. Few immigrants during this (or any other) era made contributions to the United States on the scale which he did. Moreover, most new arrivals came on their own initiative rather than under the auspices of some organization promoting industrial growth. And, as one might expect, given the predominantly rural nature of American society, most immigrants were attracted principally by the large amounts of cheap land available.

Many immigrants at this time were more motivated by catastrophe in Europe than by the attractions of America. The political and social chaos accompanying the French Revolution persuaded many to flee across the Atlantic. Hamilton smugly noted in 1791 that the "disturbed state of Europe inclin[es] its citizens to emigration." Europe's loss could be America's gain: "To find pleasure in the calamities of other nations would be criminal," he wrote, "but to benefit ourselves, by opening an asylum to those who suffer in consequence of them, is as justifiable as it is politic." From its outbreak in 1789, the Revolution passed through several stages of increasing radicalism followed by conservative reaction. Each phase produced a new group of exiles, ranging from monarchists to Jacobins. When the Revolution spilled over France's boundaries in 1793 to become an international conflict, still more refugees were created, many of whom sought sanctuary in America. The turbulent events in France horrified conservative governments throughout Europe, prompting them to suppress their own domestic dissidents. Among those displaced in this manner was Joseph Priestley, the chemist who isolated oxygen. Priestley was forced to flee from England to the United States after his support for the Revolution had inspired a mob to attack his home.

The impact of the French Revolution was felt in the United States as well. Initially, the struggle had been universally celebrated in America, but as it increased in violence the Revolution spawned second thoughts among many observers. The pro- and anti-Revolutionary factions which appeared in the United States reflected, to a degree, other political divisions which had only recently appeared, inspired by Hamilton's financial programs. In keeping with the elitist notions which he had enunciated at the Constitutional Convention, Hamilton's policies were designed to benefit the wealthy and the powerful. The funding and assumption bills rewarded speculators who had bought up a majority of governmental debts. The Bank's short-term loan policies assisted merchants and shippers while excluding farmers. Manufacturers received a degree of protection from the tariff. But it was the obviously inequitable whiskey tax which inspired the most resentment and led directly to the Whiskey Rebellion of 1794.[9] The opposition which Hamilton's policies initially aroused was scattered and inconsistent; objection to one measure did not preclude support of another. Yet they did contribute to the polarization of American society into distinct political factions, a process which was amplified by the strains arising from the French Revolution.

These various factors led, by the mid 1790s, to the emergence of the first real political parties in America, the Federalists and the Republicans. The Federalist party generally supported Hamilton's programs and, more importantly, the philosophy behind them. In terms of foreign policy, the Federalists were frightened by the French Revolution and supported England in her struggle against it. Not surprisingly, Alexander Hamilton was one of the acknowledged leaders of the party, as were John Adams and, to an extent, George Washington. The Republicans, on the other hand, looked to Thomas Jefferson and James Madison for direction, sympathized with France in the war with England, and advocated more democratic alternatives to Hamiltonian policies. Bitter competition between the two parties intensified as the French Revolution progressed. The upheaval in Europe cast numerous political radicals and revolutionaries onto America's shores, alarming conservative Federalists. Even more disturbing was the fact that these newcomers tended to gravitate toward the Republican party. One prominent Federalist, Harrison Gray Otis, asserted that he "did not wish to invite hordes of wild Irishmen, nor the turbulent and disorderly of all parts of the world, to come here with a view to disturb our tranquillity, after having succeeded in the overthrow of their own Governments."

One method of safeguarding the Republic was extending the term of residency required of foreigners who wished to become citizens. The first session of Congress had, in 1790, established a relatively brief naturaliza-

---

[9]Their protests against the tax having availed them nothing, farmers in western Pennsylvania resorted to violent demonstrations in 1794. They refused to pay the whiskey tax, abused federal tax collectors, and briefly took over Pittsburgh. Washington summoned 13,000 militiamen from several other states and placed them under Hamilton's direction. Hamilton crushed the Rebellion by arresting several of the "Whiskey Boys" and carrying them east for trial. Washington then pardoned those who were convicted. The whole operation cost several times the amount of money the government could have collected from the tax, but Hamilton considered it well spent: the power and the will of the new federal government had been convincingly demonstrated.

tion period of just two years. That had been accomplished, however, before the effects of the French Revolution had begun to be felt in America. Even then the debate had been a sometimes heated reprise of the arguments offered at the Constitutional Convention. Five years later, as Federalist leaders warned of the dangers represented by "the great numbers of violent men who emigrate to this country from every part of Europe," Congress passed the Naturalization Act of 1795, extending the residency requirements to five years. To the mounting dismay of the Federalists, even this measure did little either to curb the rising tide of immigration or discourage the growth of the Republican party.

Exciting further alarm was the fact that America's turbulent foreign relations appeared to be on the brink of plunging her into the European conflict. Chief Justice John Jay's 1794 treaty with England had temporarily solved several problems between the two countries. England agreed to fulfill an earlier pledge to withdraw its troops from America's Northwest Territory and granted some minor trade concessions in the British West Indies. At the same time, however, the Jay Treaty undermined America's Revolutionary-era pact with France and contributed to a growing breach between the former allies. By 1798 Franco-American relations had deteriorated so far that the two nations engaged in a Quasi-War—an undeclared, but nonetheless real conflict waged on the high seas. Federalist spokesmen urged that the pretense of peace be discarded altogether and outright war declared on France. Hamilton was among those who promoted war fever, constantly urging an enormous expansion of the army. Although no longer in government service—he had returned to private practice in 1795—Hamilton retained considerable political influence. He had helped author George Washington's Farewell Address in 1796 and still functioned as a leader of the more conservative wing of the Federalist party.

Conservatives were as apprehensive about internal turmoil as they were of foreign problems. And, it seemed to some, that recent immigrants lay at the root of that turmoil. "The grand cause of all our present difficulties may be traced . . . to so many *hordes of Foreigners* immigrating to America," complained one Federalist. "Let us no longer pray that America may become an asylum to all nations." In response to such sentiments, the Federalist-dominated Congress adopted another Naturalization Act in 1798, lengthening the residency qualification to fourteen years. Moreover, arguing that the crisis in foreign relations necessitated extraordinary measures, Congress fashioned the Alien and Sedition Acts in the same year. The Alien Acts authorized the President to deport any aliens whom he considered dangerous to the United States. The Sedition Act specifically called for the imposition of stiff fines and lengthy prison sentences for those convicted of uttering false or malicious criticism of the federal government or its officials. The initial draft of the latter measure had been more repressive, forbidding even truthful criticism, but it had been modified, in part through the exercise of Hamilton's influence. The Alien and Sedition Acts were designed ostensibly to safeguard the security of the young republic from unwholesome foreign influence and incendiary domestic criticism, but in reality they represented a thinly veiled blow at the Republican party which many Federalists regarded as an illegitimate opposition.

The impact of that blow was diminished by President John Adams' refusal to invoke the Alien Acts.[10] Hamilton, who subscribed to the notion that "wild Irishmen" and foreign radicals endangered America's stability, found the President's lack of action inexplicable: "Are laws of this kind merely passed to excite odium and remain a dead letter?" He urged his fellow Federalists to "stimulate" Adams to act, but without effect. In contrast, the Sedition Act was applied by the Administration—applied with a vengeance, according to Republicans. The several dozen individuals arrested under its terms all belonged to the opposition party. It was hardly coincidental that many were also immigrants. In fact, the first victim of the Sedition Act was Matthew Lyon, a Vermont Congressman who had come from Ireland in 1765. Lyon was fined $1,000 and sentenced to four months in prison for libeling the President. Most of the others indicted under the Sedition Act were newspaper editors or publishers. James T. Callender, an unprincipled pamphleteer from Scotland, was convicted and jailed. Callender's prosecution gave Hamilton considerable satisfaction, for in 1797 Callender had exposed his adulterous affair with Maria Reynolds, a revelation that caused Hamilton considerable embarrassment. Callender was joined in jail by Thomas Cooper, an English-born editor charged with defaming John Adams in the pages of his newspaper. William Duane, the Irish editor of the Philadelphia *Aurora*, semi-official mouthpiece of the Republican party, narrowly escaped a similar fate. He was indicted under the Sedition Act but acquitted. Duane's acquittal was a disappointment to Hamilton, who had frequently been pricked by his pen. Duane charged that Hamilton had corrupted his office while Treasury Secretary and that he was a paid agent of the British government. To Hamilton's chagrin he found himself unprotected by the Sedition Act.

The repressive tactics of the Federalists backfired in 1800, at the next general election. Designed in part to discourage political participation among recently arrived foreigners, the 1798 naturalization law and the Alien and Sedition Acts instead activated previously apolitical immigrants. The results were especially dramatic in New York, where the Republicans secured a narrow victory due to an unprecedented turnout of Irish and French voters. Their triumph in New York translated into a national victory for the Republican party and its presidential candidate, Thomas Jefferson. Dismayed by the outcome, Hamilton reflected on its causes and realized that the alienation of immigrants had been a major factor in the Federalists' downfall. He concluded that his party might defeat the Republicans in the future by playing their game—paying court to the foreign vote. Hamilton therefore proposed the establishment of an organization, auxiliary to the Federalist party, to embrace and aid newly arrived immigrants, laying the foundation for their eventual incorporation

---

[10]After Washington's decision not to seek reelection in 1796, John Adams secured a narrow victory over the Republican candidate, Thomas Jefferson.

into the party. His suggestion died still-born; few Federalists could even consider—let alone undertake—such a radical alteration in their attitudes. The sincerity of Hamilton's commitment to the idea was itself in doubt. Writing in 1802 as "Lucius Crassus," he noted: "The United States have already felt the evils of incorporating a large number of foreigners into their national mass; . . . it has served very much to divide the community and to distract our councils." Reverting to the alarmist tones of a few years before, he concluded: "The permanent effect of such a policy will be, that in times of great public danger there will be always a numerous body of men, of whom there may be just grounds of distrust; the suspicion alone will weaken the strength of the nation, but their force may be actually employed in assisting an invader."

Other factors besides immigrant votes had helped account for the Republican victory in 1800: a rancorous split within the Federalist party as well as the organizational genius and limitless energies of New York's principal Republican, Aaron Burr. Burr's career had frequently collided with Hamilton's own throughout the years, resulting in an accumulation of mutual distaste for each other. As two of the most able lawyers in New York in the 1780s and 1790s, Hamilton and Burr had frequently fenced with each other in court. But it was Burr's boundless political ambition which drove a wedge between them. In 1789 Burr had allied himself with New York's governor George Clinton, a bitter rival of Hamilton and his father-in-law, Philip Schuyler. The next year Burr shamelessly made overtures to Hamilton for the latter's support in seeking the governorship. With considerable satisfaction, Hamilton was able to thwart Burr's bid for the statehouse. Burr's rampant ambition ultimately led him to seek the Presidency in 1800, a quest which Hamilton fiercely opposed. Labelling Burr "unfit and dangerous" and "an embryo Caesar," Hamilton helped secure his defeat, although at the cost of installing as chief executive his other great rival, Thomas Jefferson.[11]

Four years later, Hamilton blocked Burr's path again when he helped deny Burr the governorship a second time. These repeated frustrations left Burr in a murderous mood. Seizing as a pretext a slur Hamilton allegedly made at a private dinner, Burr challenged him to a duel. Although morally opposed to dueling—his son Philip had been killed in such an encounter four years before—Hamilton felt compelled by honor to meet Burr. Having privately resolved not to fire at his opponent, Hamilton was no match for Burr, who was an experienced marksman. Hamilton suffered a fatal wound and died on July 12, 1804.

In his brief life—less than half a century—Alexander Hamilton rose from the obscurity of an illegitimate birth on a remote island to a position of power and influence almost unrivalled in America. Far from impeding

---

[11]Prior to the adoption of the Twelfth Amendment in 1804 there were no separate elections for President and Vice President; the runner-up received the lesser post. In 1800 Jefferson and Burr, Republican candidates for President and Vice President, respectively, tied in the electoral college, forcing the question into the House of Representatives for a decision. There the deadlock persisted through three dozen more ballots until it was at last broken in Jefferson's favor.

his climb, Hamilton's foreign origins actually assisted him in formulating the nationalistic views which became his hallmark. Divided in his own attitude toward other immigrants, Hamilton personified the mood of a nation which sought them as a stimulus to economic growth but distrusted their political impact.

FURTHER READING

KETCHAM, RALPH. *From Colony to Colony: The Revolution in American Thought, 1750–1820*. New York: Macmillan Publishing Co., 1974.

KETTNER, JAMES H. *The Development of American Citizenship, 1608–1870*. Chapel Hill: University of North Carolina Press, 1978.

McDONALD, FORREST. *Alexander Hamilton: A Biography*. New York: W.W. Norton and Co., 1979.

MITCHELL, BROADUS. *Alexander Hamilton: A Concise Biography*. New York: Oxford University Press, 1976.

ST. JOHN DE CREVECOEUR, J. HECTOR. *Letters From an American Farmer*. London: J.M. Dent and Sons, 1926.

SMITH, JAMES MORTON. *Freedom's Fetters: The Alien and Sedition Laws and American Civil Liberties*. Ithaca, New York: Cornell University Press, 1956.

John Hughes

*Courtesy of Harry T. Peters Collection, Museum of the
City of New York.*

7

John Hughes

ALTHOUGH HIS HEALTH was failing, within the rusting cage of his body the old man's spirit refused to yield. After nearly half a century in America John Hughes still burned with resentment toward England. "When I was a boy," he recalled bitterly, ". . . for five days I was on a social and civil equality with the most favored subjects of the British empire. These five days [were] the interval between my birth and my baptism."

His Irish heritage and his Catholic christening condemned Hughes at his birth in 1797 to a degraded status. For centuries Protestant England had ruled Catholic Ireland in a harsh manner. The Irish, in turn, periodically rebelled, although without lasting success. In the 1640s and 1650s the English civil war afforded a brief chance for another uprising, but it was crushed by the Puritan warrior, Oliver Cromwell. Many of the Irish rebels were killed; others were sold into servitude in England's New World possessions. Land owned by Catholics was confiscated and redistributed to Protestants, so that by 1660 Ireland's small Protestant minority owned three quarters of the land.

A generation later the same rebellion which drove the Logan family to seek temporary refuge back in Scotland resulted in the imposition of the notorious Penal Laws. These measures were designed to insure the political, social and economic subordination of the Catholics who comprised 80 percent of the Irish population. They were not permitted to vote, sit in Parliament, serve on a jury, teach school, enroll in a university, work for the government, carry a gun, or publish or sell books. Catholics, under the Penal Laws, could not purchase land from Protestants. When a Catholic landowner died, his holdings had to be divided among all his sons, to promote their mutual impoverishment. If the son of a Catholic converted to Protestantism, he could dispossess his father immediately, taking over the entire estate. A Catholic was not allowed to own a horse valued above

£5; if he did, any Protestant could compel its sale for £5. Under the Penal Laws Catholic priests were confined to their parishes and severely limited in their activities. They had to register with the Anglican authorities or be physically branded. The priest who dared marry a Catholic to a Protestant risked a penalty of death.

Such restrictions, some of which persisted into the twentieth century, victimized Irish Catholics in countless ways. At the funeral of Hughes' younger sister the priest was barred from entering the graveyard; he could only bless a handful of soil outside the gate and pass it to a layman to sprinkle upon the grave. Fifty years later, his recollection of this incident still caused Hughes to cry.

John spent his boyhood on a small farm in Ulster, where hostility between Catholics and Protestants was most intense. Although his father's reputation as a peaceful, quiet man shielded the family from the violence inevitably spawned by religious rivalry, they could not entirely escape it. On one occasion when he was fifteen, John was seized by several Protestants who threatened him with bayonets before letting him go.

The Hughes family, like the overwhelming majority of Catholics in Ireland, rented the small plot of land on which they scratched out a living. The economic insecurity which had stimulated Scotch-Irish emigration in 1717 was institutionalized against Catholics: the Penal Laws prohibited long-term leases, and absentee landlords customarily raised rents with each extension of a lease. Furthermore, the flax which John's family cultivated (and made into linen during the winter months) provided them with an income that was far from secure. The year 1815 was particularly bad in the linen trade, a situation made worse by the failure of other crops. Consequently, John was forced to drop out of school to help support the family. That was, for him, a bitter disappointment, as he was an eager and hard-working student who aspired to become a priest.

Hard times extended well beyond the Hughes family. The end of the Napoleonic Wars that same year triggered a collapse in argicultural prices throughout western Europe, as American products—till then held back by a quarter century of warfare—flooded the market. The effects of this collapse were most severely felt in Ireland, which had the greatest population density and the least diversified economy in Europe. In response, some Irish landlords began to convert their land from cultivation to grazing purposes, a process which necessitated the eviction of thousands of tenant farmers. These conditions understandably precipitated a growing exodus from Ireland. For several decades prior to this, emigration from Ireland had been a mere trickle, held back by the war and by measures that restricted the departure of artisans and limited the number of passengers permitted on ships.[1] But shortly after the war ended, the British gov-

---

[1]In 1788 Parliament extended to Ireland its long-standing ban against the emigration of artisans from England. The Passenger Act of 1803 had even greater consequences. Ostensibly a humanitarian measure to relieve overcrowding on ships, the Passenger Act actually was designed to restrict emigration to the United States. As a result of the reduction in the number of passengers they were allowed to carry, ships' fares were increased, limiting emigration further still.

ernment began to loosen its regulations. In addition, the dramatic increase in transatlantic commerce produced a spectacular reduction in fares on ships returning to the United States empty of cargo. This combination of circumstances revolutionized immigration to America.

In 1816 John's father and older brother, goaded by the double curse of chronic poverty and British oppression, sailed to America. After renting a house in Chambersburg, Pennsylvania, they began working to finance the fares of the rest of the family. By mid-1818 they were all reunited and relatively secure, enabling John to revive his ambition of obtaining an education. The next year he applied to St. Mary's College and Seminary in Emmitsburg, Maryland, but was rejected. Undaunted, he secured a job as a gardener at the school, working in exchange for instruction that would qualify him for admission. In the fall of 1820 Hughes enrolled in the seminary and spent the next six years there, training to become a priest. The head of the seminary, the Right Reverend John Du Bois, himself an immigrant from France, was impressed by the younger man's dedication and took a special interest in Hughes' education and subsequent career.

Late in 1826 Hughes was ordained a priest and dispatched to Philadelphia. America's small Catholic population, made up largely of immigrants, was centered in the cities of the Northeast. Impoverished Irish men and women, arriving in the United States with little more than the clothes on their backs, usually could not afford to continue into the American interior. Their poverty not only dictated location of their settlement, it also required the Catholic Church in the United States to become more than simply an ecclesiastical organization; it also served as a social agency which established and maintained hospitals, schools, orphanages, and almshouses. In this context, one of Hughes' first projects at his new post in Philadelphia was to organize St. John's Orphan Asylum.

As an immigrant from Ireland ministering to the needs of even more recent arrivals from that country, Hughes inevitably remained closely tied to his homeland. Parliament's passage of the Irish Emancipation Bill in 1829 prompted him to observe, "It is the commencement of a new era in the history of our hapless country."[2] Hughes marked the occasion by holding a thanksgiving service at which he preached an emotional sermon. He subsequently published his remarks in a pamphlet which he dedicated to Daniel O'Connell, an Irish nationalist leader. Shortly thereafter, the *Church Register*, an Episcopalian newspaper published in Philadelphia, denounced the Emancipation Bill and warned that it would lead to aggressive actions by Catholics in America. Hughes responded with

[2]The Catholic Emancipation Bill represented something less than its label suggests. It actually *reduced* the number of Catholics permitted to vote, but for the first time allowed Catholics to seek political office. Specifically, the Emancipation Bill opened to Catholics all public offices except those of Regent, Lord Chancellor of England and Ireland, and Lord Lieutenant of Ireland. In addition it prescribed for public officials new oaths—or revised existing ones—which satisfied Catholic objections to previous oaths. On the other hand, it restricted the number of Catholics permitted to vote by raising the property requirement from 40 shillings to £10. An accompanying piece of legislation suppressed the Catholic Association, a militant organization of Catholic voters led by Daniel O'Connell.

several letters published in the *United States Gazette,* a leading local paper. Casting himself as the Catholic champion, Hughes entered the lists against any and all Protestant critics of his church, a role he would play with equal parts of skill and relish for the next 45 years.

Anticatholic sentiments, such as those expressed in the *Church Register,* were by no means unusual in nineteenth century America. In fact, they came very naturally. The American colonies, after all, had been founded during the aftermath of the Reformation. Militant Protestantism had been transplanted to the colonies by John Winthrop's Puritans and reinforced by later additions to colonial society, including Scotch-Irish Presbyterians, as well as German pietists and French Huguenots. The fact that the principal enemies of colonial Americans—the French in Canada and the Northwest, the Spanish in Florida and the Southwest—were Catholics only intensified the existing religious antagonism. These feelings had been manifested in the American reaction to the Quebec Act passed by Parliament in 1774 and quickly labelled one of the Intolerable Acts by the colonists. The Quebec Act extended the boundaries of the province of Quebec—recently conquered from France in the Seven Years War—south to the Ohio River and within that territory protected the French language, customs and institutions, including the Catholic Church. Colonists viewed this as the enlargement of a dangerous, autocratic institution which threatened their way of life. It was one of the last straws leading to the Revolution.

After the American Revolution anticatholic passions subsided for a time, but they revived during the 1820s, largely because of the rapid growth of the Catholic Church. In 1810 Catholics made up only about one percent of the total American population, but within a generation their proportions increased nearly six times over.[3] This growth was due almost entirely to the influx of immigrants, primarily from Ireland. To compound American anxiety on the subject, "evidence" began to emerge which appeared to confirm the fear that Catholicism harbored aggressive designs upon America. In 1828 Friedrich von Schlegel, a Catholic scholar and German diplomat, delivered a series of lectures in which he denounced the United States as a "nursery for revolution." This was fairly typical of the sentiments voiced by spokesmen of the reaction which gripped post-Napoleonic Europe. Von Schlegel gave a religious cast to his remarks by linking democracy with Protestantism and monarchy with Catholicism. He further urged the establishment of Catholic missions in the United States to serve as bulwarks against the spread of dangerous democratic notions. Within the next few years, in apparent response to von Schlegel's remarks, groups like the Leopold Society and the Catholic Association for

[3]In 1810, out of a population of 7,239,881, there were approximately 75,000 Catholics, or one percent of the total. By 1840, the proportion reached six percent: about 1,000,000 Catholics in a total population of 17,069,453. In 1860 the Catholic Church was the largest American denomination: its 3,000,000 members represented nearly ten percent of the total population of 31,443,321.

the Propagation of the Faith were organized in Europe to support the formation of Catholic overseas missions.

These developments inspired fears in the United States of a secret, subversive Catholic plot. Beginning around 1830 several American newspapers charged that the Catholic Church was the agent of reactionary European governments bent on overthrowing democracy in America. Variations upon this theme included claims that the Catholic Church was trying to seize control of several western states by flooding them with immigrants, and reports that the Pope was planning to move his center of operations from the Vatican to Cincinnati. Respected figures like the inventor and painter Samuel F.B. Morse and the Reverend Lyman Beecher inflamed public opinion with books entitled *Imminent Dangers to the Free Institutions of the United States through Foreign Immigration* and *A Plea for the West*. Anticatholic journals and newspapers, with alarmist titles like *Priestcraft Exposed, Spirit of '76,* and *Downfall of Babylon*, further aggravated tensions.

In order to insure that the Protestant crusaders did not monopolize the printed page in Philadelphia, Hughes early in 1833 established *The Catholic Herald*. For the first few weeks of its publication he functioned as the *Herald*'s editor, before relinquishing control to an associate. A few years earlier Hughes had utilized a less direct approach as a means for discrediting a particularly abusive New York weekly called *The Protestant*. Under the tongue-in-cheek pseudonym of "Cranmer," he submitted several outrageous and patently false anticatholic reports, including one which gave a detailed description of a nonexistent Jesuit academy in Pittsburgh.[4] *The Protestant* delightedly published these contributions as fact and editorially heaped praise upon its vigilant correspondent, whom it labelled "our friend," "this genuine Protestant." After carrying on the hoax through the first half of 1830, Hughes finally revealed the actual facts of the situation in a letter to the *Truth Teller*, a Catholic journal published in New York. Signed "A Catholic," the letter was addressed "To the 'Ministers of the Gospel' who have recommended *The Protestant* to the patronage of a Christian public." Hughes commented upon the "editorial depravity" of the paper and noted that "it is remarkable that the greater the slander the greater the eulogium bestowed upon me by the editor, and the better Protestant he said I was! . . . He saw in my anonymous communications a number of falsehoods which I rendered obvious and palpable *on purpose;* but they were against Catholics, and he immediately pronounced me a 'genuine Protestant'. . . . In this, gentlemen, you pay a dear-bought compliment to your religion."

Hughes was, if anything, even more aggressive in campaigning under his own name. One of his most noteworthy skirmishes took place in 1832 when he crossed pens with the Reverend John Breckinridge, a prominent Presbyterian minister, former chaplain of Congress, and the editor of a

---

[4]Thomas Cranmer, the first Archbishop of Canterbury, was one of the leaders of the Protestant Reformation in England.

"The American River Ganges"

By Thomas Nast, Harper's Weekly, 1871.

religious newspaper. Their inconclusive exchange took place in the pages of *The Presbyterian*, a Philadelphia weekly. Out of this epistolary confrontation there emerged a more direct one: early in 1835 Hughes and Breckinridge met in a public encounter to wrestle with the question "Is the Protestant/Catholic Church inimical to civil or religious liberty?" Their debate generated more heat than light, conducted as it was in vicious, personal terms.

The efforts of Hughes and other Catholic defenders were to no avail, as the Protestant attacks continued. Inevitably the hostility which these verbal assaults revealed also found expression in violence. Public meetings and debates sometimes degenerated into demonstrations and riots. Mobs motivated by anticatholic hatred and fear were naturally drawn to the most visible symbols of their enemies. In 1831 St. Mary's Cathedral of New York was burned to the ground by Protestant rioters. Three years later another mob attacked and destroyed one of the best-known Catholic institutions, the Ursuline Convent and school in Charlestown, Massachusetts, a Boston suburb. This incident occurred the day after Lyman Beecher preached especially inflammatory sermons in three different churches.

Anticatholic demonstrators often justified their attacks upon convents and cathedrals by claiming that those institutions were dens of iniquity which housed all sorts of obscene activities. Attention had first been focussed on the Ursuline Convent by the accusations of Rebecca Reed, a vindictive, recently fired servant at the convent, who charged that the nuns engaged in sexual relations with priests. She expanded upon these charges in an 1835 book, *Six Months in a Convent*. The following year *Awful Disclosures of the Hotel Dieu Nunnery of Montreal* appeared, authored by a supposed nun named Maria Monk. Monk improved upon Reed's story, claiming that a secret tunnel connected the Canadian convent with a nearby monastery, enabling lecherous priests to have free access to the nuns. She further charged that the babies born of such illicit unions were baptized, then murdered and buried in a pit in the convent's cellar. Monk's credibility was aided by the fact that she was quite pregnant, the result, she said, of being raped by a priest.

The success of *Awful Disclosures* inspired a host of imitations, authored by an avalanche of purported nuns recently fled from convents. They were, for the most part, little more than thinly disguised pornography. Typical of the genre was *Rosamond, or a Narrative of the Captivity and Sufferings of an American Female, Under the Papish Priests in the Islands of Cuba*. In addition to the standard exposé of sexual licentiousness, *Rosamond* revealed how Cuban priests captured and killed young blacks, ground them into sausage, and sold them to the unsuspecting Protestants. This was, needless to say, wildly sensational stuff which defeated all attempts by Hughes and other Catholic spokesmen to address the issues in a rational and honest way.

His visibility as a defender of the faith helped Hughes to climb rapidly up the hierarchical ladder of the Church. Already recommended (but passed over) for the bishopric of Philadelphia, he was in 1837 named co-adjutor to the Bishop of New York, his former mentor, John Du Bois. Scarcely two weeks after Hughes assumed his new post, Du Bois suffered a paralytic stroke from which he never fully recovered. As a result, most of the Bishop's duties devolved upon his new assistant. These developments symbolized what was taking place on a larger scale within the Church. Since the 1790s, when revolutions in France and Santo Domingo had sent a wave of French refugees to America's shores, the Catholic Church in the United States had been dominated by French clerics like Du Bois. But with the surge of immigrants from Ireland some thirty years later, the French began to be replaced by the Irish in the offices of the Church.

For most immigrant groups the church played an important role. It represented order, continuity, and tradition in lives that were disrupted by change. It provided a link with the past for people cut off from their roots. It offered consolation, guidance, charity, and assistance. But for Catholics from Ireland, their church was especially important; they were particularly close to it. On the European continent the Catholic Church was rich and powerful, part of the establishment. In Ireland, however, it was as impotent and persecuted as the Irish people themselves. The result of their mutual misery was an extremely tight bond between the Catholic Church and the Irish, a relationship that was transplanted from Ireland to the United States. The Church exercised an enormous amount of influence over the lives of its Irish members: it presided at their births, marriages, and deaths; it saw to their education and their spiritual nourishment. Conversely, the Irish had a tremendous impact upon the Catholic Church in America: they filled its ranks as nuns, priests, and bishops and transformed it from a small and despised sect into the largest religious organization in the country.

As *de facto* head of the New York diocese (which included much of New Jersey) Hughes in 1838 presided over nearly 200,000 Catholics, about two dozen churches, and some 40 priests. Reflecting his earlier dedication to learning, one of Hughes' first actions was to authorize the establishment of a college in western New York. This represented a miscalculation on his part; the rural location proved too remote to attract or serve the overwhelmingly urban Catholic population. He moved to correct this problem in 1839 by planning the establishment of St. John's College (later renamed Fordham) in New York City. Since only some of the funds for his projects could be raised locally, Hughes felt compelled to go abroad to seek more support. Late in 1839 he sailed for Europe. His travels took him, among other places, to Paris, where he was presented to King Louis Philippe; to Rome, where he was received by the Pope; and to Vienna, where he met Prince Metternich, the architect and symbol of the reactionary mood which dominated official Europe. While in Vienna, Hughes appealed for financial aid to the Leopold Society, so dreaded by American Protestants, and was rewarded with a substantial grant. His letter to the Society succinctly spelled out the relationship between his immigrant flock and the Catholic Church and described their mutual poverty.

> There are many privations, especially of a moral character, incident to the life of the poor emigrant in America, even when he is conscious of improving his temporal comforts. The wealth, the manners, sometimes the language, and generally the more elevated condition in society of the people by whom he is surrounded, remind him constantly that he is not in the land of his fathers nor among the companions of his youth. It is only when he has the consolations of his religion within his reach that he feels comparatively happy in his new position. . . . The people contribute liberally according to their means, but it must be remembered that they are only poor emigrants, just commencing in a new country.

Just two months before his departure for Europe, papal instructions directed Hughes to replace the ailing Bishop Du Bois as administrator of the diocese. For the next three years Hughes served as Bishop in all things except name. Du Bois' death in December of 1842 would enable Hughes to assume the official title as well.

Upon his return from Europe in July 1840, Hughes found himself suddenly plunged into a bitter dispute over an issue of enormous importance to him and his followers—the place of Catholics in the public school system. In New York, public funds were distributed to various charitable agencies which bore the responsibility for maintaining the public schools. The funds in New York City were largely controlled by the Public School Society, an organization dominated by Protestants. The result was a school system in which the books used (including the King James version of the Bible) were often offensive to Catholics and the teachers were sometimes militantly and outspokenly anticatholic. Consequently, only a handful of Catholic children attended public schools; others were enrolled in a few inadequate parochial schools, but as Hughes had noted in his letter to the Leopold Society, the Church was simply too poor to offer this alternative to all Catholic children. Many of them, therefore, did not go to school at all—Hughes estimated that as many as one half of the Catholic school-age children were being denied an education. According to Governor William H. Seward, "one-fourth or one-fifth of the children of New York [are] left to grow up without education." The same problem existed in other states as well.

This was a matter of considerable concern for Seward, who believed that education held the key to the realization of America's democratic ideals. In his annual message of 1840, he therefore urged revision of the school system to permit the establishment of public schools staffed by teachers "speaking the same language . . . professing the same faith" as their students. This essentially meant contributing public funds to schools that would be administered by Catholics. Seward's proposal touched off an explosion of popular indignation. The governor was denounced for "sapping the foundations of liberty" and charged with "plotting the ruin of the State." Public anger burned even more intensely when Catholics applied to the city council of New York for a share of the public school funds.[5] Hughes scornfully denounced the public outcry over this petition by noting "we are citizens when they come to us to gather the taxes, but we are Roman Catholics when we look for a share of the fund thus contributed."

In support of the petition Hughes appealed to Protestant New Yorkers' sense of fair play: "in Ireland [the Catholic] was compelled to support a church hostile to his religion, and here he is compelled to support schools in which his religion fares but little better, and to support his own schools besides." In addition he held several rallies to demonstrate Catholic support for the petition and argued forcefully before the city council for its approval. Despite his efforts, the application was rejected by the council. The issue was then carried to the state assembly, but there it stalled, pending the outcome of the 1841 election, which would determine the composition of the legislature's next session.

The political scene was not particularly promising to the Catholics: neither of the two major parties appeared very supportive of their application for aid. The Federalist Party of Alexander Hamilton had long since

---

[5]This issue was not resolved until the Supreme Court ruled in June 1977 that public funds could be used to support parochial education, provided the funds were paid directly to students rather than to schools.

gone into eclipse, but it had been replaced by the Whigs, who were, if anything, even less inclined to sympathize with the aspirations of immigrants. The old Republican organization had metamorphosed into the Democratic Party, but while it retained both its posture of solicitude for immigrants and their consequent support, in this particular instance the Party appeared unwilling to risk losing any Protestant votes in its effort to wrest control of the legislature away from the Whigs. Neither party, therefore, nominated candidates who publicly favored providing support for parochial schools.

With less than two weeks to go before the election, Hughes staged a rally of the city's Catholic voters at which he exhorted them to ignore party affiliations and instead vote only for advocates "of the free and unrestricted education of your children." Having prepared the ground with this speech, Hughes four days later held a meeting to announce the formation of a city-wide ticket favorable to the Catholic position, consisting of ten of the candidates already on the Democratic ticket and five new candidates. He urged the cheering crowd to seize control of their political destiny and secure the establishment of an educational system that reflected their interests.

> You now, for the first time, find yourselves in the position to vote at least for yourselves. You have often voted for others, and they did not vote for you, but now you are determined to uphold with your own votes, your own rights. Will you then stand by the rights of your offspring, who have for so long a period, and from generation to generation, suffered under the operation of this injurious system?

The Democrats endorsed by Hughes, horrified at the prospect of a Protestant backlash, immediately disavowed any connection to his scheme. Furious editorials condemned his threat to the American principle of free elections and the separation of church and state. "Will the people of this Protestant country stand this?" asked one newspaper angrily. Another saw in Hughes' action confirmation of the dreaded Catholic conspiracy to seize control of the United States. "The foot of the beast [is] trampling on the elective franchise and His High Priest [is] standing before the *ballot box*, the citadel of American liberties, dictating to his obedient followers the ticket they must vote."

The election resulted in a statewide victory for the Democrats. In New York City the ten Democrats supported by Hughes won election; however, the other five, who had been opposed by his independent candidates, were defeated by their Whig opponents. This was a lesson which was not lost on the Party's leaders. Shortly after the legislature began its 1842 session a bill was introduced which would essentially establish local control over the public schools, enabling the Catholic wards in New York to elect their own school boards and control their own schools. The measure's Democratic sponsor quietly conferred with Hughes before submitting it to the Assembly, the legislature's lower house. Word of their meeting leaked out, causing a minor flap, but it did not impede the rapid passage of the measure. In the Senate, however, the bill encountered considerable opposition and stalled. Once again, Catholic voters flexed their political muscles. Shortly before an April election in New York City to choose a mayor and other municipal officials, Catholics held another rally to select their own candidates. Just three days before the election, nervous Democrats managed to squeeze the school bill through the Senate by a one-vote margin. The Catholic candidates then withdrew from the race, enabling the relieved Democrats to secure their usual quota of immigrant votes.

Election day found the city in the grip of tension, which that evening exploded into violence. Thousands of people milled around in the streets as Protestant and Catholic gangs clashed with each other. One anticatholic mob made its way to St. Patrick's Cathedral and attacked the official residence at its rear. Rioters bombarded the house with brickbats and paving stones, shattering several of the windows. The door was smashed in and much of the furniture demolished. Hughes was not at home, but Bishop Du Bois was, confined to his sickbed. The mob broke all of the windows in his room before being driven off by the police.

Although passage of the school bill represented a victory for Hughes and offered relief for Catholic children, he saw it as only a "partial redress." It insured that Catholic students would no longer be subjected to a Protestant-flavored curriculum in the public school, but it also meant that their training would be devoid of Catholic instruction. Hughes did not believe that religion should be removed from the schoolroom; in fact, he regarded religious instruction as the foundation for a proper education, provided that the religious instruction was of the "correct" sort. So he viewed the school bill as merely a temporary expedient, useful until the Church could afford to develop and adequately fund a system of parochial schools. Catholics would be "obliged to tolerate the attendance of our poor children at these schools, until we should, with time and the blessing of Almighty God, be enabled to erect schools of our own for their exclusively Catholic training."

It would be a long time before that ambition could be realized. In the next few years the already strained resources of the Church would be taxed even further by the necessity of ministering to a rapidly growing flood of immigrants from Ireland. The economic insecurity and political oppression which had persuaded the Hughes family to emigrate had in fact grown even worse over the next several decades. As a result, the annual volume of Irish immigration to the United States had steadily increased, from about 9,000 in 1817 to over 90,000 by 1842. In the late 1840s a further deterioration of conditions drove even larger numbers of Irish from their homes.

Famine was no stranger to Ireland, but it had never before visited the island on the scale on which it appeared shortly before mid-century. A blight destroyed the potato crop for four successive years, from 1845 through 1848, depriving Irish peasants of their principal source of food. Prior to this they had usually existed on the brink of starvation. According to a report prepared for Parliament shortly before the Great Famine (during a time of "comparative plenty") "their food commonly consists of dry potatoes; and with these they are at times so scantily supplied as to be obliged to stint themselves to one spare meal in the day. . . . They sometimes get a herring, or a little milk; but they never get meat, except at Christmas, Easter, or Shrove tide." Compounding the tragedy, a cholera epidemic ravaged the already weakened population in 1846 and 1847. The result was that in just five years out of a total population of eight and a half million, at least a million Irish died of starvation or fever.

Horrified by the reports that reached it, the Irish community in the United States offered what little relief it could. Bishop Hughes diverted $14,000 from his carefully hoarded education fund to help alleviate the distress, noting, "It is better that seminaries should be suspended than that so large a portion of our fellow-beings should be exposed to death by starvation." The Philadelphia Irish dispatched seven ships loaded with food for the famine victims. But those and other contributions from America were mere drops in an otherwise empty bucket.

The only real prospect for salvation lay in escape from Ireland, and as many of the Irish as were able to do so fled their homeland. From 1846 to 1854, more than one and three quarters million Irish emigrated, the vast majority going to the United States. The 1860 census would reveal that more than 5 percent of America's population had been born in Ireland.

The wretched conditions in Ireland owed a great deal to that land's occupation and exploitation by the English. Hughes stressed this point in an 1847 lecture, "On the Antecedent Causes of the Irish Famine" (his remarks were originally titled "The Tyrant and His Famine; or, the Irish Tragedy of Six Hundred Years"). Inevitably, the tragedy helped inspire in 1848 another of the periodic rebellions against British rule. And just as inevitably, the uprising was crushed. Although Hughes believed "if ever there was a country that could be justified for such an attempt in the sight of heaven and man, it would be Ireland," he opposed the rebellion because there was "no rational prospect of success." Yet the rebels so clearly reflected his own views that, against his better judgment he attended, in August of 1848, a fund-raising rally held on their behalf in New York. Caught up in the excitement of the moment, Hughes declared, "I come among you, gentlemen, not as an advocate of war—it would ill accord with my profession. . . . My object in coming here was to show you that in my conscience I have no scruple in aiding the cause in every way worthy a patriot and a Christian." After concluding his speech, Hughes ceremoniously contributed $500.

The Irish rebellion of 1848 sprang not only from domestic causes; it was also part of a wave of revolution which swept through Europe in that year, toppling the government of France and shaking others in Austria, Italy, and throughout Germany. The common denominator in each of these uprisings was the involvement of liberal, often middle-class, ideologues organized variously as Young Italy, Young Germany, and Young Ireland. Hughes, bitterly disappointed by the failure of the revolution, blamed Young Ireland, claiming that it had divided the rebels and confused their efforts. "The curse of Young Ireland is more calamitous than the potato famine," he thundered, and hinted that only a fraction of the contributions made to the organization had actually gone to support the struggle.

Following the revolution, many of the rebels fled to the United States. In an attempt to explain their failure, some of them blamed the Catholic clergy for betraying them outright or at least withholding support. Hughes furiously resisted such accusations, engaging in another of his frequent newspaper debates. Few of the refugee revolutionaries abandoned hope for the liberation of their homeland; instead, many of them organized nation-alist clubs and revolutionary societies to continue working toward that end. Hughes, who took a back seat to no one in his devotion to Ireland, nevertheless cautioned against membership in such groups. "Never forget your country; love her, defend her when the time comes," he advised. "But let this love of old Ireland affect you only individually. In your social and political relations you must become merged in the country of your adoption."

The Bishop's instructions notwithstanding, Irish immigrants fre-quently found it difficult to "become merged." Overwhelmingly peasants, their lack of marketable skills greatly restricted their employment possi-bilities. For the most part they became unskilled laborers or, in the case of women, domestic servants. Large numbers of Irish men found employ-ment on canal construction projects—hard, killing work that required them to stand waist-deep in icy water. Jobs in construction or household service often involved extended absence from home and contributed to reducing the importance of the nuclear family. This merely amplified a tendency toward diminished family life which was already evident in Ireland, where a pattern of delaying or even forgoing marriage had evolved in response to the extreme poverty so common there.

The proportion of unskilled workers among America's Irish exceeded that of any other immigrant group by a considerable margin at mid-century. The heaviest, dirtiest, most dangerous jobs were habitually re-served for the Irish. The wages they received were at the subsistence level, fifty cents or a dollar for a long day's labor. Sometimes construction bosses gave their Irish workers part of their pay in whiskey, a policy designed to keep them drunk, broke, and dependent.

So the Irish settled into eastern cities, where they lived jammed into ramshackle tenements, shanties, and cellars in the worst parts of town. For most of them, living and working conditions were such that some sort of escape was a necessity; many of them found that escape in the bottle. The saloon, in fact, became a focal point of Irish life in America. The inescapable companion to their drinking was violence, a problem ampli-fied by the fact that many Irish men and boys belonged to gangs. Actually gang membership was not unusual among other ethnic groups as well. Gangs offered opportunities of association for people who were often excluded from the American mainstream; they provided a means for combatting the feeling of alienation and isolation common to many immigrants.

Because of their drinking habits, their sometimes violent behavior, their lack of skills, their adherence to a despised religion, and the generally miserable condition of their lives, a stereotype rather unfavorable to the Irish took root in America. They were viewed as rowdy, unproductive, disease-ridden, and dangerous. Prejudice against the Irish, reflecting this stereotype, was widespread. They were excluded from the better hotels and restaurants, which posted signs declaring "No Irish allowed." They were prevented from seeking many jobs by the ever-present proscription "No Irish need apply." Of course American cities were not noted for their decency, safety, order, cleanliness, or sobriety *before* the Irish arrived *en masse*. The standards of American society were still, to a considerable degree, defined by the frontier; the behavior of the Irish was not fundamentally different from that of society as a whole. But because they were newcomers, the Irish were subjected to a close—and critical—scrutiny.

Their increase in numbers was matched by a proportional intensification of nativist passions. In some quarters the Irish were regarded as a major threat to the American standard of living. They also appeared to pose a political menace: by 1855 one third of the voters in New York City had been born in Ireland. And always there was the religious issue. Protestant fears on that subject were not allayed by the outspoken Archbishop Hughes (a post to which he was elevated in 1850) who expansively, but rather diplomatically, declared, "The object we hope to accomplish in time is to convert all Pagan nations, and all Protestant nations." With the escalation of anti-immigrant feelings in general, and anti-Irish sentiments in particular, Hughes once again found himself at the center of controversy in the early 1850s. The problem revolved around the question of whether control over Church property resided with the clergy or with the lay trustees. During the 1840s Hughes, who of course insisted that the clergy ruled the Church, had wrestled with recalcitrant trustees throughout his diocese, gradually bringing them under control by threatening to withdraw the priests from their churches and lay the parishioners under an interdict. By 1850 the lone holdout against his authority was the Church of St. Louis in Buffalo. At last Hughes, frustrated by his inability either to persuade or bully the trustees into submission, excommunicated them.

This was strictly a Catholic quarrel; no Protestant interests were involved. But Protestant spokesmen intruded anyway, denouncing the Archbishop's tactics. They portrayed the issue as one which not only pitted clergy against laity, but by implication, autocracy against democracy. Hughes' behavior, they charged, demonstrated once more the basic incompatibility of Catholicism with America's democratic traditions and ideals. Hughes countered with the claim that "the great elements of our institutions, namely, representative government, electoral franchise, trial by jury, municipal polity, were all the inventions of Catholics alone."

Finally in 1853, a papal emissary, Monsignor Gaetano Bedini, arrived to resolve the dispute. Hughes had met Bedini in 1840 during his trip to Europe and welcomed the Monsignor's intervention in the matter. But Bedini's involvement only made the situation worse. He had played a prominent role in helping to suppress the Italian revolution of 1848, a well-publicized fact which seemingly confirmed the fears of some Protestant Americans. So everywhere Bedini went in the United States he was greeted by demonstrations and riots. Upon his departure from New York the situation appeared so threatening—a mob awaited him at the dock—that the Monsignor had to be sneaked aboard his steamer by way of a tugboat.

The increase in nativist feelings eventually led to organized political action against immigrants. In the 1830s and 1840s dozens of local anti-catholic societies had arisen, primarily in the eastern cities where the Irish were settling. Some of these evolved into fledgling political parties, but none of them proved lasting. Finally in the early 1850s the American Party appeared, although it was more frequently called the Know-Nothing Party. The Know-Nothings were so named because of the Party's dedication to secrecy at its beginning; members, when queried about the organization, were supposed to respond only with a cryptic "I know nothing." The Know-Nothing platform captured the essence of nativist fears and complaints. It demanded that the public schools not be subject to any religious sect, while at the same time insisting that the King James Bible be used in the schools. It proposed extending the naturalization period from the existing five years to twenty-one. It would also deny the exercise of any political rights to immigrants or their offspring who had not been educated in American schools.

The Party grew rapidly in 1854 and 1855, dominating a half dozen state governments and even sending a few representatives to Congress. The Know-Nothings' apparent success is a bit misleading, however. Their sudden growth was in part due to the collapse of the Whig Party, which was torn apart by the increasingly divisive slavery issue. The political situation was very much in flux in the mid-1850s—the Democratic Party was just a few years away from splitting in two; the new Republican Party was springing up in the North, an outgrowth of intensified sectionalism. The Know-Nothing Party profited from this political confusion, serving as a sort of political way station for former Whigs uncertain of their future direction.

Despite their electoral victories in some states, the Know-Nothings were able to achieve only limited legislative success. In Connecticut a literacy requirement was imposed upon prospective voters as a means of reducing political participation by immigrants. Nativists in Massachusetts secured passage of a law that prohibited immigrants from voting until two years after they were naturalized. The legislature of New York, responding to the quarrel between Hughes and the Buffalo church, enacted a bill which vested control of all Church property in the trustees. As it turned out, the measure was never enforced and was ultimately repealed in 1862. For the most part, instead of pursuing a legislative program, the Know-Nothings allowed themselves to be seduced by their own anticatholic rhetoric and spent their time investigating convents and monasteries.

The nativist bubble burst in 1856. In that year's election the Know-Nothings offered their first candidate for the White House, former President Millard Fillmore. He carried only one state and captured just 21 percent of the popular vote, finishing a poor third behind the victorious Democrat, James Buchanan, and the Republican nominee, John C. Fremont. The Republican Party, also making its first run at the presidency, was clearly a more viable alternative than the Know-Nothing Party, which soon collapsed and disappeared.

Throughout the political turmoil of the 1850s, the Irish remained doggedly Democratic, even though other immigrant groups were increasingly drawn to the Republican Party. One reason the Democrats commanded Irish loyalties was the Party's unyielding pro-slavery position. Ranking as they did at the bottom of the social and economic scale, the Irish often found themselves in competition with free blacks for jobs and status. They believed that their position would be damaged even further if slavery were abolished, because the millions of blacks released from bondage would then pose an even greater threat to the Irish. Hughes made no secret of his opposition to emancipation. On his European tour in 1840, he met the Irish patriot Daniel O'Connell, whom he chided for criticizing American slavery. O'Connell responded, "It would be strange indeed, if I should not be the friend of the slave throughout the world—I, who was born a slave myself." An abashed Hughes later confessed, "He silenced me, although he did not convince me." Maintaining that emancipation would represent a tragedy for the slaves, who were ill-prepared for freedom, Hughes continued to oppose any attempt to interfere with the South's peculiar institution.

A further explanation for the consistent support given Democrats by the Irish lies in the fact that, increasingly, the Democratic Party *was* Irish. As early as 1820 Tammany Hall, the Democratic machine in New York, opened itself to the Irish. By the late 1850s the Irish were on the verge of making Tammany their own political vehicle. Machine politicians had early seen in the Irish a combination of qualities which promised political dividends. Their numbers—substantially greater than those of any other immigrant group in the first half of the nineteenth century—afforded the sort of mass base required by a successful political organization.[6] Moreover, the Irish concentration in cities gave their votes an impact disproportionate to their numbers. In addition, their membership in a

---

[6]The United States did not keep any reliable statistics on immigration before 1820, but for the years 1820–1850 the 1,042,436 Irish who arrived represented 42 percent of the total number of immigrants. The next largest contingents came from Germany (24 percent) and the United Kingdom (15 percent).

church with an autocratic structure suggested a predisposition to accept direction by a political boss. Irish familiarity with the English language and with Anglo-Saxon political traditions also promoted their political mobilization.

The fact that the Irish, and other immigrants as well, were insecure, confused, and often needy made them readily exploitable. By furnishing a little assistance or rendering a few services, politicians could secure their loyalty and cooperation. But it was a system which was mutually beneficial. The notion that government owed the people any responsibility for such things was just beginning to take root. Political machines, therefore, often took up the slack, helping immigrants fill out naturalization papers, arranging for jobs, providing a bucket of coal during the cold of winter, or supplying a turkey for Thanksgiving dinner. The Irish responded gratefully, repaying their benefactors with votes and support. Their political sophistication, however, increased so rapidly that by the eve of the Civil War they were more than mere cogs in a machine.

With the outbreak of the Civil War in 1861, immigrant loyalties were largely determined by geographical location. Those in the North identified with the Union; immigrants in the South tended to support the Confederacy. Consequently the Irish were overwhelmingly in the Union camp, ultimately contributing as many as 160,000 soldiers to the Northern cause.[7] As was true of other immigrant groups, the Irish soldiers were frequently organized in ethnically uniform units. Hughes initially had reservations about this practice, worrying that it would cause "trouble among the troops even before the enemy comes in sight." His fears proved groundless; instead the all-Irish units distinguished themselves with their ferocity and valor in battle after battle.

Although many of the Irish who enlisted did so out of loyalty and gratitude toward the nation which had taken them in, some had other reasons. Some were influenced by enlistment bonuses which represented as much as a year's pay for an unskilled worker—a powerful inducement for people as poor as they were. Others, Hughes noted, nursed hopes that they might one day apply their military experience in the struggle to liberate Ireland: "[they] entered into this war partly to make themselves apprentices, students as it were, finishing their education in this, the first opportunity afforded them of becoming thoroughly acquainted with the implements of war."

The Archbishop himself, an ardent advocate of the Union, flew the American flag from his cathedral as a demonstration of his support. When the conflict first erupted he excitedly wrote, "Let the question of the rights of the Federal Government over the whole country be settled once and forever. Let there be no compromise until the States shall be disposed to return to their allegiance to the Federal Government." Hughes was a frequent correspondent of William Seward, Secretary of State, offering advice

---

[7]A much smaller, but nonetheless substantial, number of Irish immigrants did fight for the South—perhaps as many as 40,000.

on troop movements, military strategy, and personnel matters. In a more practical vein, Hughes acceded to President Abraham Lincoln's request that he go to France late in 1861 and use his influence in that Catholic country to forestall its intervention in the conflict.

Although the Civil War was fought to preserve the Union, it resulted as well in the emancipation of the slaves—and the realization of Irish fears. Hughes labored mightily to avert linking the two issues together. "We despise, in the name of all Catholics," he declared, "the idea of making this war subservient to the philanthropic nonsense of abolitionism." His efforts proved unsuccessful; on January 1, 1863, Lincoln issued the Emancipation Proclamation. A short time later, a strike of New York's largely Irish longshoremen was broken by the use of blacks, dramatizing the rivalry between the two groups. Tensions between the Irish and blacks exploded in July of 1863, as New York witnessed one of the most violent riots in American history. Ostensibly the riot was in protest of the Conscription Act, which had been imposed just a few months before. It was a measure which clearly was both unfair and discriminatory. Under the Act, draftees could avoid military service by paying a commutation fee of $300—an option denied most Irish and other immigrants by their poverty. Furthermore, because the law was administered by Republicans, who were in power, its burden was often more heavily felt in Democratic— that is, Irish—wards.

For several days rioters controlled the streets of New York and several other Northern cities before they were finally subdued by federal troops. Antiblack feelings lay at the root of the violence. The principal targets of the rioters were blacks who, because of the recent Emancipation Proclamation, were regarded as responsible for the continuing war and the conscription which it necessitated. Throughout the city they were attacked and beaten, in some instances killed. The Colored Orphans Asylum was burned to the ground as were several black churches and a number of private homes. In the space of three days, over 1,000 people were killed. Despite the Archbishop's failing health—Hughes had for several months been unable to say Mass—the governor appealed to him for help. During the height of the disturbance, Hughes had notices posted around the city, inviting the protesters to meet him at his residence. By the appointed time a crowd of several thousand had gathered and, at the Archbishop's appearance, it burst into cheers. From a chair on the balcony Hughes delivered a long, rambling speech in which he pleaded for order.

According to one New York newspaper, the mob which devastated the city was composed of "a large body of Irishmen and Irish women of the very lowest class," an impression which did little to improve the Irish image. Yet on the whole, their service in defense of the Union conferred upon immigrants—including even the Irish—a greater degree of acceptability than they had enjoyed in the past. As one Irish officer exultantly proclaimed, "Know-Nothingism is dead. This war, if it brought no other excellent and salutary fruits, brought with it this result, that the Irish soldier will henceforth take his stand proudly by the side of the native-born, and will not fear to look him straight and sternly in the face, and tell him he has been equal to him."

The speech which Hughes made during the draft riot proved to be his last public appearance. Half a year later, in January of 1864, he died of a kidney ailment. Although Hughes had never lost sight of his own Irish origins, his concerned leadership had assisted thousands of his countrymen in more readily finding a place in their adoptive society.

FURTHER READING

BILLINGTON, RAY ALLEN. *The Protestant Crusade, 1800–1860; a Study of the Origins of American Nativism.* New York: Macmillan, 1938.

DINER, HASIA R. *Erin's Daughters in America: Irish Immigrant Women in the Nineteenth Century.* Baltimore: Johns Hopkins University Press, 1983.

DOLAN, JAY. *The Immigrant Church: New York's Irish and German Catholics, 1815–1865.* Baltimore: Johns Hopkins University Press, 1975.

ERNST, ROBERT. *Immigrant Life in New York City, 1825–1863.* New York: King's Crown, 1949.

GREELEY, ANDREW M. *That Most Distressful Nation: The Taming of the American Irish.* Chicago: Quadrangle Books, 1972.

LANNIE, VINCENT P. *Public Money and Parochial Education; Bishop Hughes, Governor Seward, and the New York School Controversy.* Cleveland, Press of Case Western Reserve University, 1968.

McCAFFREY, LAWRENCE J. *The Irish Diaspora in America.* Bloomington: Indiana University Press, 1976.

RYAN, DENNIS P. *Beyond the Ballot Box: A Social History of the Boston Irish, 1845–1917.* East Brunswick, N.J.: Fairleigh Dickinson University Press, 1983.

THERNSTROM, STEPHAN. *Poverty and Progress: Social Mobility in a Nineteenth Century City.* Cambridge: Harvard University Press, 1964.

WITTKE, CARL. *The Irish in America.* Baton Rouge: Louisiana State University Press, 1956.

8

Gro Svendsen

*Photo courtesy of the Norwegian-American
Historical Association.*

8

Gro Svendsen

SHE STARED DOWN THE ROAD long after her man had disappeared from sight. The biting wind tugged at her clothes, but she refused to move. Her husband had been conscripted to fight in a war whose complexities neither of them comprehended—but she understood the possibility that he might never return. Gro Svendsen "stood there like a frightened bird, with [her] young, alone, bewildered, forsaken." At that moment she regretted that they had ever come to America.

Ole and Gro Svendsen were part of a swelling movement from Norway to America around the middle of the nineteenth century. Between 1849 and 1865 approximately 65,000 of their countrymen braved the journey.[1] Only two generations before, in 1825, the first 52 Norwegian immigrants had sailed from Stavanger, aboard the *Restauration*, a tiny sloop one fourth the size of the *Mayflower*. Like John Winthrop's Puritans, they came to America for religious reasons: that initial group of Norwegians was made up primarily of Quakers who chafed under restrictions imposed by the Lutheran state church. Their three-month voyage to New York paved the way for other pilgrims who trickled out of Norway in the 1830s. Sectarian discontent motivated some of these as well. They were Haugeans, pietistic Lutherans whose fundamentalism set them at odds with the religious establishment.

Increasingly, however, economic factors dictated departure. The mid-1830s yielded poor harvests, 1849 and 1850 witnessed a serious depression, and by the early 1860s ruined crops and falling agricultural prices imposed almost irresistible pressure on much of Norway's population. Conditions

[1]The real flood of immigrants from Norway began in 1865. In the next half-century nearly three quarters of a million Norwegians came to America—a significant loss for a country which numbered only about 1,800,000 inhabitants in 1865.

were not as desperate as those which existed in some other parts of Europe, most notably Ireland. Nor were Norwegian peasants as severely affected by the march of industrialization and the social dislocation which inevitably accompanied it as were their counterparts in Germany and England. But their society was characterized by an increasing concentration of wealth in the hands of a few, the subdivision of ancestral lands into inefficiently small plots, and a growing number of forcible evictions.

These unhappy circumstances contrasted sharply with the image of America which emerged from the correspondence of the earliest Norwegian immigrants. One recent transplant wrote home, "We have gained more since our arrival here than I did during all the time I lived in Norway. . . . I do not believe that any who suffer oppression and who must rear their children in poverty could do better than to come to America." Other writers enthusiastically commented upon the political freedom, social equality, and unlimited economic opportunity which existed in the United States. These "America letters" had a dramatic impact, not only in Norway but throughout Europe. Their glowing descriptions held out prospects of a new life far away from the miseries of the present and induced many who had lost hope of any improvement at home to gamble their futures in America.

The bleak prospects which faced many of her fellow Norwegians were largely foreign to Gro Svendsen. Her family was part of the rural aristocracy. Her father, Nils Knudsen Gudmundsrud, was a teacher who was respected as a leader in his community. The family's long tradition of independent land ownership rendered it relatively safe from the economic setbacks which plagued so many others. Her father's profession enabled Gro to acquire an education that was uncommon for her time and sex. Attractive in many ways and well-liked locally, she was known as "the rose of Hallingdal," after the valley in which her family lived. From her birth in 1841 until she left home twenty-one years later, Gro led a comfortable and sheltered life.[2]

The same could not be said of Ole Svendsen, the man whom she married in 1862. The combination of America's attraction and the restricted opportunities in Norway convinced him his future lay in the United States. This decision placed a terrific burden on Gro who was torn between love for Ole and devotion to her parents. "I am not sure that I shall be strong enough to leave my parents forever," she told him. "I love them; I am their child. . . . I must be obedient to them." Her departure, she feared, would cause them "unspeakable sorrow." Dutiful though she was to her parents, Gro recognized that her place now was with Ole. In the spring of 1862, therefore, accompanied by her twenty-one-year-old husband, his aging mother, and a few other of his relatives, she sailed for America. As Gro watched Norway disappear beneath the horizon, the finality of her

---

[2]While atypical of immigrants in some respects, Gro was representative in others. The Hallingdal region, near Oslo in southeastern Norway, furnished a large proportion of the Norwegian immigrants during this period.

departure struck home. "I shall never again see my beloved homeland," she grievingly wrote in her journal. "O God of Mercy, my fatherland! O forgive me for causing my dear ones this anguish! O God, do not forsake us!"

Transatlantic travel had changed remarkably little in the more than two centuries since John Winthrop had come to America. The average crossing still took two months or more, although wide variations were possible. Despite the recent invention of the steamship, the overwhelming majority of immigrants still traveled in small, wooden sailing vessels which moved at the pleasure of the wind. The Svendsens' ship, in fact, lay becalmed in port and was forced to delay its departure by a day. Once the ship was under way, many of the passengers became ill. Stormy weather increased their misery and in the first week several of the voyagers died. Gro's mother-in-law was among those who were seriously ill. When the Svendsens arrived in Canada after a voyage of two months, they learned that another boatload of 300 Norwegians—about 40 of whom had died in a shipboard epidemic—had preceded them by two days.

The uncertainty of ocean travel posed other problems to passengers. Food and water supplies were sometimes exhausted before land could be reached. On the Svendsens' ship, barrels containing ale and milk were damaged during a storm, spoiling their contents and necessitating the rationing of water. A shortage of food developed as well. In this crisis Gro observed that most of her fellow immigrants were unwilling to share their supplies with those who had run out. Since passengers were required to furnish (and in some instances prepare) their own food, miscalculations as to the quantity needed regularly occurred. Crossings that were slower than expected or delays in port while additional cargo was loaded compounded the problem.

Women—particularly those traveling alone—sometimes faced harassment and even sexual attack from male passengers and members of the crew. Accompanied by her husband, Gro escaped any such unpleasantness on the ocean crossing, but after transferring to a steamboat for the journey from Quebec to Montreal she was pestered by sailors, whom she labelled "most annoying and disgusting. I more than the others had to suffer unwelcome attentions," she complained.

Gro and Ole traveled at a time when ocean traffic was on the verge of being revolutionized. A combination of circumstances would bring about a spectacular change within the next dozen years. Obviously the advent of the ocean-going steamship was instrumental in that change. But so, too, was the American Civil War. During the conflict, Confederate commerce raiders constructed in English shipyards largely destroyed America's merchant fleet, which up until that time had carried a large percentage of the immigrant trade. German and British steamship lines like Hamburg-Amerika and Cunard seized the opportunity which beckoned by building fleets of steamers to fill the void caused by American losses. Because these new vessels were specifically built for passenger traffic, they offered greater comfort. Made of steel, they were also bigger, stronger, and safer than the ships they replaced. Steam power made them independent of the wind and faster than sailing ships—transatlantic crossings were reduced to just ten days' duration. The new ships were far from perfect, but in 1873 a Congressional committee was able to report that "the cruelty, ill-usage and general discomfort of the steerage belong to the . . . past." It is little wonder that in view of all this, by the mid-1870s steamships carried well over 90 percent of the immigrants bound for America.

The Svendsens' intermediate destination, Canada, lay along the route taken by the vast majority of their countrymen bound for the United States after mid-century. Initially, Norwegian immigrants had followed the track of the original Stavanger Quakers to New York, or had journeyed to Le Havre, France, proceeding to New Orleans and up the Mississippi River. But in 1849, just as substantial numbers of Norwegians for the first time began to leave home, England repealed the Navigation Acts. This opened her colonies to foreign ships on the same terms enjoyed by English vessels, resulting in a considerable traffic of Norwegian ships carrying timber from Quebec to England and transporting immigrants back in the other direction.[3] The last leg of the journey, from Canada to the United States, was usually accomplished by railroad. Gro and her husband boarded a train at Hamilton, Ontario, entered the United States at Detroit, and continued to Chicago.

There the Svendsens were besieged "by people who urged us to go here, there and everywhere." Known as "runners," they had made a profession of preying on confused and helpless immigrants. Under the guise of offering assistance, runners (who were frequently recent immigrants themselves) steered newcomers to cheap hotels or boarding houses where they would be overcharged or robbed of their baggage. Swindlers also posed as employment agents, taking commissions on the pretext of securing nonexistent jobs for unsuspecting immigrants. Runners were not, of course, indigenous merely to Chicago. They haunted every city which received substantial numbers of immigrants. New York was their Mecca. There they posed a problem so acute that in 1855, when city officials opened Castle Garden as a compulsory landing place for all new arrivals, runners were excluded from it in no uncertain terms.[4] But no such protection existed in Chicago, where innumerable immigrants found themselves fleeced in one manner or another, often by unscrupulous travel agents who overcharged them for inadequate tickets. Gro and Ole were cheated in such a manner, so that after leaving Chicago they found themselves dumped off the train short of their destination. "There are many frauds and deceptions here," Gro angrily concluded.

[3]This increased volume of traffic led to a considerable reduction in fares so that by 1860 the cost of a ticket from Norway to Quebec was about $12 to $15.

[4]So angry were the runners over this development that they staged a riotous demonstration outside Castle Garden, during which they launched flamming rockets into the facility!

Finally, in August of 1862 Gro and her husband arrived at St. Ansgar in north-central Iowa. Founded less than a decade earlier, St. Ansgar was a village numbering over 500 Norwegians. Its small population, however, belied the town's importance to immigrants. St. Ansgar functioned much as Germantown had when Johann Buettner passed through it—serving as a sort of receiving and distributing center for many Norwegian newcomers who paused there to catch their breath before moving on to other parts of Iowa or Minnesota. Back in the mid-1830s the focus of Norwegian settlement in America had shifted from New York to the Midwest when pioneering immigrants had established a colony in the rich Fox River Valley of Illinois. Subsequent arrivals had settled there, as well as spilling over into Wisconsin, Iowa, and Minnesota, creating a fairly compact population pattern. Although some Norwegians settled in cities, the large majority lived on farms.[5] Initially they had chosen sites along streams and near forests, settings that reminded the immigrants of the land they had left behind them. But after mid-century, Norwegian settlers increasingly ventured out onto the open prairie, having discovered that the richness of the soil there offset the strangeness of their surroundings.

Still, the American frontier represented a shock for nearly all newcomers except the Scotch-Irish. In writing her mother Gro spoke for many pioneers when she noted, "Life here is very different from life in our mountain valley. One must readjust oneself and learn everything all over again, even to the preparation of food." Not only was the work unfamiliar, it appeared to be never-ending. "We are told," she wrote, "that the women of America have much leisure time, but I haven't yet met any women who thought so!" Frontier life was not merely hard, it was frequently aggravating and even dangerous. Gro's letters to her parents described plagues of locusts that were of biblical proportions, temperatures so hot that keeping milk or making butter was an impossibility, as well as the unnerving sight of "thousands" of deadly snakes. In addition, the power of the elements encountered on the prairie was awesome. "The thunderstorms are so violent," Gro reported, "that one might think it was the end of the world. The whole sky is aflame with lightning. . . . Then there is the prairie fire. . . . It is a strange and terrible sight to see all the fields a sea of fire."

These and other hardships quickly molded the attitudes of even recent settlers into a wary and often unforgiving pattern. Gro readily adopted the pioneer's principle that the only good Indian was a dead one. Her arrival on the frontier had coincided with an uprising among the Santee Sioux. Angered by the federal government's failure to abide by treaty terms which committed it to provide them with food and supplies, the starving Sioux in August of 1862 vented their rage in attacks upon several isolated Minnesota farmhouses and villages. One of the principal targets was New Ulm, a largely German settlement located little more than 100 miles to

[5]Chicago attracted more Norwegians than any other city. In 1860 about one percent of the city's 110,000 inhabitants had been born in Norway.

Sod Cabin, Kansas, 1872

Photo courtesy of Culver Pictures, Inc.

the northwest of St. Ansgar. At least 500 whites were slaughtered in the initial attacks and more were killed before the Indians could be subdued. The Sioux uprising frightened Gro very badly and kindled within her the fires of revenge. "It isn't enough merely to subdue them," she insisted. "I think that not a single one who took part in the revolt should be permitted to live. Unfortunately, I cannot make the decision in the matter. I fear that they will be let off too easily."

The menacing strangeness of her surroundings sharpened the homesickness which Gro inevitably felt. In her nostalgia she magnified America's shortcomings and exaggerated Norway's advantages. To her the weather in Iowa seemed too extreme and violent, whereas the Norwegian climate was "invigorating." As a consequence, Gro felt that in America people were "not so strong and healthy as in Norway." Perhaps it was because Norwegian clothes were "better and much warmer" than those worn by Americans. "So it is with everything," she concluded after a few months in the United States: "shoddy and careless workmanship everywhere." Her attitude led Gro into "heated arguments" with other immigrants whose lives in Norway had not been as comfortable as her own, but she steadfastly insisted, "I shall never be able to place this country above my own fatherland. . . . My love for my native land is far too deep and too sacred."

Yet, inevitably, her new home wrung concessions from Gro. In an early letter to her parents, Gro admitted "the day's wage is better than in Norway," and urged them to tell her friends "they ought to be here."[6] As she grew more familiar with American ways, Gro's feelings of discontent subsided and in time she gained insights that made unfamiliar situations more comprehensible. At first overwhelmed by America's chaotic financial structure in which "currency fluctuates constantly . . . [and] paper money is printed in every town," the Svendsens soon discovered "it is better to have cattle than cash," since the value of livestock remained more or less constant.

Their adaptation to such a foreign culture was enormously eased by the Svendsens' settlement in an ethnically uniform community. There the impact of a new world was cushioned by the vestiges of the old. Customs, traditions, language, food, attire, and music were preserved, although often in modified form. The routines of a lifetime could be roughly reconstructed, if not duplicated exactly. Friendships persisted because immigrants from the same regions in their homeland tended to settle together in America—neighbors remained neighbors. Gro, in letters to her parents, frequently relayed greetings from people she had known in Norway and encountered again in Iowa.

Yet immigrant communities were rarely as tightly knit or stable as those of the old country. America was, after all, a rootless society, characterized by perpetual motion. This was especially true on the frontier, where even new arrivals pulled up stakes and pushed farther west. And while some immigrants were baffled by such restlessness, others were themselves seized by the same fever. In April of 1863, after less than a year in the United States, the Svendsens moved to a farm near Estherville, Iowa, about 100 miles west of St. Ansgar. The influence of the community was further diminished by the American credo of the individual. Individualism was more than an overworked cliché, particularly on the frontier. There, American farms were larger and more isolated than the tiny plots worked by European peasants. As a result, frontier families were frequently thrown onto their own resources, without assistance or support from neighbors.

The family was, of course, the elemental social unit. This was especially true for Norwegians, who tended more than most other ethnic groups to immigrate as families. Moreover, in America the Norwegian family structure remained largely intact, in contrast to that of groups like the Irish, whose family ties were often weakened by the type of jobs available and the male-oriented nature of their social organizations. Among immigrants the family represented a curious combination of forces which at the same

[6]A laborer earned about a dollar a day, a farm hand made fifteen dollars a month and a domestic servant one dollar a week.

time preserved traditional values and promoted assimilation. In urban settings in particular, the immigrant wife or mother was often confined to the home, insulated from the mainstream of American society. As a result she was the family member least exposed to the forces of assimilation. Her role was, therefore, that of the repository of the past, the preserver of custom. The husband or father usually worked outside the home and inevitably absorbed more of American culture as a consequence. But it was the children who were the real agents of assimilation. The old ways were not so deeply ingrained in them, nor were they so resistant to change. Schools and playmates afforded them wider contact with the host society than their parents experienced, the effects of which were then inescapably transmitted to their elders.

These general patterns did not always hold up among the Svendsens. Gro was a singular person—independent, intelligent, and outgoing. For all of her fervent loyalty to Norway, she did not deny herself the opportunity to learn more about America. Instead, she sought it out, sometimes attending public school when her chores permitted. But in other respects the Svendsen family did conform to the immigrant model. If children were the principal instruments of assimilation, Gro and Ole assured themselves of every opportunity to become Americanized: in the sixteen years following her arrival in 1862, Gro bore ten children. Concern for their welfare involved her in educational affairs, exposing her as well as them to the indoctrinating effects of the public school. Likewise, attention to their interests prompted Gro to discard seemingly small but symbolically significant aspects of her Norwegian heritage. In explaining to her parents why she had christened her sixth child Steffen instead of a more traditional name, she declared, "I thought I'd choose one that was a little more in conformity with American so that he would not have to change it himself later in life."

Gro's interest in public education reflected the thinking of many Norwegians in America, since schooling represented an almost certain means of getting ahead. According to one immigrant, "The greatest difficulty for the Norwegian is his deficiency in the [English] language," a shortcoming curable by education. Countless letters from America and Norwegian-language newspapers hammered away at this same theme. But a recognition of the importance of an American education did not necessarily constitute a rejection of the Norwegian past. In fact, the public schools were frequently paralleled by privately financed "Norwegian schools," established to preserve the immigrants' native language and culture. Within a few months of her arrival in St. Ansgar, Gro adopted her father's calling and began teaching at one such institution. After moving the next year to Estherville, she taught at another Norwegian school for $12 a month. Gro met her pupils three times a week for a short term. Little else was possible since her chores and those of the children, as well as their American education, permitted few spare moments. Her efforts were further hampered by a lack of suitable materials. It is no wonder, then, that even

Gro's own children were further behind in their native studies than if they lived in Norway. "We so seldom have Norwegian school," she dejectedly explained to her parents, "and it is slow work to teach the boys at home."

Norwegian schools like those which Gro conducted were hardly unique. Other ethnic groups made similar efforts to preserve their traditions and resist assimilation. Sometimes, however, their attempts collided with the fears and programs of American nativists, provoking serious trouble. In the mid-nineteenth century many who advocated free public education did so because they viewed it as a means of breaking down ethnic distinctions which they felt threatened the stability of American society. Some nativists even proposed withholding political rights from naturalized citizens unless they had been cleansed by the purifying medium of the public school system. But because of their relatively small numbers, their isolation on the frontier, and especially their Protestant religion, Norwegian immigrants never encountered the hostility and violence reserved for the more numerous—and Catholic—Irish.

Although they escaped nativist persecution for the most part, Norwegians nonetheless confronted other obstacles to the pursuit of their religious beliefs. In the old country the Lutheran church had been state-supported, its functions financed through tax assessments. No such system existed in America, however, which meant that those whose souls required spiritual nourishment had to defray its expense themselves. In Estherville, money to establish a church was collected with agonizing slowness, causing considerable frustration for Gro, a devout woman. "In America, money was said to be so plentiful, and it may be," she complained. "But it's hard to get any of it when it's to be used for the common good, for such as . . . ministers' salaries, and other expenses connected with the church." A lack of money and the smallness of congregations combined to discourage trained, ordained pastors from leaving Norway to minister to the needs of their countrymen in America. As a result, several communities often shared the services of a "circuit preacher," who periodically visited each of them while following a fixed route. Estherville was visited in this manner by one Pastor Torger Torgerson two or three times a year.

Despite the difficulties which these circumstances entailed, Gro derived a great deal of comfort from her religion. Among immigrants, the church was one of the most important factors in stabilizing their disrupted lives and easing adaptation to American society. Ethnic churches reinforced traditions, and their services and prayer books promoted literacy in native languages. They strengthened the bonds of community by providing a focal point for social activity; religious holidays afforded welcome variations from a routine that was often drab and monotonous. Churches sometimes offered relief and charitable assistance to the poor and infirm in an era when such activities were not accepted as the responsibility of government.

To Gro it seemed that Americans were less devout than Norwegians. She was shocked to discover that in the United States some people worked on Christmas just as they did on any other day. But religion was taken as seriously in America as it had been in Norway, although the equalitarian nature of American society sometimes obscured that fact. One Norwegian immigrant observed, "The minister dresses just like other members of the congregation. He wears no cassock in church, as in oppressed Europe, to call attention to differences of station in society." He concluded, "In America the Sabbath is observed very rigorously, that is to say, among the native Americans. . . . they have not forgotten that fear of God is the strength of nations."

Some immigrants—particularly those from countries which had state churches like Norway—were taken aback by the diversity in American religion. Almost infinite varieties of denominations and sects competed for attention and membership. Inevitably some of the immigrants who were visited only rarely by Lutheran circuit riders were attracted to more active and accessible churches. In particular, the Baptists and Methodists made inroads within the Norwegian community. Religious diversity was not unknown to Norwegians; in fact, sectarian differences had prompted their earliest immigration to America. The conflict between "high" and "low" church views was transplanted into the United States, where it was intensified by the absence of any state church structure. Congregations split up, rival synods were organized, and bitter doctrinal debates were waged. The overall effect of the quarreling, paradoxically, was the reinforcement of a sense of community and ethnic identity as the participants scrutinized traditional beliefs and reexamined their heritage.

The bonds of community were further strengthened by the Norwegian press in America. Shortly after arriving in St. Ansgar, Gro and Ole subscribed to *Emigranten*, the foremost Norwegian language publication in the United States. It provided them with a comforting connection to their homeland: "There is always one article about Norway," Gro reported to her parents. Immigrant newspapers accomplished much more than that, as they also informed newcomers about American life and advised them on various subjects. In establishing *Nordlyset* in 1847, one of the first Norwegian papers in America, its editors shouldered broad responsibilities for their enterprise: "Besides information about the constitution of this country and reports from Scandinavia, historical, agricultural, and religious news, we intend to bring contributions from private individuals and everything else that is suitable and useful for the information and use of our readers."

Despite—or perhaps because of—its ambitious aims, *Nordlyset* ceased publication after only a few years. *Emigranten*, launched in 1852, fared much better. By the time the Svendsens arrived, its circulation numbered in the thousands. *Emigranten* provided a link among isolated Norwegian settlements by soliciting literary contributions from their residents. Gro authored a couple of short articles for the paper after it became *Emigranten og Faedrelandet* as a result of a merger with another newspaper. Although *Emigranten* resembled its ill-fated predecessor in several respects, there was one significant difference. Whereas *Nordlyset* had pledged to "make every effort to preserve the strictest possible neutrality in matters of politics," *Emigranten* was an openly partisan journal and after 1854 was enthusiastic in its support for the newly established Republican Party.

Gro had little personal interest in politics. She could not, however, help noticing the extent to which political activity pervaded her new society. Shortly after her arrival in America, Gro commented in amazement upon the large number of elected officials. Moreover, public office was not the exclusive preserve of native-born Americans. With evident pride she informed her parents that "the Norwegians are well represented in the county offices." Norwegian immigrants had for several years already exerted a considerable influence on government at the local level, electing their countrymen to a variety of offices in Wisconsin, Minnesota, and Iowa. As early as 1848, *Nordlyset* had urged its readers: "We must run our town governments ourselves; there is no one else who can do it for us. The time has come for us to assume the duties and enjoy the privileges of every American citizen. It is our privilege to rule ourselves, our own township, and make our voices heard in the affairs of the county, even in the State as a whole. Let us undertake this affair with all our zeal."

National issues also attracted the immigrants' attention. At mid-century the United States was in the throes of a bitterly passionate sectional debate over the institution of slavery. Primarily inhabitants of the upper Mississippi valley, most Norwegian immigrants were not directly affected by the peculiar institution. But they involved themselves nonetheless, overwhelmingly reflecting the sentiments of the section in which they lived. Some Norwegians based their opposition to slavery upon moral objections and called for its elimination. Most, however, were not abolitionists, mirroring instead the free-soil sentiments of the northern majority. As frontiersmen interested in the future of western settlement, they were more concerned that slavery be prevented from extending into the territories than they were with abolishing it altogether. These views inclined Norwegians inevitably toward support of the Republican Party. In the 1860 election the party's presidential candidate, Abraham Lincoln, received considerable support from the Norwegian community.

Little more than a month after Lincoln took office, South Carolina's bombardment of Fort Sumter signalled the outbreak of the Civil War. The President's call for volunteers to serve their country was enthusiastically received by adoptive as well as by native Americans. Many immigrants viewed service in the army as an opportunity to demonstrate their gratitude to a nation which had given them a second chance in life. Colonel Hans Christian Heg, commander of the predominantly Norwegian Fifteenth Wisconsin Regiment, appealed to such sentiments in his drive for recruits: "Let us show that we also love our new fatherland—that we, too, are prepared to defend our government, our freedom and the unity of our country." Others volunteered in order to receive the enlistment bonuses, which ranged up to $300, equal to a year's pay for the average worker. In all, 4,000 to 6,000 Norwegians served in the Union army, relatively few when compared to the Irish, but a significant number in comparison to the total Norwegian community in America.

To Ole and Gro Svendsen, the conflict at first seemed remote, even abstract. They had, by 1864, a 160-acre farm to tend and a young son to care for, so Ole elected not to volunteer, even though several of his Norwegian neighbors did. Increasingly, however, the war touched their lives in the form of higher prices for many goods, Gro's fears of a famine, and what she termed "many other problems." Suddenly in October of 1864, the war intruded cruelly when Ole was drafted into the army. Having just delivered her second child, Gro was deeply distressed by Ole's conscription. The day her husband left to report for duty, she stared after him, her heart as desolate as the empty prairie. The same day, Gro christened her new baby Niels Olaus to commemorate the man whom she feared she would never see again.

Gro's fears were well-founded. A bloody, murderous conflict, the Civil War proved especially deadly for Norwegians. The Fifteenth Wisconsin, which fought at Chickamauga and other battles, and accompanied General William T. Sherman on his "march to the sea," suffered the loss of one third of its troops by the time the war came to an end. Fortunately for Ole, he joined Sherman's forces in the closing stages of the campaign and saw action only once. It was several months, though, from the time that the South surrendered until Ole was mustered out of service, but at last he was able to return to Iowa. Gro was of course happy to have her husband home safely, and—somewhat after the fact—rather proud of his military service. Ole, she informed her parents, had been "discharged as an honorable soldier." Gro even had a photograph taken of him in uniform, which she enclosed in her letter. While insisting that Ole looked better as a civilian, she explained, "I am sending you [this] so that you can see what American soldiers look like."

Ole's brief military career resulted indirectly from his desire to qualify for a land grant under the terms of the Homestead Act. That measure awarded government land free of charge to American citizens or immigrants who had filed their declaration of intent to become citizens. In conformity with the law, Ole had taken out his initial citizenship papers, but in the process he rendered himself vulnerable to the draft. Still, in view of the relatively painless nature of Ole's service and the quarter-section farm to which he gained title, the exchange was ultimately quite a beneficial one from the Svendsens' viewpoint.

The passage of the Homestead Act in 1862 marked the culmination of a twenty-year campaign in Congress. The vastness of America's uninhabited domain, the equalitarian ideology which had emerged from the Jacksonian era, and the general inability of authorities to prevent the occupation of public lands by squatters had combined to give life to the dream of free land. Political expediency played a hand as well: the Homestead Act was a Republican-sponsored measure, opposed by Democrats sensitive to southern fears that it would flood the western territories with "free state" settlers. The homestead plank in the Republican platform was at least as important as the slavery issue in securing the support of Norwegian immigrants and other land-hungry groups.

Specifically, the measure provided that any head of a family who was at least twenty-one years old or a veteran of military service to the United States, who had not borne arms against the Union and who was either an American citizen or had filed for citizenship, could claim 160 acres of land. Within six months of filing a claim, an applicant was required to move onto the land and undertake its improvement. In addition, he had to take an oath, swearing that the land was for his use and for no one else. After a continuous residence of five years on the claim, the applicant could take out his final papers and receive title to the land upon official verification. Essentially the land was free: modest filing and verification fees totalled approximately $20.

The passage of the Homestead Act very nearly coincided with the Svendsens' departure for America. Although their journey had not been prompted by the Act, Gro and Ole availed themselves of its terms within less than a year of their arrival. In April of 1863, Ole staked a claim to "a fine piece of land" near Estherville. Their venture entailed separation for the Svendsens. While Gro remained with her in-laws for several months, Ole moved west and worked as a hired farm hand. Ole lived on their new land and guarded the claim, a precaution made necessary "because quite often others come around, pull up the stakes, and claim the land."

Stolen claims were by no means the only problem associated with the Homestead Act. Despite its generous conception, the Act nevertheless failed to fulfill popular expectations for it. Speculators, cattlemen, and other interests fraudulently obtained millions of acres under its provisions, to the obvious detriment of legitimate homesteaders. All told, only a little more than 10 percent of the federal lands dispensed in the third quarter of the nineteenth century were granted directly to pioneers and small farmers. Yet despite its failure to provide the "free homes for the millions" advertised in promotional literature, the Homestead Act did result in the issuance of 600,000 claims. It represented an opportunity unparalleled anywhere else in the world.

Needless to say, the Homestead Act greatly magnified the already alluring image of the United States. When reports of its passage reached Norway, they were at first dismissed as hoaxes. But letters from excited immigrants and the advertising efforts of American promoters quickly confirmed the news. Shipping lines anxious to fill their holds with human cargo advertised in European newspapers and distributed pamphlets filled with glowing descriptions of life in America. Sparsely populated western states established special immigration bureaus to draw settlers from Europe and to direct them westward from the Atlantic ports of entry. As an additional inducement to immigrants, they sometimes offered voting rights to aliens who had not yet completed the naturalization process. The most systematic efforts to attract immigrants, however, were those mounted by the railroads. The recipients of nearly two hundred million acres of land from the federal and state governments, western railroads of course had a vested interest in selling that land to newcomers. But even if the settlers claimed homesteads instead of purchasing railroad land, the railroads benefited: western settlement under any auspices created increased traffic in passengers and goods. Consequently the Northern Pacific, Santa Fe, Burlington, Union Pacific, and numerous other railroads competed with each other in offering inducements to immigrants, including reduced ship and railroad fares, temporary housing while the settlers selected their land, free seed, and lessons in the techniques of prairie agriculture.

The relationship between the railroads and settlers was in some respects a symbiotic one: for many western farmers railroads offered the only feasible route to market. Establishing oneself near a rail line was, therefore, an important consideration for a pioneer. Ole staked his claim in an area then under survey by a railroad. A half year later when the study was completed, Gro reported with obvious pleasure that the tracks would run only about six miles from their farm.

A combination of good fortune and hard work brought the Svendsens success. After a year on their homestead, Gro took stock of their situation: "We are self-sufficient and can even help others. . . . We are by no means rich, but we cannot be called poor; that's just as certain." The next year brought them a bountiful harvest of wheat, corn, potatoes, sorghum, and fruit (including watermelon). Their inventory also included four cows, some pigs, and a sheep. Fate was not uniformly kind, however. On several occasions over the next few years, "the locusts came like a blinding sheet of snow," causing considerable loss. In other years bad weather damaged crops and reduced the harvest. Despite such setbacks, Gro became increasingly attached to her new home. Once she had scoffed at the notion that she would ever be completely satisfied in the United States: "The statement that one often finds in letters from America—that one wouldn't care to be back in Norway for all the world, or words to that effect to assure those at home that they like it here—such a statement I could never make as I should not be telling the truth." Yet only a few years later Gro confided, "This place has become very dear to us." She seemed almost surprised that she was sinking new roots into the rich soil of the Iowa prairie. Her concessions had been slow, grudging—and inevitable. They were revealed in small but significant ways: a son named Steffen, a pony named Greeley—American, not Norwegian names.

Gro's acceptance of America enabled her to realize the satisfaction she had once despaired of achieving. In one of her last letters to her parents, Gro in 1877 declared, "We are now well housed, both man and beast. This means a great deal to a pioneer because during the first years he is deprived of many comforts previously enjoyed. Nobody must doubt that we are living comfortably. We have whatever we need. . . . We are satisfied and happy with this life." Prematurely worn out by child-bearing and the hardships of frontier life, Gro died the next year, survived by Ole and nine of their ten children.[7] Ole buried her in a grave bordered by a white picket fence and planted a tree as a living memorial to the woman who had shared so much of his life. He then gathered up his children and struck out for the Dakota Territory, where he claimed a new homestead, settling among "many of our old friends" from Norway.

Although she was only 37 years old when she died, Gro's short life offers a complete chronicle of the immigrant experience. In the agony she felt upon leaving her native land, in her stubborn adherence to tradition, in her concessions to the irresistible pull of assimilation, and in countless other ways, Gro's story personifies the saga of millions.

FURTHER READING

ANDERSEN, ARLOW W. *The Norwegian Americans.* Boston: Twayne Publishers, 1974.

BLEGEN, THEODORE C., EDITOR. *Land of Their Choice: The Immigrants Write Home.* Minneapolis: University of Minnesota Press, 1955.

————. *Norwegian Migration to America, 1825–1860.* New York: Arno Press, 1969.

FARSETH, PAULINE AND THEODORE C. BLEGEN, EDITORS. *Frontier Mother: The Letters of Gro Svendsen.* New York: Arno Press, 1979.

LOVOLL, ODD S. *The Promise of America: A History of the Norwegian-American People.* Minneapolis: University of Minnesota Press, 1984.

NEIDLE, CECYLE S. *America's Immigrant Women.* Boston: Twayne, 1975.

SEMMINGSEN, INGRID. *Norway to America: A History of the Migration.* Minneapolis: University of Minnesota Press, 1978.

---

[7]Their eighth child, Sigri, died in November of 1876 after living only twenty months. The other nine children and the years in which they were born were: Svend (1862), Niels Olaus (1864), Carl (1866), Ole (1867), Albert Olai (1869), Steffen (1871), Bergit (1873), Sigri Christine (1877), and Gurine Louise (1878).

9

San Francisco's Chinatown

Arnold Genthe photo courtesy of Library of Congress.

9

Huie Kin

HUIE KIN[1] AND THE WOMAN he loved stood nervously but defiantly before her father. The young Chinese immigrant had just asked for her hand in marriage. Visibly agitated, her father recoiled at the thought of his daughter "living under the stigma of having married a Chinaman." The family's pastor made no effort to conceal his disapproval. "You marry a Chinaman?" he scoffingly asked Louise Van Arnam. "Why, you could marry any man . . ." Clearly he intended to suggest that virtually any man would be preferable to her chosen suitor. Then the minister triumphantly posed the question which he was certain would put an end to the couple's foolish plan: "Have you considered where would your children stand?" Despite such objections, Huie Kin and Louise Van Arnam married and shared a long, loving, and fruitful life. But the undisguised opposition of her family exemplified, in microcosm, the enormous difficulty which Chinese immigrants would encounter in trying to make their way in American society.

The intense animosity directed toward Chinese immigrants was not reflective of their overall numbers. During the second half of the nineteenth century the Chinese constituted less than two percent of America's total volume of immigrants, although their concentration in California frightened some westerners.[2] Not only were they relatively few in number, the Chinese were often merely temporary immigrants. More than half of them ultimately elected to return to their homeland rather

---

[1]The Chinese practice of listing the surname first is followed here.

[2]During the latter half of the nineteenth century only 305,409 Chinese arrived in the United States among a total of 16,657,406 immigrants.

than settle permanently in the United States. Although this would seem a natural response to the scorn and violence which they encountered in America, the departure of the Chinese was even more indicative of the fact that most had from the outset regarded the United States as only a temporary haven from their country's poverty and turmoil.

The great majority of Chinese immigrants to America came from a rather limited area. Overwhelmingly, they hailed from Kwangtung Province, the most populous of China's more than two dozen provinces and one of its poorest. In fact, the focus of emigration from China was even more narrow than that suggests: about one half of the immigrants came from Toi Shan District, one of 98 districts in the province. Most of the other immigrants came from a half dozen or so districts which neighbored Toi Shan.

Huie Kin came from Toi Shan (then called Sunning). He was born in 1854 in the tiny village of Wing Ning, not far from the sea and about 90 miles distant from the provincial capital, Canton. Like most of the peasants in the region, the Huie family struggled to scratch a living from the barren, rocky soil, but their efforts were barely enough. Their two room hut provided insufficient space for the two adults and their five children— "for lack of room, my two brothers stayed at the ancestral temple at night," Huie later recalled. His two sisters also slept away from home, "but the family cow, because of its importance, shared the rooms with the family."

> We knew what poverty meant. To toil and sweat year in and year out, as our parents did, and to get nowhere; to be sick and burn or shiver with chills without a doctor's care; always to wear rough homespun; going without shoes, even in cold winter days; without books or time to learn to read them—that was the common tale of rural life, as I knew it.

Such hardships were compounded by social and political chaos, as the structure of Chinese society and government rapidly decayed. Shortly before the middle of the nineteenth century, China suffered a violent collision with the modern world. Prior to 1842 contact with outsiders had been discouraged, with only the port of Canton open to foreign merchants. But as a consequence of its defeat by Great Britain in the Opium War (1839–42), China was forced to open its doors further, allowing foreigners access to more ports. The ensuing economic depression in Canton was amplified in its impact by severe crop failures in the surrounding districts from 1847 to 1850. Famine and destructive floods added their weight to the peasants' burden during these same years.

The aftershock of the Opium War also contributed to the Taiping Rebellion, a massive upheaval which wracked China from 1850 until 1864, claiming at least 20 million lives and perhaps as many as 30 million. Obscure in its origins, the Rebellion was focused in Kwangtung Province and led by a Christian convert who had come to regard himself as the younger brother of Jesus Christ. In addition to religious factors, the Taiping Rebellion was fueled by demands for agrarian reform, hatred for the ruling dynasty, resentment of government inefficiency and corruption, ethnic rivalries, and uncounted local issues. Its effects, exemplified by, but by no means limited to, the staggering death toll, were enormous. Civil order broke down completely. "Marauding tribes," as Huie Kin called them, "now and then came down into the plain and pillaged farmhouses. Then the villagers would beat loud gongs, muster all the grown-up men, and fight them off" while the rest of the villagers hid. Bandits ravaged the countryside; pirates plagued the coast and rivers.

Racial rivalry intensified the turbulence. The region where Huie Kin lived was inhabited by three distinct ethnic groups. The Punti, to which the Huie clan belonged, and who were the original inhabitants of the area, constituted the majority. The Hakka had migrated into the area from northeastern provinces several centuries before. The third group, the Tanka, were "boat people." Antagonism between Punti and Hakka came to a head during the Taiping Rebellion, whose leader Hung Hsiu-ch'uan was a Hakka. Although they were outnumbered by his own people, Huie remembered the Hakkas as "good fighters" and noted "we had to flee for safety." When government troops at last appeared near Wing Ning village it was the Hakkas' turn to flee. Finally, after more than a dozen years of turmoil, and with the intervention of several European powers, order was restored by the Chinese government.

Against this background of political upheaval and economic hardship, word reached China of the discovery of gold in California. Exciting tales about the "Mountain of Gold" swept through Kwangtung Province, stimulating an outbreak of gold fever. Elsewhere in China, however, the news had virtually no impact. For one thing, most Chinese were disdainful of foreigners, whom they dismissed as barbarians. Since they viewed their own land as the Celestial Empire, it is understandable why few Chinese would wish to leave home to live among barbarians, despite the chance of finding gold. This attitude was reinforced by religious belief. The teachings of Confucius emphasized devotion to one's parents; deserting them for an extended period was virtually a cardinal sin. Imperial law, which forbade emigration under penalty of death, posed a further obstacle. This restriction was not formally removed until the 1890s, although it was modified in 1860. Of course, while the domestic turmoil of the Taiping Rebellion raged, the restriction on emigration was impossible to enforce; nevertheless, such official disapproval discouraged emigration by adding its weight to the ethnocentrism and religious attitudes of the Chinese.

The main exception to this was Kwangtung Province. Its people historically had encountered foreigners more frequently due to the fact that Canton had long been open to the outside world. The prospect of living among foreign barbarians was consequently less disturbing to them than it was to other Chinese. In fact peasants from Kwangtung Province had already for two centuries temporarily emigrated to Southeast Asia in search of economic opportunity. When California's golden promise beckoned, they readily transferred their aspirations.

By the time fortune hunters from China arrived in California the Gold Rush was already well under way. The discovery of gold in California virtually coincided with that territory's annexation by the United States. America formally acquired California in February of 1848 under the terms of the Treaty of Guadalupe Hidalgo, which ended the Mexican War.[3] The previous month, unknown to the outside world, gold had been discovered on the American River not far from present-day Sacramento. These events had a tremendous impact upon the size and nature of California's population. When the war broke out in mid-1846, California had a non-Indian population of about 8,000,—more than 90 percent of whom were Mexican. By the end of 1849, the population had reached nearly 100,000, with Americans in a clear majority.

The Gold Rush was an international movement, attracting people from around the world. Not surprisingly California contained a higher proportion of immigrants than did the rest of the United States. According to the 1850 census, about 10 percent of the American population was foreign-born. In California, however, the number was closer to 25 percent. Among the earliest outsiders to reach California were a small group of Hawaiians and a much larger contingent from Latin America. By the spring of 1849 approximately 5,000 South Americans, most of them Chileans, were in California. By 1852 as many as 50,000 Latin Americans had arrived. Although they kept mostly to themselves, they nonetheless suffered considerable discrimination and even violence at the hands of gold seekers pouring in from the eastern United States. In July of 1849 more than three dozen Chileans were assaulted during a riot in San Francisco. A few months later about a dozen Chilean miners were murdered during the "Calaveras County War."

In part, these attacks were inspired by economic jealousy—American prospectors feared that foreign miners would carry off their country's mineral wealth. The early arrival of the Chileans did in fact enable them to stake out many of the most promising claims. Even more than economic competition, however, racism lay at the root of the tensions. The presence of racism in American society was demonstrated rather clearly by the existence of a system of slavery based on race. Moreover, racial passions were particularly inflamed at mid-century by a widely held ideology called Manifest Destiny. Advocates of Manifest Destiny maintained that the United States was foreordained by God to spread its authority across all of North America, bringing civilization to the supposedly inferior people who inhabited the region and extending the area of democratic government. Combining democratic idealism with notions of racial superiority,

---

[3]As a consequence of the war, the United States also acquired the present-day states of Nevada, Utah, New Mexico, and Arizona; established its southern boundary along the Rio Grande River; and added a Hispanic population estimated at 75,000.

Manifest Destiny both inspired and justified the rapid territorial expansion of the United States. The fact that Americans fought a war against the darker-skinned Mexicans from 1846 to 1848 merely served to arouse even more racial antagonism against Latin Americans.

Just at this time nativist feeling, exemplified by the Know-Nothing Party, was swelling to a peak. Easterners who came to California looking for gold brought their prejudices with them. But the European immigrants—especially the Irish—who were treated so scornfully on the Atlantic coast encountered significantly less opposition in California. The nativist passions of white Americans in California for the most part focused narrowly upon those immigrants who were perceived as racially distinct: Mexicans, Chileans—and Chinese. Discouraged by the violence of their reception, Latin American prospectors stopped coming to California by 1852, and most of those who were already there returned to their homelands. Their exodus coincided with the beginning of substantial immigration from China. In 1851 only about 2,700 Chinese arrived at San Francisco, the principal gateway to California. The next year more than 20,000 poured in. As their numbers rose, the Chinese became the almost exclusive objects of nativist scorn and violence in California.

Even more racially distinct and culturally removed from the American mainstream than Latin Americans, the Chinese excited even more prejudice. They also aroused widespread economic concern. The Chinese represented competition, not only in the gold mines. Moreover, the Chinese appeared to contribute little to the state's economy other than their labor. A reporter for the San Francisco *Daily Alta* labelled them the "least profitable of miners. Their wants are few and supplied in a cheap and peculiar manner," he continued, "and as they are saving, penurious and apt at trade, society seldom gets the benefit of their earnings."

Resentment for the Chinese was brought sharply into focus by a measure introduced in the legislature in 1852. As a means of addressing California's chronic labor shortage—wage work held little appeal as long as there was gold to be mined—State Senator George A. Tingley proposed a bill to permit Chinese immigrants to sign labor contracts committing them to their employers for up to 10 years. Governor John Bigler, running for re-election, seized upon the Tingley bill, warning it would create a class of "coolie laborers" which would undercut the economic prospects of free white men. Bigler's opposition contributed to the measure's defeat. The inflammatory nature of his remarks is particularly apparent when viewed in the context of the increasingly bitter debate over slavery. Throughout the gold country mobs of white miners attacked the Chinese, driving them from their claims. A mass meeting of prospectors near Marysville adopted resolutions barring any Chinese from staking claims and ordering them out of the area. Mob action enforced the measures. Similar steps were taken at Columbia, Indian Bar, Sonora, Mariposa, Horseshoe Bar, and elsewhere. Most Chinese prudently complied with these prohibitions; those who did not had their cabins burned, were

Anti-Chinese Cartoon of 1880s

Courtesy of Library of Congress.

beaten, or were even killed. Murders of Chinese usually went unpunished. Authorities exhibited little inclination to extend legal protection to them and in 1854 the state Supreme Court voided what minimal safeguard the law had offered by ruling that no white man could be convicted of a crime solely on the basis of testimony by Chinese witnesses.

Where they were not completely driven away from the mines, the Chinese were reduced to working claims already abandoned by whites. Yet so exhaustive and painstaking were they in their efforts that Chinese miners were often able to extract gold from these supposedly unproductive mines. When they were excluded from working claims, the Chinese often took on the menial but profitable jobs that abounded in mining camps—preparing food or doing laundry. Even these endeavors aroused complaints that, by taking over work ordinarily done by females, the Chinese were driving women into prostitution. Performance of traditionally male jobs prompted other objections: "I do not want to see Chinese . . . carpenters, masons, or blacksmiths, brought here in swarms . . . to compete with our own mechanics," declared Senator Philip Roach.

Despite these problems, the "Mountain of Gold" continued to exert a magnetic attraction for the people of Kwangtung Province. Even as the Gold Rush tapered off they continued to arrive in California in increasing numbers. And as white miners abandoned prospecting for other work the Chinese constituted a growing percentage of the state's miners. In 1860 fewer than a fifth of California's 100,000 miners were Chinese; by 1870 Chinese comprised about three fifths of the 30,000 miners in the state.

Even though Huie Kin was not born until after the Gold Rush had passed, California exercised its pull on him. He observed how other members of the Huie clan had gone to America and returned: "Every one of them went away poor . . . but came back with the beautiful gold pieces in their pockets." Their experience infected his thinking. With his playmates Huie "concocted ambitious exploits, one of which was to go together across the great sea to that magic land where gold was to be had free from river beds and men became rich overnight." Finally in 1868, when he was fourteen, Huie Kin decided to make his dream a reality. With three of his cousins, ranging in age from 14 to 25, he made his plans to go to America.

Their decision coincided with a sudden surge in Chinese immigration to the United States. In 1868 China and the United States signed the Burlingame Treaty, which recognized the inalienable right of the two countries' people to cross national boundaries and change their place of residence. This agreement was actually designed to facilitate the penetration of China by American missionaries and merchants, but in fact it encouraged Chinese immigration by superseding several California statutes which had aimed at curtailing that movement, and, for the first time in international law, by signalling the Chinese government's acceptance of its subjects' right to emigrate.

The cost of Huie Kin's ticket was $30, which was more than his family had. His father, who was by no means immune to the lure of California's gold, borrowed the money from a neighbor, pledging his small farm as security. The family's sacrifice insured that Huie Kin would be able to make his way in America free of the sort of economic obligations which burdened many of his countrymen. Most Chinese immigrants were too poor to pay for their passage, so they depended on the credit-ticket system. Under this system Chinese merchants—usually in Hong Kong or San Francisco—furnished the ticket on credit, but those who traveled in this manner remained under contract to the merchants until their debts were paid. The position of the immigrant under this arrangement was not unlike that of the indentured servant of the colonial era. The credit-ticket system therefore inspired some objection in the United States, particularly among opponents of slavery who feared that the peculiar institution might be revitalized by Chinese debt bondage.

Once their fathers had arranged to purchase tickets for them, Huie Kin and his three cousins packed their meager possessions and, in high spirits, took a junk to Hong Kong. To their disappointment they learned that no ship would be sailing to America for the next month, so the two older adventurers returned to their village to work. Left in Hong Kong with his youngest cousin, Huie Kin haunted the waterfront. There he saw his first

Westerners—"strange people," he would recall, "with fiery hair and blue-grey eyes." At last the day for their departure came and, reunited, the four Huie cousins boarded a large sailing ship manned entirely by the odd-looking Westerners.

For the next two months they were at sea, an average Pacific crossing in terms of its duration. Typical, too, were the conditions they faced aboard ship, which were, if anything, worse than those confronting transatlantic immigrants of the same period. A water shortage developed. Carefully rationed, the precious liquid was used only for drinking. "Not a drop was allowed to be wasted for washing our faces," Huie later wrote, "and so, when rain came, we eagerly caught the rain water and did our washing." En route to America Huie Ngou, the eldest cousin, suddenly contracted a fever and, after a brief illness, died. With the nonchalance which accompanies a routine act, sailors wrapped his body in a sheet and threw it overboard. For hours afterward the three young boys stood silently by the railing, staring into the night. Sad and frightened, Huie Kin mourned his cousin and wondered uneasily, "What [is] to become of the party now that our leader [is] gone?"

Huie's concern about their fate was largely unfounded due to the tight structure of the Chinese community in California. It was characterized by organizations based upon family ties or clan relationships. People with the same surname were presumed to be related to each other and even though they may never have met before, they joined together to assist one another. In addition, there were benevolent societies which united Chinese immigrants from the same district. Since people from different districts spoke in different dialects, identifying a member from the benevolent association was an easy matter, even in the confusion of the San Francisco waterfront. Because of the Gold Rush, San Francisco had grown from a sleepy fishing village of perhaps 800 in 1848 to a bustling city of about 35,000 just two years later. By the time Huie Kin arrived in 1868 it had a population of nearly 150,000 and was the third busiest port in the United States.

As the three anxious Huie boys descended the gangplank they were at first overwhelmed by the noise and the press of humanity on the pier. Then they heard a voice calling out in their local dialect. "Like sheep recognizing the voice only," Huie Kin and his cousins "blindly followed, and soon were piling into one of the waiting wagons." The wagon took them slowly up a hill, rumbling over cobblestones, to Chinatown. There it stopped before the headquarters of their district association, a benevolent society, where the three boys spent the night.

To a greater or lesser degree, all immigrant groups benefited from similar organizations. New York's Irish community had established the Irish Emigrant Assistance Society in 1825; Germans could turn to the Deutsche Gesellschaft for help. The Society for Italian Immigrants was founded in 1901 in New York; the Hebrew Benevolent Society was established there in 1822. Although such organizations assisted only a tiny fraction of European immigrants, virtually every Chinese newcomer had contact with a mutual benefit association.

At the time of Huie Kin's arrival, San Francisco had six such district organizations, known as the Six Companies. They constituted the unofficial government of the Chinese community, serving as intermediaries between it and American authorities. The Six Companies also exerted considerable influence over the residents of Chinatown—controlling commerce, making loans, arranging for jobs, enforcing order, settling disputes, paying death benefits, offering protection. The existence of these associations was not merely a response to the needs of overseas Chinese; it reflected the structure of society in China itself, where comparable organizations were fundamental to most social and economic activity. They formed the basis for craft and labor guilds, they provided a means for charitable work, and they served as intermediaries which represented their members in dealing with other associations or the government. If a person had a dispute with his neighbor or a problem with the tax collector, rather than trying to resolve these difficulties himself he took them to his association.

Of course one consequence of this pattern was the isolation of the individual from the larger aspects of Chinese society. And since this structure was transplanted to their overseas communities by Chinese immigrants to the United States, Malaya, Jamaica, and elsewhere, it also served to isolate them from the mainstream of their host society. A further aspect of the structure of the Chinese community was the strong bonds which linked overseas associations with those in China. Although separated by thousands of miles or dozens of years, members of a clan were part of the same organization. After Huie Kin had lived in America over half a century the Huie clan in the United States sent him back to China to help settle a dispute over some land between the Huies of Wing Ning village and the Wong family from a nearby village. Nor was there, as Huie Kin described it, any question about the strength of the ties which bound him—and his children—to the clan.

> All the Huies abroad are registered with their local Benevolent Society and a similar list is kept in the ancestral halls of their native villages in China. My three sons, Irving, Albert and Arthur, although they were born in America and have never set foot on Chinese soil, have their names duly recorded in Wing Ning village.

In addition to clan and district associations, Chinese immigrants sometimes belonged to tongs. Tongs were secret societies composed of people whose clans were too weak to represent their interests effectively, who came from remote districts, or who shared a common interest, as well as those who were outcasts from other associations. Although they functioned in much the same way and for the same reasons as the other types of association, the tongs were also sometimes involved in criminal activ-

Toy seller in San Francisco's Chinatown

Photo by Arnold Genthe. California Historical Society, San Francisco.

ity—prostitution, gambling, and the like. This fact points to the uglier side of the Chinese community's structure: benefit associations did not merely assist their members; they also often oppressed them, sometimes literally holding them in bondage.

After Huie Kin had spent his first night in America at his district association's headquarters, relatives from nearby Oakland picked him up and took him to their home. He stayed with them briefly until he found work as a house servant, earning $1.50 per week plus board. Huie later worked on a dairy farm near Oakland, making $2.00 a week and living in a tent. In both occupations he reflected the experience of his countrymen in California. The Chinese were sought after by households which could afford servants or cooks. They were also widely employed in the state's increasingly important agricultural sector. It was estimated in the 1870s that Chinese workers cultivated two thirds of the vegetables, planted and harvested most of the grain, and tended, picked, and packed virtually all of the fruit grown in the state. Their labor in reclaiming swamps and the Sacramento delta, as well as digging irrigation ditches, greatly expanded the quantity of productive farm land. Chinese workers were also employed in manufacturing, operated fishing boats, and dominated the laundry business. Their contributions were particularly obvious and noteworthy in construction of the western railroads. As many as 14,000 Chinese were employed in building the Central Pacific Railroad, lifting, hammering, drilling, blasting—and dying. A Chinese crew laid ten miles of track in one day in 1869, a record never broken.

By the early 1870s, however, most of the great railroad construction projects were completed and thousands of Chinese laborers were released into the western workforce. This development aggravated a job market that was already intensely competitive due to a severe depression triggered by the Panic of 1873. White workers feared displacement by Chinese immigrants willing to work for lower wages. Their fears were not without some basis in fact. In addition, groups of Chinese employed as strikebreakers were shuttled from one labor dispute to another and were used to smash the unions organized by desperate workers. These circumstances led to a further deterioriation in the perception and treatment of Chinese immigrants by many Americans. Anti-Chinese feelings, held somewhat in check by the relative prosperity of the 1860s, exploded. Huie Kin reported a "sudden change of public sentiment towards our people. . . . The useful and steady Chinese worker became overnight the mysterious Chinaman, an object of unknown dread."

The most dramatic expression of intensified anti-Chinese feeling was offered by the Workingmen's Party and its leader Denis Kearney, himself a recently naturalized immigrant from Ireland. Haranguing crowds of unemployed workers on San Francisco's sandlots, Kearney preached a gospel of racial intolerance, ending each speech with the exhortation "The Chinese must go!"[4] In the mid-1870s, the slogan was taken up and acted upon throughout California. A riot in Los Angeles ended with 19 Chinese hanged or shot to death. In San Francisco mobs destroyed more than two dozen Chinese-owned laundries. Five Chinese tenant farmers were mur-

---

[4]The Workingmen's Party denounced monopolistic railroad, land, and mining corporations, as well as the Chinese laborers they employed. Its anti-Chinese stance attracted enough support to the Party so that it could affect the political balance of power in California for several years.

dered in Chico, reportedly on orders from the Party. Armed parties drove Chinese farmworkers out of Oroville, Grass Valley, and Colusa, burning their homes. None of California's Chinese felt safe. "We were simply terrified," Huie remembered later. "We kept indoors after dark for fear of being shot in the back. Children spit upon us as we passed by and called us rats."

Huie Kin conceded that the Chinese immigrants were to a degree responsible for the abuse directed toward them because of their refusal to accommodate themselves to American society. "Our people were too slow in adapting ourselves to the life of the people among whom we lived, moved and had our material well-being," he observed. "We remained a clannish people. We kept to our native dress and carried on our daily life as if we were back in our old villages." Huie was no different from the rest of his countrymen in this respect: throughout his first 15 years in the United States, he continued to wear his native costume.

But the ethnocentrism of the Chinese is only a partial explanation for the way that they were treated. They did not merely keep themselves aloof from American society, they were held at arm's length by it. Even if they had rejected their past and attempted to immerse themselves in the nation's cultural mainstream, they might not have been permitted to do so. From the beginning of Chinese immigration to the United States, they were the objects of discriminatory measures which singled them out and kept them socially separate. California's Foreign Miners Tax, first imposed in 1850, was for 20 years enforced almost exclusively against the Chinese. Other taxes, like one assessed against foreign fishermen, were similarly applied mainly to the Chinese. This practice culminated in the adoption of a measure in 1862 which required all adult "Mongolians," if they hadn't paid the miners tax or were not engaged in the production of exempted crops, to pay a tax of $2.50 per month. They were taxed, in other words, simply for being Chinese! Although Governor Leland Stanford admitted the tax was "stringent and oppressive," he nevertheless hoped that other measures of a like nature would be enacted to achieve "the object desired, the discouragement of Chinese immigration."

California also passed a number of laws designed to accomplish that end in a more direct manner. In 1852 the legislature required the masters of ships bringing Chinese passengers to the state to post a $500 bond, ostensibly to defray relief and medical costs but in actuality to discourage the traffic altogether. The adoption in 1858 of a measure entitled "An Act to Prevent the Further Immigration of Chinese or Mongolians to This State" needs no explanation. Another law, under the guise of combatting prostitution, attempted to prohibit immigration by Oriental women. Many of these measures, as well as other laws like them, were found to be in violation of federal law. Quite a few which were thrown out in court ran afoul of the Burlingame Treaty of 1868, which apparently guaranteed unrestricted access to the United States by the Chinese. The federal courts were by no means uniformly kind, however. As early as 1854 one federal judge ruled that Chinese immigrants could not become American citizens.

Much of the legislation which directly affected the Chinese clearly had no other object than their humiliation and harassment. San Francisco's Queue Ordinance, which required that anyone arrested have his hair cut short, caused much anxiety for the Chinese. Their braided hair was symbolic of their loyalty to the Manchu dynasty; without their queues, re-entry into China might be difficult. A basket ordinance prohibited carrying bundles on bamboo poles; a cubic air ordinance outlawed the close quarters customary in Chinese sleeping rooms; a cemetery law discouraged the shipment of bodies back to China for interment. The same sort of racial discrimination mandated against Southern blacks by the Jim Crow laws—barring them from attending school with white children, for example—was practiced against the Chinese in California.

Despite these legal obstacles and their own cultural inhibitions, many Chinese immigrants did attempt to accommodate themselves to American life. Overcoming the language barrier was basic to any adjustment, and to that end it was a common practice for Chinese immigrants to attend Sunday services in Christian churches. Few who listened to the sermons were seriously interested in the ministers' messages; they simply sought more exposure to the language. In Oakland Huie Kin subscribed to this strategy with a vengeance: each week he attended Sunday school at three different churches, literally running from one to the next in order to improve his command of English. The first American family he worked for generously assisted his efforts, teaching him to read and write, as well as granting him time off to attend an evening class. For all his eagerness, Huie nonetheless found that some adjustments were impossible to make. Eating in his employers' household imposed a severe test upon him. Over half a century later he still professed to be haunted by "the vision of the ubiquitous applesauce on the table" and declared "I soon got so sick and tired of that I would have given anything for a Chinese meal."

No amount of exposure to applesauce could overcome Huie Kin's resistance to it; but such was not the case with religion. In 1874, after half a dozen years in the United States, Huie was baptized and formally joined the Presbyterian Church. This stamped him as a member of a distinct minority among his countrymen—relatively few Chinese immigrants converted to Christianity. Yet the role of the Western church within the Chinese community was not insignificant. It was, in a way, like the clan organizations and district associations which assisted the newcomers in dealing with the confusing complexities of American life. Years later, when he directed a Presbyterian mission in New York's Chinatown, Huie Kin would extend himself and the mission's facilities to all his countrymen, whether they belonged to the church or not.

One reason that Christian churches did not make better headway among Chinese immigrants is that many of the missionaries, for all their good intentions, were misinformed about, and prejudiced against, Orientals. In fact, the distorted image of the Chinese as diseased and vice-ridden savages—an image that was widely held in the United States—had been given circulation by the first American missionaries to China when they returned to the United States. The contradictory feelings of some missionaries, who wanted to help the Chinese and yet were horrified by them, often alienated the objects of their solicitation. Huie Kin was particularly upset by one fervent but ill-informed woman who "in her desire to bring out the contrast between Christian and heathen civilization, overdid herself in painting a black picture of Chinese homes without a ray of redeeming love." With growing irritation he listened as she described "little children crushed under inhuman cruelty, women denied an education and treated as the plaything of the predatory male, etc." When she added that all Chinese men beat their wives without provocation, Huie felt compelled to rise and declare that in his village he had never seen a man beat his wife. Unabashed, the woman then inquired how many wives Huie's father had had! After acidly assuring her that the Chinese were as devoted to monogamy as Americans were, Huie pointedly remarked that "even preachers in Christian America sometimes could not avoid difficulties with their wives." This jibe brought laughter from the crowd, for the city's newspapers were just then full of stories detailing the domestic embarrassment of a prominent clergyman.

Despite his impatience with the ignorance of some of his new associates, Huie Kin was firm in his commitment to Christianity. That commitment, in turn, gave a new direction to his life in America. Shortly after his baptism, Huie was appointed assistant superintendent of the Chinese Sunday School at Oakland's First Presbyterian Church. The mutual attachment which grew up between the young convert and the Church's pastor, the Reverend James Eells, continued even after Eells left California in 1879 to assume a professorship at Cincinnati's Lane Theological Seminary. The next year, in fact, Eells arranged for Huie, now twenty-six, and another young Chinese immigrant to enter the seminary.

In leaving California for Ohio, Huie Kin and his companion were undertaking an adventure scarcely less dramatic than their move from China to the United States. Over 90 percent of the Chinese population in America was concentrated on the West Coast; only a handful of Chinese immigrants had penetrated the nation's interior. Some of those who had done so followed the mining frontier as it moved north into Oregon and east into Nevada and Wyoming. Railroad construction projects had also scattered some Chinese around, although most of the workers had returned to California when the railroads were completed. Other Chinese workers wound up in the industrial centers of the East as a consequence of being imported from California to break strikes during the strife-torn depression years of the 1870s and 1880s. Uncertainty about the reliability of the newly emancipated slaves prompted some interest in the Chinese as a labor force in the post-Civil War South. Several conventions were held to promote this idea, including one in Memphis in 1870 which adopted a resolution "that the introduction of Chinese labor would be of great benefit" to the region, since the Chinese were "industrious, frugal, obedient, and attentive to the interest" of their employers. Little came of this particular effort, however.

Under the guidance of an enterprising classmate at Lane Seminary, Huie Kin capitalized upon this novelty by embarking on a lecture tour during summer vacation. But while his mastery of English was sufficient to satisfy the curiosity of listeners at his lectures, it was inadequate to permit Huie to pursue his theological studies unhindered. As a result, in 1882 he enrolled at Geneva College in Beaver Falls, Pennsylvania, in order to improve his knowledge of English. Five years before, Beaver Falls had been the site of a bitter strike by workers at a cutlery plant. The strike had eventually been broken when hundreds of Chinese workers were brought in to replace the strikers. Although the strikebreakers had long since moved on, scars from that conflict were still evident when Huie arrived. He encountered difficulty finding a landlady willing to take him. And even though he tried to make himself inconspicuous by wearing American clothes for the first time in his life and hiding his distinctive queue inside his coat collar, it was impossible for Huie to disguise his ethnicity. Letters from the Reverend Eells addressed simply to "Huie Kin, Chinaman, Beaver Falls, Pennsylvania" invariably found their way to him.

In the same year that Huie began his studies at Geneva College, the Chinese Exclusion Act became law. Adoption of the Exclusion Act marked the culmination of several years of political agitation and maneuvering at the national level. In 1876 both the Democratic and Republican Parties had adopted anti-Chinese planks in their platforms as they competed for votes in the volatile western states. Simultaneously a special Congressional committee held hearings in California, taking testimony from opponents of Chinese immigration. Its report recommended legislation to save the Pacific Coast from the Chinese "scourge." Congress finally acted upon the committee's recommendation in 1879, passing a bill to prohibit Chinese immigration, but President Rutherford B. Hayes vetoed it as contrary to the terms of the Burlingame Treaty. Bowing to political pressure, the Hayes Administration in 1880 renegotiated the Treaty to permit the United States to "regulate, limit or suspend" but not prohibit immigration by Chinese laborers. California Senator John F. Miller immediately introduced a measure to "suspend" entry by Chinese laborers for 20 years, although other types of immigrants—scholars, merchants, travelers—would still be permitted to enter. By the time Miller's bill passed Congress, the White House was occupied by Chester A. Arthur, who vetoed it as contrary to the spirit of the renegotiated treaty. The Miller bill was hastily revised, the suspension reduced to 10 years, and signed into law by President Arthur.[5]

---

[5] The Exclusion Act of 1882 was extended for 10 years in 1892 by the Geary Act, and renewed again in 1902. In 1904 it was extended without limitation. Not until 1943 was the prohibition on Chinese immigration and naturalization rescinded.

The 1882 measure also specifically prohibited Chinese immigrants from becoming naturalized citizens. In this it marked a turning point in American immigrant history: the United States repudiated its traditional policy of accepting immigrants regardless of their ethnic origins. This new approach would be carried to its logical conclusion with the adoption in 1924 of the racially discriminatory National Origins Act. The Chinese Exclusion Act opened the floodgates of restrictive legislation: the first general federal immigration law in American history was enacted by Congress just a few weeks later.[6] Over the next several decades, other measures would define various categories of immigrants as undesirable on the basis of ethnic, political, economic, and medical standards.

The Chinese Exclusion Act had an impact that was much more immediate than that, however. Chinese immigration dropped dramatically. In the dozen years preceding passage of the Exclusion Act, an annual average of over 14,500 Chinese immigrants had entered the United States. In the first full year under the new law, there were only 279, and the year after that just 22! Some Chinese attempted to see a bright spot in this gloomy picture. Ch'en Lan-pin, Chinese ambassador to the United States, hoped that the measure would at least satisfy nativist passions and make life easier for those of his countrymen already in the United States. But the Exclusion Act appeared to aggravate, rather than relieve, anti-Chinese feeling. The violence reached a peak in 1885. Bloody riots forced many of Seattle's Chinese to flee the city; in Tacoma the entire Chinese population was forced into boxcars and shipped out of town. The worst incident took place in Rock Springs, Wyoming, where Chinese coal miners were attacked by a mob of whites. Before order was restored by federal troops the local Chinatown had been burned down, at least 28 Chinese killed, and most of the rest driven out of the Wyoming Territory.

The same year that these tragedies struck his countrymen, good fortune smiled on Huie Kin. In 1885, after two years at Geneva College and a third at another school, the Presbyterian Board of Foreign Missions called him to New York to begin missionary work in that city's Chinatown, a community of perhaps 5,000. Immediately upon assuming his new post, Huie immersed himself in the problems of a people whom he described as "strangers in a strange land, unknown beyond the narrow circle of their own nationality . . . [and] without significance." His days were taken up with helping them settle disputes with landlords, restoring domestic harmony, tending to the sick, or solving legal difficulties. These tasks were complicated by several factors, including the ever-present prejudice against the Chinese. This extended even to his associates in the Presbyterian Church—one leading minister bluntly informed Huie that he was "not favorably disposed to receiving Chinamen, in strange Oriental garb, into his church." A further problem was posed by the Chinese whom Huie

---

[6]The Immigration Act of 1882 barred convicts, lunatics, idiots, or persons likely to become a public charge from entering the United States. In addition, it imposed a tax of fifty cents upon each immigrant.

hoped to assist—what he termed their "natural diffidence . . . to come forward" made them extremely reluctant to avail themselves of the mission's facilities.

Huie Kin overcame the latter obstacle by taking several months to familiarize himself with the Chinese community and people in greater New York. He tirelessly visited all the Chinese shops and factories in the area, making himself known. As a result, many of New York's Chinese inhabitants eventually came to view Huie as they would a kinsman—with absolute trust. Prior to his arrival in New York, the city's Chinese who became seriously ill often suffered without benefit of medical attention, due to poverty, ignorance of the available charities, and an inordinate fear of American doctors and hospitals. By convincing suspicious Chinese that the doctors would not remove their eyes, by personally accompanying prospective patients to Presbyterian Hospital, by visiting them while they remained at the institution, and by escorting them home again after they had been discharged, Huie Kin insured medical care for literally hundreds of people who otherwise would have been without it. Since many of these patients were indigent, much of his time was spent collecting charitable contributions and seeking cancellation of hospital costs.

But Huie aspired to more than merely saving lives; he hoped to save souls as well. To this end, he was ordained as a Presbyterian minister in 1895, New York's first Chinese clergyman and one of only three in the entire country. Huie Kin's desire to save souls led him to embark upon campaigns to eradicate the prostitution, drug use and gambling for which Chinatown was notorious. These activities—particularly prostitution—were to a great extent reflective of the largely male nature of Chinese society in America. Only a small proportion of the total number of Chinese immigrants consisted of women; the possibility of family life existed for relatively few American Chinese. This became even more true with the passage of the Chinese Exclusion Act. And since American women were essentially unattainable for Chinese males, their only prospect for female companionship lay with prostitutes.

The tragedy of prostitution resided in the fact that few of the young Chinese women engaged in it did so by choice. Some had been kidnapped in China, others in effect "sold" to settle a debt, while still others had immigrated freely to America in response to what they believed were proposals of marriage. Although some managed to escape their situation without any help, assistance was often required. Among those active in this effort was Huie Kin, whose mission sometimes served as a refuge for former prostitutes. There was some element of risk in this—prostitution and other vice activities were controlled by powerful tongs which resented any intrusion into their affairs. The willingness of the tongs to resort to violent means to retain control of vice operations was illustrated in spectacular fashion by the "tong wars" which raged in New York's Chinatown around the turn of the century. Huie Kin was given a more personal demonstration when several thugs invaded his home in search of a prostitute he had helped escape. After threatening Huie's wife and oldest son, the thugs ransacked the house. Nor was this an isolated incident. Huie Kin's campaign against vice led to several threats against him and even to attempts upon his life.

The overt vice of Chinatown and the violence frequently associated with it fed popular prejudice against the Chinese. In 1889 Huie encountered the most painful exhibition of this prejudice when he married Louise Van Arnam over the angry protests of her family. Louise Van Arnam had come to the city from upstate New York in 1886 to be a missionary. Because of their parallel callings, her path soon crossed that of Huie Kin. Completely smitten, Huie invited her to assist him at the Chinese mission. When Louise's devotion to her work ripened into affection for her coworker, Huie Kin proposed marriage. Despite her family pastor's concern about the children of mixed marriages, the Huies eventually produced nine. The children's names indicate just how far Huie Kin had come in adjusting to American culture: Irving, Harriet, Alice, Caroline, Helen, Ruth, Dorothy, Albert, Arthur.

In addition to raising a family, the couple continued to work together: Louise Huie made their home the center of the mission. She frequently filled in for her husband when crises arose in his absence, dealing with tong "hatchet-men" and unsympathetic police officers with equal aplomb. Confrontations with the police were not infrequent, due both to the mission's role as the champion of a powerless group and to the increasingly severe nature of the federal restrictions upon Chinese immigration. One of the most stringent measures was the Scott Act, passed in 1888, half a dozen years after the Chinese Exclusion Act. The Scott Act absolutely prohibited entry into the United States by Chinese laborers, including even those who had already established American residence and were merely temporarily out of the country. As a result of this measure, more than 20,000 laborers visiting their families in China—and carrying American re-entry permits—were stranded, cut off from their homes and jobs in the United States. Although this measure clearly violated the 1880 treaty with China, federal courts refused to disallow it. And since the Chinese government was too weak to command the respect of western nations, its nationals were subjected to continued harsh treatment by other countries.

When the Chinese Exclusion Act expired in 1892 it was replaced by a more stringent law called the Geary Act. This measure not only extended the existing exclusion, it struck at Chinese already resident in the United States. They were required under the Geary Act to register with the federal government and carry certificates confirming their right to reside in the United States. Anyone arrested without such documentation had to prove he was entitled to remain in the country. It was their responsibility, in other words, to demonstrate their right to be in the United States. This clearly represented a reversal of the traditional standard of American justice—that a person is innocent until proven guilty. Those accused of violating the Geary Act were, because they were Chinese, presumed guilty unless they could establish their innocence. The Geary Act seemed also to contradict the Constitutional prohibition of "excessive bail," by barring altogether alleged violators from posting bond.

The increasing severity of their treatment under the law generated considerable dissatisfaction among Chinese immigrants. However, instead of directing their anger against an American government over which they had no influence, they focused their resentment upon their own leadership. In the late 1880s and 1890s San Francisco's Chinatown, home of the nation's largest Chinese community, was shaken by violent protests. Believing that the Six Companies no longer effectively represented their interests, many Chinese cast their lot with several tongs which were challenging for control. But protest by the Chinese, no matter whom it was directed against, was futile. They were simply irrelevant to most Americans.

Huie Kin made no secret of his opposition to the Geary Act. When possible he assisted those who became entangled in its provisions. In one such instance Louise Huie was horrified to find her husband harboring in their kitchen four Chinese laundrymen who lacked proper registration papers—she had just finished insisting to the police that she had no knowledge of the men. With obvious delight, Huie recounted another incident in which the unfair law and an unsympathetic bureaucrat had unwittingly combined to assist a Chinese immigrant:

> A Chinese had bought a ticket for China and was on his way. At Buffalo, he was arrested and detained, because he could not produce his registration paper. I was asked to go and straighten up the case. I called on the Commissioner of Immigration and explained that the man was really on his way to China; he had no registration paper, but there was his ticket for the journey. The Commissioner would not believe us and said that the United States Government would deport the person. So I got the man to give me his ticket and collected the refund for him, while the United States provided him with a free trip back to the old country.

Despite his stance on the Geary Act, Huie remained on the good side of authorities. He was invaluable as their intermediary in dealing with New York's Chinese. And at hospitals those people identified as "Huie's patients" received the best treatment. In addition to arranging medical care for the sick, Huie Kin directed a boy's day school. This institution was so highly thought of that it not only served the children of Chinese living in America, it began to attract students directly from China. Huie's mission also functioned as a sort of way-station for homeless Chinese in transit. Among those whom Huie accommodated at the mission was Sun Yat-sen, the scholarly future president of republican China. Huie later claimed that Dr. Sun wrote the first draft of the Constitution of the Chinese Republic while at the mission.

Few individual Chinese had as stunning an impact upon their country as Sun Yat-sen did, but the collective weight of the Chinese who immigrated to America and later returned to China was enormous. The skills and knowledge they brought back with them proved essential for China's modernization. The savings which they sent or brought home provided China with capital desperately needed for development. And, according to a former Chinese foreign minister, "our revolutionary movement, which resulted in the founding of the [Chinese] Republic, drew its main support from the overseas Chinese national." Since the beginning of settlement in America, some immigrants had returned to their homelands. But few peoples did so in such proportions as did the Chinese. Well over half of the Chinese who immigrated to the United States before 1943 later returned to China. In fact, from 1908 (when the federal government began to keep track of alien departures) until 1943 (when the Chinese Exclusion Act was repealed), the number of Chinese departing the United States exceeded those entering by a margin of 90,299 to 52,561. In view of the treatment to which they were continually subjected in America, this is hardly surprising. Nor is it surprising that Huie Kin was, toward the end of his life, part of this exodus.

In 1932, having spent 64 of his 78 years in the United States, Huie wrote, "My work in America is finished." China, in the throes of entering the modern world, seemed to have greater need of him. Devotion to his family also tugged at Huie—China was not only the land of his ancestors, it was also by that time home to six of his nine children. All of his daughters had married Chinese, or Chinese-American, men and by then lived in China where their husbands were engaged in religious, educational, or medical work. In contrast, all three of his sons (two of whom went by the surname Van Arnam rather than Huie) had married American women and remained in the United States. There was, perhaps, something symbolic in this: Huie Kin was leaving in America something very valuable in exchange for what he had gained in the United States. As he prepared to depart for China, Huie recalled how in 1868, as "a rustic of fourteen," he had left his native village in order to make his fortune. "I came to America for gold, as many of my cousins had done before me," he mused, "but I have found riches that never rust and a fortune that cannot be stolen."

FURTHER READING

Barth, Gunther. *Bitter Strength: A History of the Chinese in the United States, 1850–1870.* Cambridge: Harvard University Press, 1964.

Chen, Jack. *The Chinese of America.* San Francisco: Harper and Row, 1980.

Kung, S. W. *Chinese in American Life: Some Aspects of Their History, Status, Problems and Contributions.* Seattle: University of Washington Press, 1962.

Miller, Stuart C. *The Unwelcome Immigrant: The American Image of the Chinese, 1785–1882.* Berkeley: University of California Press, 1969.

SAXTON, ALEXANDER. *The Indispensable Enemy: Labor and the Anti-Chinese Movement in California.* Berkeley: University of California Press, 1971.

STEINER, STAN. *Fusang: The Chinese Who Built America.* New York: Harper and Row, 1979.

TSAI, SHIH-SHAN HENRY. *China and the Overseas Chinese in the United States, 1868–1911.* Fayetteville: University of Arkansas Press, 1983.

10

Emma Goldman

Photo courtesy of Library of Congress.

10

Emma Goldman

OUTSIDE THE SHIP'S CABIN the winter wind howled relentlessly. The icy blasts, the uniformed guards, the harshness of her treatment, all conspired to play a trick on Emma Goldman's imagination—briefly she supposed herself to be in the Russia of her youth. "But no," she realized with a start, "it was New York, it was America, it was the land of liberty. . . . repeating the terrible scenes of tsarist Russia!" Peering intently through a port-hole, she could see the city's skyline and then, suddenly, looming large above her, the Statue of Liberty. As she watched, the city and its towering symbol, which had welcomed so many millions of immigrants to America, receded into the distance. Emma Goldman was being deported.

Fully a third of a century had passed since Emma Goldman had come to the United States, a mere drop in a tidal wave of Jewish immigration from Russia. During that period more than two million Jews had fled Eastern Europe for America, exchanging a life of economic hardship, social insecurity, and political repression for one of opportunity and hope. The event which triggered this exodus was the assassination of Tsar Alexander II in 1881. It spelled the end of his moderately liberal regime and signalled the beginning of policies which were frankly and unremittingly anti-Jewish.

Even prior to that time, life was a struggle for Eastern Europe's Jews. The rise of Pan-Slavism stamped them as an impediment to racial unity, establishing anti-Semitism as the litmus test of nationalistic expression. Russian Jews were buffeted by the same forces of economic modernization which created such widespread distress among Europe's masses; the social dislocation which accompanied industrial revolution was blind to ethnic distinctions. But because the administrators of governmental policy were not, the suffering of Jews was amplified. Their economic prospects were severely limited by countless restrictions: Jews were barred from the new industrial cities where factory jobs offered some chance of salvation. Because they were also prohibited from owning or renting land, many Russian Jews entered into petty commerce or trade. Increasingly, however, this brought them into competition with gentiles, especially peasants forced off their land by the new industrial order. Jews were restricted in terms of where they could live, confined to an area known as the Pale of Settlement, a strip of territory stretching from the Black Sea to the Baltic. Within the Pale population pressures quickly became acute: In 1800 fewer than 1,000,000 Jews lived there; by 1890 there were nearly 5,000,000— over 90 percent of Russia's Jewish population. Other regulations restricted their movement, imposed special taxes and established educational barriers.

Under Tsar Alexander II these strictures were eased somewhat, but his assassination by revolutionary socialists inspired an anti-Jewish reaction. The fact that many socialists were Jewish furnished a convenient excuse for the repression. A wave of *pogroms*—officially-sanctioned massacres of Jews—produced widespread terror and destruction, as well as several thousand deaths. The implementation of the May Laws in 1882 imposed further burdens upon them. Jews were prohibited from the professions, public office, and industry; additional restrictions hampered their pursuit of education or their practice of religion. The Pale residency requirement was reinforced. The obvious purpose of all these, and similar measures, was nothing less than the destruction of Russia's Jewish community as a social and religious body. One government official boasted that as a consequence of this program one third of the Jews would convert, one third would die, and one third would flee the country. He was correct in at least one of his predictions: By the outbreak of the First World War approximately one third of Eastern Europe's Jews had emigrated.

A tiny part of that anonymous mass was named Goldman. Emma's parents, Abraham and Taube, struggled futilely for some years against their fate, then bowed to it. Their life in the Pale was one which Emma would later describe, in unvarnished terms, as "poverty-stricken." Late in 1881, only a few months after the Tsar's assassination, the Goldmans sneaked out of the Pale, bribing their way past soldiers, and journeyed to St. Petersburg. Their change of habitation brought no improvement to the family's circumstance. Abraham Goldman was stalked by economic failure and social humiliation. The psychological impact of this was devastating. Her father, Emma would recall, "smarted under daily indignities from the officials he had to deal with. The failure of his life, the lack of opportunity to put his abilities to good use . . . embittered him and made him ill-natured and hard towards his own."

Her father's harsh treatment of his children helped kindle in Emma the keen sense of personal injustice which would characterize her subsequent career. Late in 1885 sixteen-year-old Emma left home, rebelling against her father's attempt to arrange a marriage for her. Accompanied by an older sister, Helena, she journeyed to Rochester, New York, where another sister lived. Within a year Emma's parents and two brothers would follow, because, she later recalled, "conditions in St. Petersburg had become intolerable for the Jews, and the grocery business did not yield enough for the ever-growing bribery Father had to practise in order to be allowed to exist." This aspect of the Goldmans' experience ran somewhat counter to the pattern among Jews, who tended to migrate in family units rather than as individuals. Among other ethnic groups, however, immigration was more often than not a movement of individuals, particularly young men.

Emma and Helena travelled overland to Hamburg, one of the foremost ports of embarkation for immigration from central and eastern Europe. There they booked passage on a steamer. Years later Emma vividly remembered being "herded together like cattle" with the other passengers in steerage. But as their ship steamed into New York harbor in early 1886, her spirits soared. Hopeful immigrants crowded onto the deck, watching as the Statue of Liberty magically appeared from the mist. As her eyes filled with tears, it seemed to Emma that the silent colossus made her a promise that she "would find a place in the generous heart of America." Abruptly the calm scene disintegrated into bedlam. Uniformed guards pushed their way through the confused mass of immigrants, shouting incomprehensible commands. Clutching their few possessions, the immigrants were herded ashore at Castle Garden, New York's reception center for new arrivals.

Castle Garden was a municipal facility, opened by New York in 1855 in what had once been a fort. It represented the city's response to the federal government's abdication of responsibility for screening or processing immigrants. A few services were provided to assist the newcomers: a labor bureau for locating jobs, ticket offices for those continuing their journey into the American heartland, a currency exchange, a small hospital. But overall, Castle Garden offered a very rude welcome, packed as it was with bewildered immigrants and manned by harried, unsympathetic officials. Emma would remember her reception at Castle Garden as "a violent shock," an experience that left her only with the overriding desire "to escape from the ghastly place." For more than a third of century, from 1855 until 1892, Castle Garden introduced the vast majority of immigrants to their new life in the promised land. Finally, in the latter year, the federal government belatedly assumed responsibility for their reception and opened a facility for that purpose at Ellis Island in New York harbor. This development signalled little improvement in conditions, merely an enlargement of scale. The crowds of immigrants became larger, the tempers of officials proportionally shorter. Long lines, bad food, confusing questions, and embarrassing medical exams added to the discomfort. The newcomers were driven from one crowded holding pen to another, where officials fastened tags to them or wrote directly on their clothes with chalk. Years later, when Emma was deported through Ellis Island, she "marvelled that things had changed so little since [her] Castle Garden days of 1886."

Following their ordeal at Castle Garden—or later, Ellis Island—many immigrants remained in New York. The city's Jewish population, approximately 80,000 in 1880, exceeded 1,100,000 thirty years later. Other ethnic groups were similarly represented: By the outbreak of World War I, New York contained more Italians than any other city except Rome. Those immigrants who chose to move elsewhere in America tended to concentrate in the urban industrial centers of the Northeast and the upper Midwest: Buffalo, Pittsburgh, Cleveland, Chicago. Not surprisingly, cities grew spectacularly.[1]

The Goldman sisters continued to Rochester where their older sister, Lena, lived. Emma quickly found work in a clothing factory, sewing overcoats 10½ hours a day. A majority of Jewish immigrants joined Emma in the "needle trades," so much so, in fact, that by 1912 about 85 percent of America's garment workers were Jewish. Some labored in large factories, as she did. Emma found the work monotonous, the discipline iron-clad (permission was required even to go to the toilet), and the pay low. If anything, however, conditions were even worse for those immigrants who worked in tiny sweatshops, crowded apartments in which as many as ten or twelve workers hunched over sewing machines for up to 16 hours a day. For the sake of profit, factory owners and sweatshop contractors reduced wages and cut corners on their workers' safety. The consequences were tragic, often dramatically so, as in the case of the Triangle Shirtwaist factory fire in 1911. About 150 garment workers, most of them young girls, died horribly when fire swept through the factory. Locked doors, to prevent the workers from leaving their jobs early, blocked the escape of many, some of whom then hurled themselves—already ablaze—from the upper floors of the ten-story building.

Rebelling against being exploited, Emma called upon Leopold Garson, owner of the factory where she worked, and asked for an increase in pay. He contemptuously cut off her plea and suggested that Emma seek work elsewhere if she were dissatisfied. Leopold Garson's exploitation of his Russian Jewish workers seemingly flew in the face of his own ethnic background. He was, after all, a pillar of the Jewish community, chairman of the United Jewish Charities of Rochester. But Garson was also a German Jew, significantly distinct—both in his eyes and in theirs—from the

---

[1]In 1880 the five largest American cities were, in order of size, New York, Philadelphia, Chicago, Boston, and St. Louis. The figures below offer a clear indication of the dramatic pace of urban growth over the next few decades:

	1880	1890	1900	1910
New York	1,911,698	2,507,414	3,437,202	4,766,883
Philadelphia	847,170	1,046,964	1,293,697	1,549,008
Chicago	503,185	1,099,850	1,698,575	2,185,283
Boston	362,839	448,477	560,892	670,585
St. Louis	350,518	451,770	575,238	687,029

During this same period Cleveland grew from 160,146 to 560,663; Buffalo from 155,134 to 432,715; and Pittsburgh from 235,071 to 533,905.

Russian Jews starting to pour into the United States. In 1880, when that flood began, there were perhaps a quarter million Jews in the United States, most of whom, like Garson, were of Germanic origin. They or their parents had been an indistinguishable part of the wave of German immigrants to arrive in America in the mid-nineteenth century. Largely unnoticed, unimpeded by racial prejudice, they had moved quickly toward the social mainstream.

The established Jewish community, therefore, regarded the tide of Russian Jews with some uneasiness. The newcomers were seen by American Jews as poor cousins, a likely source of social embarrassment and a probable economic burden. Many therefore attempted to distance themselves from the Russian Jews, fearing that the new immigrants' strange appearance, superstitious behavior, and threatening numbers would inspire anti-Semitic feeling among Protestant Americans, to the detriment of all Jews. In most instances, these reservations diminished within a short time, and American Jews of German descent pitched in to help their East European cousins. A large number of support organizations, the most important of which, the Hebrew Immigrant Assistance Society, was established in New York in 1892, offered a wide range of services to the newcomers: language instruction, help in finding work, medical care, cultural programs, funeral arrangements, and more. But the divisions did not disappear entirely. They were kept alive by religious differences (the new arrivals were Orthodox Jews, whereas those already established in America tended to be Reformed) and by distinctions of social and economic status (Russian Jews like Emma worked for German Jews like Garson). Even in her later career as an anarchist agitator, Emma would encounter—and sometimes be frustrated by—the rivalry of German and Russian Jewish radicals.

After Garson refused to grant her a raise, Emma analyzed her situation. Of the $2.50 she earned each week, she paid $1.50 to Lena for board. Transportation to and from work took nearly sixty cents, leaving only forty cents for incidental expenses. Emma therefore decided to quit Garson's and look for better-paying work. Within a few days she was once again employed as a seamstress, this time in a small shop which paid her $4.00 per week. There she met a young man named Jacob Kershner, who was also a Jewish immigrant from Russia. Following a brief courtship, the two became engaged. By this time, late 1886, Emma's parents had arrived from Russia and she and Helena moved in with them. Even with the girls' contributions, the family found it difficult to make ends meet, so Jacob Kershner was added to the household as a paying lodger. The practice of boarding in was common among turn of the century immigrants, few of whom earned enough to afford their own apartments. As many as a dozen might share a single room, the lucky ones sleeping in shifts in the same bed, the others stretching out on couches or sprawling on the floor. The Goldman flat, consisting of two small bedrooms, a living room and a kitchen, was home to seven people—not particularly crowded in comparison to the lot of many immigrants. And in February of 1887 the number of its occupants was reduced by two, when Kershner and Emma—not yet eighteen—married and moved out.

Their marriage failed from the first. On their wedding night Emma discovered that Kershner was impotent. Moreover, he seemed to be without ambition, content to work in a factory by day and play cards at night. Bitterly disappointed, Emma obtained a divorce within a year. For a short time she moved to New Haven, working in a corset factory, but before long she returned to Rochester. A second marriage to Kershner proved no better than the first and ended the same way when Emma was twenty. Her unhappy marital experience left a mark on Emma which would endure throughout her life—she never married again. Instead she determined to pursue relationships with men outside the restrictions and sacrifices demanded by marriage. During the space of her few troubled months with Kershner, Emma's life took on a new direction, and not merely in terms of her attitude toward men and marriage. It was during this period that the Haymarket Riot and the execution of four men charged with inspiring it occurred. These events left an indelible impression on the young immigrant girl, activating her politically.

The Haymarket Riot capped a turbulent labor confrontation at Chicago's McCormick Reaper factory, where striking workers had been violently handled by police. On the night of May 4, 1886 a public meeting was held in Haymarket Square to protest the killing of four of the workers. Following some angry speeches, the crowd was about to disperse when a squad of police entered the Square. The ensuing confrontation erupted into violence when a bomb exploded in the midst of the policemen. The bomb blast and subsequent shooting left about a dozen killed and more than 100 injured. In the hysterical aftermath of the incident, authorities rounded up virtually every anarchist in Chicago, eventually bringing eight of them to trial. The judicial proceedings proved a grim farce. The prosecution failed to identify the source of the explosion, nor could it link any of the defendants to the bombing. Indeed, several of the eight had not even attended the rally. Nonetheless, all of them were convicted. Four were hanged, a fifth committed suicide in his cell, and the other three received long prison sentences (although they were commuted in 1892). The obvious injustice of the judicial proceedings shocked Emma.

On a grander scale, the Haymarket Riot had two major results. It plunged the Knights of Labor, a promising union, into an immediate and irreversible decline, severely setting back the growth of organized labor in the United States. Clearly only a relative few Americans shared Emma's view. In addition, the Riot triggered an upsurge in nativist feeling that far surpassed in intensity the Know Nothingism of the 1850s. Six of the eight men convicted following the Riot were immigrants, easily identifiable as such by "foreign-sounding" names like August Spies and Adolph Fischer. The whole episode aroused alarm among many Americans over the prospect of revolution and anarchy imported by immigrant radicals. That fear assumed even greater proportions as the volume of immigration increased toward the end of the century. In the years from 1871 to 1880, more than

2,800,000 immigrants entered the United States, a record number. That figure was eclipsed in the next decade when over 5,200,000 immigrants arrived. And in the first decade of the twentieth century nearly 8,800,000 immigrants poured in. It seemed inevitable that this influx of foreigners would have an impact upon the United States.[2]

But what sort of impact, Americans anxiously wondered? Deleterious, surely—because these new arrivals appeared so different from native Americans and even earlier immigrants that they were believed incapable of assimilation into the nation's mainstream. During the last quarter of the nineteenth century the focus of European emigration shifted from the north and west—Germany, Scandinavia, the British Isles—to southern and eastern countries like Italy, Austria-Hungary, Russia, and the Turkish Empire. However much they had been despised at first, the earlier immigrants—who were fair-skinned, largely Anglo-Saxon, and (except for the Irish) Protestant—had been readily absorbed into American society. But the newer immigrants appeared to *threaten* that society. America was still overwhelmingly Protestant; but the more recent immigrants were Jews from Russia, Catholics from Poland and Italy, Muslims from Syria. America's dominant ethnic strain was Anglo-Saxon, but the new immigrants were Slavs, Italians, Jews, and Arabs. The immigrant masses were largely poor and illiterate, raising fears that they would degrade American social standards. And even though most were peasants who were almost by definition politically conservative or apathetic, the relative handful of radicals attracted the attention and aroused the fears of Americans. In view of this, a nativist reaction to the Haymarket incident was almost inevitable, but Emma was stunned by what she described as "the violence of the press . . . [and] the attacks on all foreigners." Determined to fight back, she embarked upon the path that would make her the most hated woman in America.

Ostracized by her friends and even by her family because of her second separation from Kershner, Emma left Rochester in 1889. She arrived in New York, possessing only five dollars, a handbag, and the sewing machine with which she hoped to earn her living. In addition, Emma had the address of *Freiheit,* an anarchist newspaper published by a German immigrant named Johann Most. Gravitating naturally to the city's Jewish ghetto on the Lower East Side, Emma was immediately swept into the political ferment which characterized it. On her first evening she met eighteen-year-old Alexander Berkman, another Russian immigrant, who would become her lover and closest political associate. That night Berkman took her to a lecture by Johann Most. Caught up by Most's condemnation of the Haymarket verdict, Emma joined his circle of radicals. Although in ideological terms she was still little more than a blank

[2]Population figures for the United States are as follows:

1880	1890	1900	1910
50,155,783	62,947,714	75,994,575	91,972,266

slate, Most recognized in Emma great potential as a political organizer and public speaker. Under Most's tutelage Emma consumed mountains of political literature, as well as occasional tastes of the theatrical and musical worlds. After six months, Most judged Emma ready and sent her on a short lecture tour.[3]

Despite Emma's new sense of direction, her life was complicated by several factors. As anarchism was hardly a proposition which paid for itself, Emma had to struggle to survive. That meant hunching over her sewing machine, stitching together women's blouses for up to 18 hours a day. The rivalry for her affection which grew up between Berkman and Most caused Emma a different sort of distress. The contest was finally resolved in Berkman's favor, as Emma reacted against Most's inclination toward domineering and possessive behavior. And always, there was the disappointing realization that her speeches and lectures accomplished little in practical terms. The mass of workers, engaged in a desperate struggle merely to survive, ignored anarchist exhortations. Even members of the tiny labor unions, bent on achieving respectability, were intimidated by newspaper attacks and editorials which demanded that they purge their ranks of "foreigners and criminals who came to our country to destroy its democratic institutions."

Although immigrant radicals and their American-born counterparts shared many of the same complaints about social and economic conditions in the United States, their methods of addressing problems differed markedly. The latter, familiar from birth with the workings of the American political system, tended to seek change within it. In contrast, Emma, Berkman, and other foreign-born radicals mounted their protests as if they still operated in the repressive context of tsarist Russia. Their rhetoric and actions, often overblown and extreme by American standards, alienated the very masses which they sought to "liberate."

Discouraged by their insignificance in America, and aroused by a new outbreak of atrocities in Russia, Emma and Berkman resolved to return to the old country, seeing there a better chance for effecting political and social change. They saved what money they could and in early 1892 were on the brink of carrying out their plan when the Homestead Strike changed their minds.

A walkout at the Carnegie steel works in Homestead, Pennsylvania, prompted Carnegie's partner, Henry Clay Frick, to attempt breaking the striking union with armed force. He hired strikebreakers and a private army of some 300 Pinkerton detectives, a force soon supplemented by the state militia. In the ensuing violence, more than a dozen men were killed

[3]Ironically, the first stop in Emma's tour was Rochester. From there she traveled to Buffalo and Cleveland. Denouncing labor movement agitation for an eight-hour workday as a dangerous distraction from the real struggle against capitalism, she merely parroted arguments she had picked up from Most. But Emma could offer no response to a white-haired worker who pointed out that while neither he nor his contemporaries would live to see an anarchist society, the more readily achieved eight-hour day could make their declining years more bearable.

and many more injured. These events convinced the two young Russians that their war should indeed be fought in America—and that Homestead was the battlefield. To avenge the murdered workers, Berkman decided to assassinate Frick. Emma, the experienced orator, would be responsible for explaining the meaning of his deed to the public.

Frick survived Berkman's attack, although he was seriously wounded. Berkman received a prison sentence of 22 years. And Emma Goldman emerged as a public figure. She published a eulogistic article about Berkman in the *Anarchist*, a radical weekly, explaining and praising his act to a horrified public. Emma also organized a rally to help finance his legal defense. As a consequence, she became a target of attacks in the conventional press and harrassment by police. The police broke into and ransacked Emma's apartment while she was at a meeting; two days later she was evicted by her frightened landlord. Several of Emma's anarchist colleagues were arrested. All this she expected, but what surprised her was the reaction of Johann Most. He at first ignored, then belittled Berkman's act and used the columns of his newspaper to heap scorn upon Emma, Berkman, and those who sympathized with them. Emma responded in the *Anarchist* and then confronted Most when he delivered a public lecture. After issuing a futile demand that Most explain his behavior, Emma suddenly produced a horsewhip and lashed him repeatedly across the face. Her furious attack dramatically showed how Alexander Berkman's attempted assassination of Frick divided the anarchist movement in the United States. A further result was that it embarrassed the Homestead strikers, turning public sentiment against them, which eventually led to their defeat.

But for Emma there was no turning back. She became more outspoken—and more an object of police attention. Following a Baltimore lecture late in 1892 in which she condemned the "ferocious sentence" given Berkman, Emma was arrested for the first time in her life. A few months later, she helped organize a mass meeting in New York's Union Square to dramatize the plight of the unemployed.

Never had the problem of unemployment been so severe. Between 1860 and 1900 the United States experienced unparalleled industrial expansion: The amount of capital invested in manufacturing increased ten times over; the number of industrial workers quadrupled; the gross national product rose by nearly 700 percent. The primary fuel for this spectacular rise was the immigrant labor flooding into the country. According to a Congressional report published in 1911, 58 percent of America's industrial work force was made up of immigrants, about two-thirds of whom were "newer" arrivals from southern and eastern Europe. An even higher proportion of immigrants could be found in riskier or more physically demanding industrial jobs such as coal mining, steel production, meat processing, and construction. But the expansive economy surged upward in fits and starts, its climb interrupted by panic or depression. The economic collapse which began in 1893 was more severe than any the nation had yet experienced. By the year's end there had been about 8,000 business failures; perhaps 4,000,000 workers had lost their jobs, while thousands more were idled by often violent strikes. Immigrants, disproportionately important to the economy's growth, suffered disproportionately when it contracted.

Even those fortunate enough to continue working faced a desperate situation. Wages hovered near the subsistence level in response to the glut of labor. The Massachusetts Bureau of Statistics estimated annual living costs for a family of five at $754. But the annual earnings of an adult male from southern Italy were $368, from Poland $365, and from Syria $321. Women made roughly half of what men made; children earned even less. On average the workday lasted twelve to sixteen hours. The standard in the steel industry was twelve hours a day, seven days a week. Every month workers were given a day off, but in order to make up for it they had to work three straight shifts—36 hours! Hazards abounded: Between 1880 and 1900 35,000 workers were killed on the job, many times that total injured and maimed. Soap powder, coal dust, chemical agents, and other unseen killers accomplished their work with less speed or drama, but with no less effect. Labor unions, small and weak, offered little prospect of salvation. Strikes and other organized action crushed by an alliance of capital and government, proved uniformly unsuccessful. In 1870 less than three percent of America's non-agricultural workforce belonged to unions. To the limited extent that unions did attract support, they depended disproportionately on immigrants. According to an 1886 survey, only 21 percent of union members in Illinois were native Americans. Immigrants were prominent not merely in organized labor's rank and file; they also furnished valuable leadership through the likes of Samuel Gompers and Mother Jones.

But the modesty of union demands—an eight-hour workday, for example—infuriated Emma. The futility of appealing to the government for assistance seemed no less absurd to her. Instead, she urged the thousands of jobless men and women who jammed Union Square to take a bolder approach: "Demonstrate before the palaces of the rich; demand work. If they do not give you work, demand bread. If they deny you both, take bread. It is your sacred right!"

Emma's intemperate exhortation earned her the nickname "Red Emma" and, after a sham of a trial in 1893, a one-year prison sentence for "inciting to riot." At New York's Blackwell's Island Penitentiary, she worked first in the sewing shop, then as a nurse assisting the prison doctor. Upon her release from prison, Emma found that her newly acquired nursing skills liberated her from the drudgery of sewing. "The joy of no longer having to grind at the machine, in or out of a shop, was great," she exulted. "Greater still [was] the satisfaction of having more time for reading and for public activity." Her interest in reading was stimulated and encouraged by Edward Brady, a scholarly anarchist from Austria. He introduced Emma to the works of Rousseau, Voltaire, Goethe, Shakespeare, and a host of others. Brady provided Emma with more than just intellectual companionship—although she rejected his proposal of marriage, the two of them professed their mutual love and lived together for several years.

At Brady's instigation, Emma spent a year (1895–96) in Vienna, studying midwifery and nursing. Upon returning to New York she employed her new expertise in the immigrant slums of the city's East Side. The terrific congestion there, and its predictable results, afforded Emma ample opportunity to apply her medical training. By 1900 the Tenth Ward, which bordered the city's central factory district, had a population density exceeding 700 per acre. The "dumbbell" tenement, so named because of its shape, made a bad situation even worse. The six-to-eight story dumbbell was designed to provide about two dozen apartments, all with ventilation, on a standard 25 × 100-foot city lot. But when two such buildings stood side by side (and there were rows and rows of them), it meant that the only ventilation for two-thirds of the apartments came from a narrow air shaft, often no more than two feet wide and usually filled with rotting garbage. It is little wonder that outbreaks of scarlet fever, diptheria, measles, typhus, and cholera were commonplace. At the turn of the century, the mortality rate in New York's slums was 38 per 1000—nearly twice the national rate of 20 per 1000. Among children under five, it was a horrifying 136 per 1000. The staggering mortality rate among their children was in part an expression of the tremendous birth rate among immigrant women. Emma was especially struck by what she termed "the fierce, blind struggle of the women of the poor against frequent pregnancies." Among her patients were desperate women who had attempted to induce abortion in an effort to escape the trap.

Emma later testified how revealing an experience her service in the slums proved:

> It brought me face to face with the living conditions of the workers, about which, until then, I had talked and written mostly from theory. Their squalid surroundings, the dull and inert submission to their lot, made me realize the colossal work yet to be done to bring about the change our movement was struggling to achieve.

She also concluded that she had been misdirecting her efforts to secure that change. To this point, Emma had addressed innumerable meetings and rallies, but only in German or Russian—her listeners had for the most part been immigrants who, however much they might support her ideas, lacked the means to implement them. Belatedly Emma resolved to reach a new audience:

> From now on I meant to devote myself to propaganda in English, among the American people. Propaganda in foreign circles was, of course, very necessary, but real social changes could be accomplished only by the natives. Their enlightenment was therefore much more vital.

Emma's new strategy not only broadened her audience, it increased her visibility. Press attacks on "Red Emma" became more frequent. Reporters

Tenements, 24 Baxter Street,
New York, c. 1889

Jacob Riis photo courtesy of Jacob A. Riis collection,
Museum of the City of New York.

seized upon a chance remark by Emma to link her to the assassination of the Spanish prime minister by an anarchist in 1897. She was similarly blamed for the murder of the Empress of Austria a year later. Emma's growing notoriety translated into increased attention from the police. During a rally in Providence, Rhode Island she was arrested and jailed.

As her interests expanded, so did Emma's scope. Her speeches were not limited to attacks upon capitalism or diatribes against an American government she regarded as repressive. Drawing upon her own unhappy experience, Emma delivered feminist lectures condemning marriage as an institution which limited and exploited women—and found herself branded an advocate of "free love." She inspired even greater antagonism by denouncing America's declaration of war against Spain in 1898. While pronouncing her sympathy for the Cuban rebels, on whose behalf the war was ostensibly fought, Emma expressed skepticism about the motives of the United States. Because her antiwar message ran contrary to the patriotic fervor which gripped the nation, Emma's lectures across the country were frequently disrupted by jeers and violence. Indignant Americans failed to understand that her target was not their nation but war itself. Two years later, while visiting some of her anarchist colleagues in London, Emma seized the opportunity to denounce publicly the Boer War.[4] She did so over the protests of her hosts, who feared her remarks might undermine the position of Russian refugees in England. Indignantly, Emma declared, "I'm not here as a Russian, but as an American."

Emma's remark was a revealing assertion of how she had come to view herself. She had, at this point, spent nearly half of her 30 years in the United States, having long since abandoned any intention of returning to Russia. She had intently analyzed American social, economic and political institutions, mounting a critique of them in English, for an American audience. There was no doubt in Emma Goldman's mind that she was an American. Few Americans shared that opinion, however. To them, "Red Emma" represented everything that was dismaying and dangerous about the new immigrants from southern and eastern Europe. During one of her increasingly frequent court appearances the prosecutor denounced Emma as one of the "aliens who would just as soon as not run a knife into anyone or blow up half the town with dynamite bombs."

No single event brought these views more clearly into focus than the assassination of President William McKinley in 1901. While greeting visitors to the Pan American Exposition in Buffalo, McKinley was shot several times in the chest and abdomen at close range by an anarchist named Leon Czolgosz. Public officials and newspaper reporters immediately attempted to connect Emma to the tragedy. In fact, she had met Czolgosz earlier that year, recommending some anarchist literature to him and introducing him to several of her radical colleagues. McKinley's assassin readily acknowledged their casual acquaintance, but he rejected attempts by authorities to implicate Emma in his crime. Nevertheless, she became the object of a nationwide search by police.

Fearing for her life after McKinley was shot, Emma quickly went underground. She travelled to Chicago, where several of her associates had already been rounded up by police. She later insisted that she had planned to surrender to authorities there, but before she could do so Emma was arrested. Police officials questioned her incessantly, deprived her of sleep and nourishment, and threatened her with physical harm. The threats were not idle—one policeman knocked Emma down with a blow to her

[4]In the Boer War (1899–1902) Great Britain defeated the Transvaal Republic and the Orange Free State, south African states peopled by settlers of Dutch descent.

jaw, bloodying her face and dislodging a tooth. A hearing was finally held after about a month, but because no evidence had surfaced to tie Emma to the assassination, she was set free.

Emma Goldman was the most prominent victim of the hysteria and rage which followed McKinley's death, but she was by no means the only one. Johann Most was sentenced to a year in prison for reprinting a 50-year-old article on murder. Other anarchists were attacked by mobs or harassed by police. Almost inevitably a connection was drawn between anarchist violence and immigration. Leon Czolgosz was not an immigrant, but Emma Goldman was. A prominent Senator and the Assistant Attorney General both suggested that if Emma had been barred from the United States, President McKinley would not have been shot. The logical consequence of such thinking was the passage in 1903 of "An Act to Regulate the Immigration of Aliens into the United States," which prohibited entry by anarchists and persons advocating the violent overthrow of government or the assassination of public officials. The 1903 law also barred epileptics, prostitutes, and professional beggars from entering the country.

This bill represented an expansion of the first general federal immigration law, enacted in 1882. That earlier measure, which in turn had reflected the racial restrictionism of the Chinese Exclusion Act, denied entry by lunatics, convicts, idiots, and anyone else likely to become a public charge. With the passage of time, the definition of "undesirable" had been broadened: An 1891 law extended the ban to paupers, polygamists, and those who suffered from "loathsome or contagious diseases." These measures expressed the Social Darwinist ideas of groups like the Immigration Restriction League, founded in 1894. Social Darwinists, convinced of the superiority of Anglo-Saxons, reacted fearfully to the rising tide of immigrants from southern and eastern Europe. They therefore attempted racial preservation and improvement by specifically culling out immigrants whom they regarded as weak, sick, undesirable, and inferior.

Emma had at first foolishly fanned the flames which fed passage of the 1903 immigration law by publishing an article which eulogized Czolgosz and rationalized his deed. But the price of her notoriety soon forced Emma to assume a lower profile. She discovered that merely finding a place to live in New York required her to adopt an alias—"Miss E. G. Smith"—for no landlord wanted "Red Emma" as a tenant. Such subterfuge afforded only incomplete protection, however; over the next few years she was evicted from one apartment after another as her disguise was penetrated. Not until about two years had passed did Emma begin cautiously to emerge once more. Soon she was more active than ever, travelling around the country lecturing on subjects ranging from anarchism to birth control and modern drama, rallying support for striking workers, and helping to operate *Mother Earth*, a political review with literary aspirations.

For the next dozen years or so, Emma continued at a frantic pace, conducting her various crusades. One tour alone took her to 25 states, where she delivered 120 lectures in 37 cities. Run-ins with the police became an accepted fact of Emma's life. When not arrested outright by them, Emma could virtually count on indirect interference—the denial of a speaker's permit, or the lecture hall padlocked for code violations. On a tour in 1909 she was detained by police eleven times during the space of one month. Emma Goldman was fair game, no matter what the nature of her remarks: Her attempt to lecture on "Henrik Ibsen as the Pioneer of Modern Drama" resulted in a police raid and her arrest! The fact that Emma was an immigrant left her especially vulnerable to harassment by authorities: Fearful that immigration officials would prevent her from re-entering the United States following a 1907 anarchist conference in Amsterdam, Emma quietly sneaked across the border from Canada. The next year she was detained briefly at the border after making an appearance in Winnipeg, but because Emma was an American citizen by virtue of her marriage to Jacob Kershner, she could not be denied entry. In 1909, however, this protection was removed when federal authorities quietly denaturalized Kershner. Since Jacob Kershner was believed dead, it is obvious that Emma was the real object of this proceeding. On the verge of a visit to Australia, Emma canceled her tour for fear she would not be permitted to return.

Not all of Emma's problems during this period arose from official sources. She and her supporters continued to be attacked by mobs, sometimes under the watchful eyes of police. During one particularly violent episode in San Diego, Emma was threatened by vigilantes and her companion savagely beaten. And on occasion Emma found herself frustrated not by her opponents but by those whom she would help. Following the 1914 massacre of striking miners and their families in Ludlow, Colorado, Emma hastened to the scene, only to be rebuffed by the strikers, who feared that the support of "Red Emma" would taint their cause.[5]

The outbreak of World War I in 1914 added another issue to Emma's catalog of causes. Despite the fact that the United States remained neutral for the first two and a half years of the conflict, the events unfolding in Europe commanded the attention of Americans. The enormity of the tragedy—it would claim 20,000,000 lives in four years—was riveting enough, but interest was intensified by the fact that so many Americans had ethnic roots extending to the countries involved in the fighting. According to the 1910 census, America's population of just under 92,000,000 contained about 13,300,000 immigrants, or approximately 15 percent of the total. If Americans with at least one foreign-born parent are included, the number climbs to 32,200,000 or about 35 percent of the total population. Furthermore, most of those immigrants had come from the countries caught up in the war: There were 4,300,000 immigrants from the major Allied nations (the United Kingdom, Italy, France and Russia) and even more from

---

[5]Following a long strike by the United Mine Workers against the Colorado Fuel and Iron Company, the state militia was sent in. The striking miners' camp was attacked by militia which set their tents on fire, killing two of the strikers and a boy. The next day two women and eleven children were smothered to death in a cave, where they had taken refuge from the militia. About a week of open warfare between the enraged miners and the militia followed. Order was not restored until federal troops were called in.

the principal Central Powers (Germany and the Austro-Hungarian Empire). It is therefore not surprising that many Americans had a passionate interest in the war. Yet few Americans desired to be part of it. Insulated from the conflict by the broad expanse of the Atlantic Ocean, the United States attempted to steer a neutral course. Ultimately that policy would fail, but the United States would be drawn into the conflict by factors other than the ethnic origins of its population—close economic ties to the Allies, the biased attitudes of President Woodrow Wilson and his advisors, the effects of Allied propaganda, provocative acts by the belligerent powers.

Wars always stimulate nationalism and World War I was no exception. And because nativism is a defensive expression of nationalistic feeling, the war gave rise to that as well. Even before the United States finally entered the fight in April of 1917, immigrants had begun to be pressured to exhibit their "loyalty" by conforming completely to American cultural patterns. The clearest expression of this phenomenon, known as "100% Americanism," aimed at making immigrants into Americans overnight. 100% Americanism was rooted in Progressivism, a middle-class reform movement which attempted to clean up politics, regulate business, and improve the quality of life for the disadvantaged. This last aspect involved reformers like Jane Addams establishing centers in slums and immigrant ghettos, where they offered classes in personal hygiene, industrial safety, and English, helping European peasants adjust to the complexities of industrial America. World War I vastly amplified this movement, elevating "Americanization"—that is, learning English, respecting American institutions and ideals, naturalization—from a matter of choice to a patriotic duty. At the same time, the conflict narrowed the reformers' focus; the Americanizers discarded their lessons on cleanliness and safety, concentrating exclusively upon loyalty. Schools, churches, civic and patriotic organizations and businesses all lent their support to the campaign.

Emma's outspoken criticism of the "Preparedness" policy of the Wilson Administration insured her of the Americanizers' hatred. Nonetheless, she felt compelled to warn that "'readiness,' far from assuring peace, has at all times and in all countries been instrumental in precipitating armed conflicts." And even though she failed to fit the Americanizers' peculiar standard, Emma exhibited no doubt about herself. When the repressive tsarist regime was overthrown in March of 1917 and replaced by a moderately liberal government, many Russian immigrants—particularly political exiles—returned to their homeland. But not Emma. She and Alexander Berkman, finally released from prison in 1914, decided to stay in the United States. "Our lives were rooted in our adopted land," Emma explained. "We had learned to love her physical grandeur and her beauty and to admire the men and women who were fighting for freedom, the Americans of the best calibre. I felt myself one of them, an American in the truest sense."

The Russian revolution of March, 1917 removed one of the last obstacles to American entry into the war, which could now be portrayed as a contest between the democratic, enlightened Allies and the militaristic, dictatorial Central Powers. The next month the United States declared war on the Central Powers. The Wilson Administration, not content with mobilizing the nation's military and industrial might, attempted to make the war effort a total one by mobilizing the American public as well. It created a propaganda agency, the Committee on Public Information, and charged it with the task of selling the war to a public that only a few months before had been demonstrably opposed to entering the conflict.

The Committee mounted a massive effort—printing posters, publishing pamphlets, composing songs, producing movies—and succeeded in whipping up a patriotic frenzy. One consequence of the campaign was a backlash against German-Americans and their culture. Certain words, obviously Germanic in origin, were dropped from the vocabulary and replaced by more "patriotic" versions. "Hamburger" became "Salisbury steak," "dachshunds" became "liberty pups." The study of German was eliminated from the curriculum of many schools. The works of German composers like Wagner and Beethoven were struck from concert programs. The California village of Germantown was hastily renamed Artois. Laughable in retrospect, these developments had tragic implications at the time. German-Americans became the object of suspicion, hostility and even mob violence. Ironically the wave of anti-German feeling improved the standing of other immigrant groups, most of which favored the Allies. This was especially true of the immigrants from eastern Europe, who saw in an Allied victory the liberation of their homelands from Austrian or German domination. Their enthusiasm for the Allied cause, often expressed in vehemently anti-German terms, helped shift the weight of nativist hostility largely onto the backs of German-Americans.

The hysteria of wartime inspired the passage of repressive legislation. The 1917 Espionage Act imposed stiff penalties upon anyone convicted of making "false reports or statements" about the war. The Sedition Act of 1918 imposed the same punishment upon anyone responsible for "disloyal" acts or statements, a dangerously nebulous standard. Nearly 2,000 Americans were prosecuted under these measures. The principal targets were political radicals who opposed the war, many of whom were doubly jeopardized by the fact that they were also immigrants. Among the biggest fish caught in this particular net was Emma Goldman. Upon America's entry into the war she had intensified her protests against it. And when the Wilson Administration had imposed a draft in May of 1917, Emma had helped organize the No Conscription League. Within days she and Alexander Berkman were arrested for publishing antidraft articles. Following a trial which mocked American judicial standards, they were convicted, given the maximum sentence (two years in prison and a $10,000 fine), and recommended for deportation after their prison terms. The pair spent a few weeks in prison, but were then released on bail while their case was appealed. When the Supreme Court upheld the legality of conscription in early 1918 and refused to hear their appeal, Emma and Berkman returned to prison. On their last night of freedom the two of them appeared before a meeting of Russian workers in New York. They attempted to address the audience in Russian, but were forced to resort to English. "So completely had we become identified with the life and speech of America," Emma later reflected, "that we had lost the fluent use of our native tongue."

While they were waiting for the Supreme Court to review their case, another revolution occurred in Russia. In November of 1917, Bolsheviks seized power, bent on creating a communist society. This event had a dramatic impact, not only upon Russia but in the United States as well, where it triggered the "Red Scare." Many Americans feared that the Russian revolution was merely the opening salvo in a Bolshevik campaign to revolutionize the world.[6] These fears were apparently confirmed by upheavals in Hungary and Germany in 1919 and 1920 as well as by a rash of strikes in the United States. Most of the strikes which occurred—in the steel industry, among Boston policemen, among workers in general in Seattle—involved nothing more than a desire for higher wages by workers whose actual incomes had shrunk during the war while they observed a no-strike pledge. But businessmen and government officials linked their protests to "Bolshevism" as a means of discrediting them. Because these events coincided with a resurgence of immigration, which had been held in check by the war, it is not surprising that some people drew a connection: Bolshevism was being imported into the United States by the immigrant hordes![7]

Several individuals and groups fed and exploited these feelings, chief among them Wilson's Attorney General, A. Mitchell Palmer. Bent on riding the Red Scare all the way to the White House, Palmer ordered a highly publicized series of raids upon radical groups. Despite the fact that only 39 of them could be deported legally, in December of 1919, Palmer loaded 249 aliens aboard the *Buford*—popularly called "the Soviet Ark"—and dispatched them to Russia. On New Year's Day, 1920, he struck again. His agents conducted hundreds of simultaneous raids, netting 6,000 more "radical aliens." Some were, in fact, innocent bystanders, like the passersby who had stopped to gaze into the windows of Communist offices, or the Western Union courier nabbed while making a delivery! Although the hysteria would subside by mid-1920, and Palmer's political prospects with it, the Red Scare would have a lasting impact upon American immigration policies and patterns.

Emma Goldman emerged from prison at the height of the Red Scare, in the fall of 1919. After the formality of a deportation hearing, she was instructed to report to Ellis Island, gateway to the United States. There Emma surrendered to federal authorities. Over the next two weeks other prospective deportees trickled in. Finally, early on the morning of Decem-

---

[6]This fear was grounded in the Soviets' March, 1919 formation of the Third International ("Comintern"), dedicated to the promotion of worldwide revolution.

[7]In 1918, some 110,618 immigrants entered the United States. Within two years, the annual volume quadrupled, reaching 430,001 in 1920 and doubling again to 805,228 in 1921.

ber 21, 1919, Emma and the others (including Alexander Berkman) were ferried out to the *Buford*, loaded aboard and banished from the United States under the triumphant gaze of federal officials. According to one account, a gloating Congressman called out a sarcastic "Merry Christmas, Emma!" Her wordless but expressive response was to thumb her nose.

Any hopes Emma had for the new Russia were soon shattered. She found herself disillusioned by the ruthlessly centralized Soviet state and in 1921 left Russia in disgust. For the next 19 years she wandered, stateless, yet unable to shake the grip which America maintained upon her. While still aboard the *Buford*, Emma had confided in a letter to her niece, "I long for the land that has made me suffer so." Years later she confessed to Alexander Berkman, "I will never be able to free myself from the hold A[merica] has on me, nor feel at home anywheres." She traveled to Canada to be as near the United States as possible, and was even permitted to make a brief visit in 1934. But it was not until after her death in 1940 that Emma Goldman could return permanently to her adopted country. She was buried in Chicago, near the graves of her Haymarket martyrs.

FURTHER READING

DRINNON, RICHARD. *Rebel in Paradise*. Chicago: University of Chicago Press, 1961.

GOLDMAN, EMMA. *Living my Life*. 2 vols. New York: Alfred A. Knopf, 1931.

HIGHAM, JOHN. *Strangers in the Land: Patterns of American Nativism, 1860–1925*. New York: Atheneum, 1965.

HOWE, IRVING. *World of Our Fathers*. New York: Harcourt Brace Jovanovich, 1976.

KARP, ABRAHAM. *Haven and Home: A History of the Jews in America*. New York: Schocken Books, 1985.

PARMET, ROBERT D. *Labor and Immigration in Industrial America*. Boston: Twayne, 1981.

PRESTON, WILLIAM, JR. *Aliens and Dissenters: Federal Suppression of Radicals, 1903–1933*. New York: Harper and Row, 1963.

RISCHIN, MOSES. *The Promised City: New York's Jews, 1870–1914*. Cambridge: Harvard University Press, 1962.

WEXLER, ALICE. *Emma Goldman: An Intimate Life*. New York: Pantheon Books, 1984.

11

Leonard Covello, c. 1918

11

Leonard Covello

By THE UNCERTAIN LIGHT of a flickering kerosene lamp, the small boy carefully wrote out the message which his illiterate mother dictated: "My dear Husband, I am writing these few lines to let you know that we are all well and that we hope you are well too. . . ." Eight-year-old Leonardo Coviello missed his father, although he could barely remember the man. More than four years had passed since Pietro Coviello had departed for New York. Leonardo, his two younger brothers and their mother waited, with hopes that rose and fell, for a message from across the sea, for steamship tickets, for the chance to reunite the family in the promised land of America. Still more months of waiting lay ahead of them, but at last the letter came.

Pietro Coviello's prolonged separation from his family was painful for all concerned, but it was not an unusual situation for Italians to face around the turn of the century. From 1876 to 1914 at least 14,000,000 emigrants left Italy, seeking improved prospects in other European countries, northern Africa, South America, and the United States.[1] But to describe this movement as an exodus of Italians obscures its nature. Prior to its unification in 1861 Italy had been a jigsaw puzzle of independent states, foreign holdings, and territory controlled by the Pope. While not so fragmented as the Germany of Johann Buettner, Italy was divided by regional identifications which endured well past unfication.

In Italy a social system had developed which directly mirrored geography and indirectly reflected ethnicity. Northern Italians, often Germanic in appearance, regarded themselves as superior to their shorter, swarthier southern cousins. This prejudice was reinforced by the facts that northern Italy enjoyed a higher standard of living, experienced indus-

[1]The dimensions of this exodus are revealed by the fact that in 1900 Italy's population was estimated at 34,000,000.

trialization earlier, and exhibited more widespread literacy than did the *mezzogiorno*, the southern provinces.[2] The Italian scale of social acceptability declined with each step south: Piedmontese looked down upon Umbrians, who in turn despised Basilicatans, while everyone scorned Sicilians.

Political unification in the 1860s did not alter this situation. Indeed, in some respects it made the problem worse. To a great degree, the new Italian state merely represented an enlargement of the northern kingdom of Piedmont, under whose auspices unification had been accomplished. The government's policies supported northern growth, often at the expense of the more needy south. The earliest and most extensive land reclamation projects were undertaken in the north, schools were built, and industrial development encouraged there, while the pressing problems of the *mezzogiorno*—where soil erosion, unemployment, and illiteracy were widespread—went unnoticed. The government imposed a tax on grinding wheat, a largely southern crop, while corn, which was grown in the north, escaped taxation. Understandably, many southerners who had fought for unification in the hope that it would improve their political, economic, and social circumstances were disappointed by the result— power had simply passed from one elite group to another, bypassing them in the process.

Leonardo Coviello was brought up among men—"uncles, cousins, and other relatives"—who had joined in the struggle to unify Italy, and he spent many hours listening to their stories. Living as he did in the mountains of Basilicata—the very heart of the *mezzogiorno*—young Leonardo could not have avoided exposure to their disillusionment. But not all of the problems which plagued the south were man-made. The weather played havoc with the lives of southerners: Winter downpours triggered floods and the unrelenting summer heat severely limited the range of crops which could be grown. "There was suffering enough in the mere business of living," Leonardo recalled many years later. "Torrents of water ... carried the land away in the spring and the lack of water in summer ... caked the ground." Because, as he noted, "empty promises of governments and politicians to build dams and create reservoirs were never realized," it was necessary to catch and store rainwater in tubs. One reason for such devastating floods and soil erosion was the deforestation of much of the south. "Wood was scarce and hard to get," according to Leonardo.

The extreme nature of the weather created a severe health problem. Stagnant pools of water in the late spring contributed to deadly outbreaks of malaria. In 1887, the same year that Leonardo Coviello was born, 21,000 Italians died of the disease. The mortality rate from malaria in Basilicata was the highest in Italy, nearly 19 times greater than that of the northern province of Lombardy. A more common health problem was malnutri-

[2]The provinces which comprised the *mezzogiorno* are Abruzzi, Basilicata, Calabria, Campania, and Sicily.

tion, the inevitable result of the meager diet typical of the southern household. Although not of the poorest class, the Coviellos often ate only *acqua sale,* "hard bread soaked in boiling water with a little olive oil and salt added for flavor." Soup afforded an occasional variant in their diet, but the Coviellos rarely tasted meat. Although he never ate breakfast, and carried to school a lunch consisting only of a piece of bread and an onion or a tomato, Leonardo often shared his food with a poorer classmate.

There was not enough food—or too many people. Among Europe's nations only Belgium, the Netherlands, and England had a greater population density than Italy. All three of those nations were highly industrialized, rendering them more capable of sustaining such a burden than was agrarian Italy. In the south particularly, most people were peasants who owned little or no land. Instead, they were victimized by a system which resembled that of Ireland in its viciousness. Absentee landlords resided in Rome or some other distant city, insulated from—and disinterested in—the problems of their tenants. The dual curse of high rents and short leases was amplified by the landowners' refusal to invest any of their profits in improving the land. Fertilizer was rarely utilized and the antiquated techniques and implements employed by nineteenth-century peasants differed little from the standards of Roman times. The combination of exhausted soil and obsolete methods guaranteed a low rate of production.

Toward the close of the nineteenth century things went from bad to worse. Land became increasingly concentrated in the hands of a few wealthy families, while the number of landless peasants living the uncertain existence of day laborers grew. In Basilicata between 1880 and 1900, the number of landowners declined by 5 percent; in neighboring Calabria it dropped 25 percent! By the turn of the century, half the farmers of Basilicata (and two-thirds of those in Calabria and Sicily) were hired laborers. If lucky enough to work regularly, male farm hands might earn from $40 to $60 per year, although they rarely received all their wages in cash.[3] Steady work was uncommon, however, especially during the winter. And because of an excess of workers, wages actually fell as the century drew to a close.

The Italian economy reeled from several severe blows in the last decades of the nineteenth century. In the 1870s, revolutionary advances in production and transportation made wheat from the United States and Russia competitive in Italy. The following decade saw the emergence of the Florida and California citrus industries—and a sharp decline in Italian citrus exports. At the same time, France's imposition of a tariff on wine shut off access to Italy's principal export market, causing further hardship. An interest rate which climbed above 50 percent aggravated the effect of these developments. When Booker T. Washington toured Italy in 1911, the American educator who had been born a slave remarked that the condition of southern Italian peasants was comparable to that of American slaves a half century before.

[3]In the United States the average annual farm income was $260.

It is little wonder that the turn of the century witnessed a swelling tide of emigration from Italy. Initially, Italians journeyed to neighboring countries: France, Switzerland, the Austro-Hungarian Empire, Germany. By the 1880s, however, the focus of interest had shifted to the New World, especially Argentina and Brazil. In the late 1880s, Argentina attracted an annual average of 57,000 Italian immigrants, Brazil nearly 69,000, and the United States about 50,000. But the early 1890s saw a crisis in the Brazilian coffee industry, while in Argentina an outbreak of yellow fever which claimed the lives of 9,000 Italians and a disruptive war with Paraguay focused the attention and hopes of prospective emigrants upon the United States.

At virtually the same time that Italian immigration to the United States increased spectacularly, the focus of emigration from Italy shifted from the northern provinces to the south. In 1870, census returns indicated an Italian population in the United States of barely 17,000, most of whom had come from the north. Over the next several decades, Italian immigration mounted dramatically: nearly 56,000 in the 1870s; over 307,000 in the 1880s; 652,000 in the 1890s. From 1901 to 1910, the peak period, 2,046,000 Italians entered the United States, 85 percent of them from the southern provinces.

Tales of success in America as well as dismal conditions in Italy helped shape and magnify this movement. It was "a big event" in Avigliano, the ancient walled town of about 8,000 where the Coviellos lived, when a former resident returned from the United States. Leonardo and the other Aviglianese could not help but be impressed: "Usually the *Americano* had a huge gold chain spread across his vest, at the end of which reposed some masterpiece of the watchmaker's art—tremendous in size." Reflecting upon such events years later, Leonardo concluded, "Everything emanating from America reached [Italy] as a distortion. . . . News was colored, success magnified, comforts and advantages exaggerated beyond all proportions." The result was that the discontented masses "believed what they wanted to believe: that if they were ever fortunate enough to reach America, they would fall into a pile of manure and get up brushing the diamonds out of their hair."

Because he was a member of the artisan class, Pietro Coviello's prospects in Italy were not quite so bleak as those of the peasant majority, but they were dim enough to convince him to seek a better life in America. Arriving in New York in 1890, Coviello found himself within a community of 40,000 Italians.[4] That 22 percent of all Italian immigrants in the United States should live in New York City is not surprising in view of the fact that more than 95 percent of the total entered the nation there. A large proportion of these were, like Pietro Coviello, unaccompanied, working-age males who either intended to send for their families after they had made a start in America, or who planned to stay in the United States for only a few years before returning to Italy. In fact, for most years

[4]The city's population at the time was 2,507,414.

between 1880 and 1910, males constituted more than 80 percent of the total of Italian immigrants.

This phenomenon often meant terrific hardship—both emotionally and materially—back in Italy. Leonardo heard his mother exclaim, "Cursed be America. Men are lured away." In order to survive she and her three sons were forced to live crowded together in one room of the house belonging to Pietro's brother. Sometimes they went without food, although Leonardo would remember that pride compelled them to conceal their distress: "We bolted the door and rattled kitchen utensils and dishes to give the impression to our close neighbors that the noonday meal was going on as usual." As the oldest child, Leonardo was expected to help out as much as possible. At the age of seven he therefore became an apprentice to his uncle, a shoemaker. Because education was "highly respected" in the Coviello family, Leonardo also managed to find time for school, although "sessions were short and irregular."

At last, after Pietro Coviello had been absent for six years, he sent for his family. Nine-year-old Leonardo and his two younger brothers relished the adventure, but their mother, who had never travelled more than a few miles from Avigliano, found the train ride to Naples and three-week voyage to New York overwhelming. Leonardo sensed the "fear and torment locked in her breast" and realized from her expression how she "longed for familiar scenes . . . and the security of a life she had forever left behind." Their reception at Ellis Island proved even more unsettling. Because of miscommunication, Pietro was unaware of their arrival.

> Two days and two nights we waited, eating the food that was given us, sleeping on hard benches, while my mother hardly closed her eyes for fear of losing us in the confusion. Once during a physical examination men and boys were separated for a short time from the women. My mother was frantic as the guard led me and my two younger brothers away. When we ran back to her, she clutched us convulsively. Still in her eyes was the disbelieving look of a mother who never expected to see her children again.

When the family was finally reunited, Pietro took them to East Harlem, one of several largely Italian neighborhoods known to Americans as "Little Italy." As distinctive as it seemed, this label implied a broader sense of ethnic identification than most Italian immigrants felt. Reflecting the fragmentation of pre-unification Italy, they exhibited an enduring sense of *campanilismo*, loyalty limited to the area within which the village bell can be heard. According to Leonardo, "Anyone who came from outside the town itself was called a *forestiere*, or a foreigner." "With the Aviglianese you are always safe," his father counselled him. "They are your countrymen, *paesani*. They will always stand by you." These loyalties persisted in the New World. The Coviellos lived on 112th Street, surrounded by other displaced Aviglianese. The Accurso and Salvatore families, neighbors from the old country, were also their neighbors in New York. In other of New York's Italian enclaves, Calabrians clustered on

*Italian Neighborhood, Smith Street,
Brooklyn, New York, 1903*

Photo courtesy of Museum of the City of New York.

Mott Street, Sicilians settled on Prince Street, Genoese claimed Baxter Street, and so on. Ironically, it was only in America that these diverse groups began to acquire the sense that they were *Italian.*

The Coviellos lived in a typical tenement—crowded, dark, airless—with a water pump and toilet in the hall to serve four apartments. As Emma Goldman had noted, congestion was a fact of life in the immigrant ghetto, but among southern Italians, especially Sicilians, it was carried to an extreme. Immigrant families were often large. When the Coviello family grew to include seven children, Leonardo was forced to share a bed with two of his brothers. Many families took boarders into their apartments; for six years before his family arrived Pietro Coviello had lived with the Accursos. In one Italian neighborhood, 3,500 people occupied a single block—the density of 1,100 per acre unsurpassed anywhere in the world. A government investigation failed to discover even a single bathtub on the entire block. The report also indicated that "all halls are cold and dirty the greater part of the time, and most of them are dark." One result of such crowded, unsanitary conditions was a tremendous mortality rate; on a single block 155 children under five years old died in one year.

The congested condition of the ghetto—and the hopelessness which sometimes accompanied it—also contributed to violence and crime.

Crime has traditionally represented one of the few avenues out of the slums open to ethnic minorities. It was a route followed by some Irish immigrants in the nineteenth century, by Jews in the early twentieth century, and more recently by Blacks, Puerto Ricans, and Mexicans. But no group has been more closely associated with criminal activities than the Italians—the image of the stiletto-wielding *mafioso* is one of the most durable ethnic stereotypes in American culture. Ironically, the image was fostered in the United States by northern Italians who carried with them their prejudice against and contempt for their southern countrymen.

At the crossroads of the Mediterranean, Sicily was at some point or other in its history attacked and overrun by nearly everyone—Greeks, Spaniards, the French, Turks, Austrians, even Vikings. The recurring chaos undermined respect for authority, loyalty to government, and the power of the law. Instead, feudal lords took matters into their own hands by creating private armies of thugs to protect their estates and control the peasantry. When the feudal system was abandoned these groups persisted, evolving into outlaw bands of *mafiosi* engaged in cattle rustling, extortion, kidnapping, and murder.

These circumstances gave rise to the "Black Hand" conspiracy scare of the 1890s, when large numbers of Sicilians began to arrive in the United States. Ambitious politicians and sensationalist newspapers promoted the fear that a secret, criminal organization—the Black Hand—was being transplanted in the United States by Italian immigrants. Although unsupported by any evidence, belief in the Black Hand spread. The late nineteenth century was a tumultuous period characterized by rapid industrialization and the extreme social and economic dislocation which it caused. And it was a violent period, marred by upheavals like the Haymarket Riot and the Homestead Strike. For Americans who sought an explanation for their nation's climate of violence, it was far easier to assert that it was a foreign importation than to consider that it might result from conditions within the United States. It was less unsettling to blame some shadowy conspiracy than to acknowledge that poverty, hopelessness, and discrimination contributed to criminal behavior.

The violent stereotype attached to Italians represented a rather cruel irony, as they were frequently the *victims* of assault. The worst such incident occurred in 1891 in New Orleans where the Black Hand was accused of murdering the police chief. Although nine Italians were charged with the crime, a jury acquitted six and a mistrial was declared in the case of the other three. Egged on by a local politician, a mob rampaged through the jail and shot ten Italians to death in their cells. An eleventh, wounded, was dragged into the street, hung, and used for target practice. Echoing the public reaction, the *New York Times* applauded the mob, asserting that "these stinking and cowardly Sicilians, the descendants of bandits and assassins, . . . are to us a pest without mitigation." The tragedy in New Orleans was not an isolated incident. In 1894 a mob drove 200 Italians out of Altoona, Pennsylvania. A year later six Italians accused of a murder in Walsenburg, Colorado were lynched. Five Italian storekeepers who had dared to pay blacks the same wages as whites were killed by a Mississippi mob in 1899. There were other, similar assaults.

But in the public view, the image of Italians as the perpetrators of violence rather than its victims was fixed. This stereotype intensified the apprehension with which many Americans regarded the apparently unassimilable, seemingly inferior Italians swarming into the United States. According to one jaundiced observer, the typical Italian dwelling in New York was a "bedlam of sounds, and a combination of odors from garlic, monkeys, and dirty human persons. They were, without exception, the dirtiest population I have met with." Even Jacob Riis, who wrote so sympathetically of New York's immigrants in *How The Other Half Lives*, complained that the Italian immigrant "promptly reproduces conditions of destitution and disorder" like those in his native land, conditions which in "a matter-of-fact American community become its danger and reproach."[5]

The considerable prejudice directed against Italians also reflected the fact that such a high proportion of them were unskilled that they seemed to have little to offer American society. Three quarters of the Italian immigrants in New York in 1880 performed manual labor; more than half were unskilled. A quarter-century later these proportions had diminished a bit, but 42 percent remained unskilled. At the turn of the century the rate of unskilled workers among Italians was twice that of Irish immigrants and nearly four times as high as among Germans. Their lack of skills meant that Italian immigrants commanded lower pay than those other groups did. But that fact, along with their reluctance to join unions, gave them a competitive edge. By 1900 they were beginning to crowd Russian Jews out of the garment industry and challenge Irish longshoremen on the waterfront.

Since so many of the Italian immigrants were unaccompanied by families, they were often employed on railroad construction projects, which placed a premium on mobility. These jobs were frequently secured through an intermediary called a *padrone*. The *padrone* system was common to all turn of the century immigrant groups, although it is most closely connected to Italians. The *padrone* was a labor contractor who, for a commission, secured jobs for immigrants as yet incapable of fending for themselves. Prior to 1885 *padroni* sometimes recruited workers in Italy for jobs in American factories, but passage of the Foran Act that year barred the importation of contract labor. Consequently, the *padroni* worked the New York waterfront, promising new arrivals steady work at good pay. Their need for work, ignorance of English, and suspicion of outsiders made Italian immigrants susceptible to the appeal of the *padrone*. All too often the arrangement proved to be one in which the workers were exploited—shortchanged in their pay, assessed unexpected "transportation charges," or even subjected to physical brutality. But the *pa-*

---

[5]Born in Denmark in 1849, Riis became intimately familiar with New York's slums as a police reporter. His vivid portrayal of conditions there shocked middle-class sensibilities and stimulated demands for reform.

drone also benefited the immigrant by acting as a translator, locating employment, arranging room and board, writing letters, even serving as a banker who collected savings or sent money overseas.

Pietro Coviello had no need of a *padrone* and, burdened as he was by the presence of a family, he was not inclined to labor at some distant construction site. Although he had worked as a cobbler and had upholstered furniture in Italy, in New York he found employment as a general handyman at a tavern and set pins in a bowling alley beneath it. Coviello made $7–8 per week, plus tips, although as Leonardo noted, he was "often without work for weeks at a time." Coviello's earnings were consistent with the norm; early in the twentieth century immigrant Italian males made an average of $390 per year (even less for southern Italians), well below the $876 which the New York Factory Commission claimed was necessary to maintain a normal family without savings. Clearly other members of the family were required to contribute as well. Women were far more likely to hold jobs among southern Italians than in any other immigrant group, although only a small minority were employed at this time. Children were also expected to do their share. While playing in demolished buildings, Leonardo salvaged lead plumbing and bricks, which he sold to dealers. At the age of twelve he got a job delivering bread several hours each day before school. Although the pay was minimal—$1.75 per week, plus coffee and a roll—it was a vital supplement to his father's wages. A few years later he secured summer work in a factory, earning $3.00 for a 60 hour week, and passed his bakery job to a younger brother. Continuing at the factory beyond summer's end was a tempting possibility; the Coviello family needed all the money its members could earn. But Leonardo was encouraged to remain in school by his father who told him: "In me you see a dog's life. Go to school. Even if it kills you. With the pen and with books you have the chance to live like a man and not like a beast of burden."

Shortly after the family's arrival in America, Leonardo's father had enrolled him in the "Soup School." Run by a Protestant mission group called the American Female Guardian Society, the Soup School derived its name from the bowls of soup served the students every day at noon. It was at the Soup School that Leonardo Coviello became Leonard Covello, his name arbitrarily changed by a teacher who had trouble pronouncing it. In a vain attempt to diminish his father's outrage, Leonard asked, "What difference does it make? Its more American." "Even at that age," he would reflect later, "I was beginning to feel that anything that made a name less foreign was an improvement."[6] After two years at the Soup School, Leonard entered a public elementary school.

Americanization of immigrant children was no less a mission of the public schools than it was of the Soup School. The process was essentially unchanged since John Hughes' time: Americanizing immigrants meant

---

[6]In similar fashion his brothers Raffaele and Michele became Ralph and Michael.

undermining their native culture.[7] In school Leonard Covello was insulated from his past:

> Throughout my whole elementary school career, I do not recall one mention of Italy or the Italian language or what famous Italians had done in the world, with the possible exception of Columbus, who was pretty popular in America. We soon got the idea that "Italian" meant something inferior, and a barrier was erected between children of Italian origin and their parents. This was the accepted process of Americanization. We were becoming Americans by learning how to be ashamed of our parents.

The Americanization of some of its members introduced tension into, or sometimes completely disrupted, the immigrant family. Generally it was the children, more impressionable and less rooted in tradition than their parents, who adapted most readily. Their greater exposure to American society, most notably through attendance at school, furthered this process. Immigrant men usually worked at jobs and engaged in other activities which assured them of at least some contact with the outside world. But immigrant women—especially those with families to care for—were often quite isolated from American society. As a result, they were slow to adjust to American life, clinging tenaciously to tradition. Inevitably this affected the relationships within families. Adults became more dependent upon their English-speaking children and were sometimes transformed from respected figures of authority into sources of shame. Leonard Covello and his classmates were acutely conscious of how "un-American" their parents seemed. Years later he confessed that "we used all our resources to keep our parents away from school—particularly our mothers, because they did not speak English and still dressed in the European way with the inevitable shawl. We didn't want these embarrassing 'differences' paraded before our teachers."

No less important in Leonard's adaptation to American life was the Home Garden mission. Situated in a small brownstone building, the mission offered the youth of East Harlem an alternative to the streets and the waterfront. At Home Garden, children were encouraged to read books, put on plays, and sing songs. Reflecting the religious inclinations of Anna Ruddy, its Protestant director, the mission also offered Sunday school and Bible reading classes. "Miss Ruddy and the Home Garden filled a need we could find nowhere else," Covello acknowledged later. "It was Miss Ruddy who gave me an idea of how important the influence of a teacher can be in the life of a growing boy." He never lost sight of that idea.

---

[7]In John Hughes' view parochial schools were needed to shield the children of Irish Catholic immigrants from the pernicious influence of Protestant-dominated public schools. In contrast, few Italian immigrants attended parochial school. An early twentieth century survey of two dozen cities indicated that southern Italians constituted less than one percent of parochial school pupils, while the Irish accounted for over twenty-six percent.

Home Garden was typical of the settlement houses established by social workers and middle class idealists shortly before the turn of the century. Designed to relieve the tedium and misery of slum life, settlement houses offered a variety of services and diversions to the disadvantaged—social clubs and hobby shops for children, day care for working mothers, classes in cooking and personal sanitation, libraries, theatrical presentations. Because the slum areas were often populated by immigrants, the settlement houses also functioned as Americanizing agencies where English classes were held and democratic principles imparted.[8]

Under Miss Ruddy's influence Leonard drifted into the Protestant orbit. Like virtually all Italians, his family was Catholic—one uncle was even a priest. But in the United States their loyalty to the Catholic Church was diminished by the fact that it was an institution vastly different from the one which they had known in Italy. In America the Catholic Church was virtually an adjunct to the Irish community, led by Irish immigrants like John Hughes or their descendants. Their cold, austere brand of Catholicism was completely foreign to Italians, who were made to feel less than welcome. One immigrant later remembered that in 1886 at the one Catholic church in East Harlem "we Italians were allowed to worship only in the basement part of the church, a fact which was not altogether to our liking."

Moreover, in Italy the Catholic Church was a part of the power structure, removed from the peasant masses by virtue of its great wealth and its resistance to the unification and liberalization of Italy. As a result, they rarely developed the intensity of commitment to the Church exhibited by Catholics from Ireland, where the Church had shared the misery and oppression of the people.

Recognizing that this distance afforded an opportunity, a variety of Protestant groups and churches mounted a campaign seeking converts among Italian immigrants. Newspapers and pamphlets were published and distributed; Protestant churches and missions were founded in immigrant neighborhoods. The Soup School and Home Garden mission were part of this effort. While most Italians in the United States remained at least nominally Catholic, Leonard Covello left the Church. Years later when he married, the ceremony would be performed in a Presbyterian church; later still, he would teach Sunday school for the Methodists.

The rivalry within the Catholic Church between Irish and Italian immigrants extended into other arenas. The two groups competed with each other for jobs and social standing. And just as Irish domination of the Catholic Church inclined some Italians toward Protestantism, the partisan identification of the Irish influenced the politics of Italian immigrants. Even though the Democratic Party was historically more sensitive to the interests and aspirations of immigrants than was the Republican, Irish

---

[8]The most famous of these settlement houses was Hull House, founded in 1889 by Jane Addams in a Chicago immigrant slum.

domination of the Democratic machines in New York and other northeastern cities persuaded many Italians to join the Republicans.

Political parties functioned as Americanizing agents in much the same
fashion as public schools and settlement houses. But the influence which
these institutions could exert was limited by the extent to which immigrants were involved with them. For many the daily struggle to survive
required so much effort that even a free public education became an un-
affordable luxury. Although education might hold out the dim prospect of
some future reward, it could hardly compare to the more immediate and
tangible benefits offered by a paying job. Compulsory education laws notwithstanding, the rate at which immigrant children dropped out of high
school was quite high. A 1911 survey in New York revealed that zero
percent of Italian immigrant children received high school diplomas![9]

Despite an unusual regard for education in his family, Leonard Covello
felt the same pressures which terminated the education of all but a few of
his fellows. Leonard and two brothers worked after school, adding their
earnings to those of their father, but it was not enough to support a family
of nine with an ailing mother. So, even though he had but one year left
before graduation, Leonard dropped out of high school in 1905. More than
economic pressure lay at the root of his decision. Leonard attended Morris
High School in the Bronx, away from the familiar surroundings of Italian
East Harlem. When he and a few companions had entered Morris, they
discovered that the other students "came from better homes in better
sections of New York." As a result, Covello noted that "the fear of ridicule, constant with us of foreign birth, was further aggravated."

After working at a variety of jobs for a year, Leonard was persuaded to
return to school by Home Garden's Anna Ruddy and Mary Accurso, an
interested neighbor. Matured by his experience, Leonard demonstrated
new confidence by excelling as a student and an athlete. He became active
in the literary club, joined the debate society, and wrote for the school
newspaper. His new-found appreciation for learning (as well as his never-
ending need for money) led Leonard to offer English lessons to Italian
immigrants in the evening and on weekends. His outstanding record and
evident promise earned Leonard a full four-year scholarship to Columbia
in 1907.

At Columbia Covello majored in French, although his inclination was
to study Italian. But as he afterwards acknowledged, "to have prepared
myself to teach Italian would have seriously limited my possibilities of
earning a living." The subject was simply not offered anywhere. Still, his
interest in Italian studies signalled a significant step in Covello's personal
growth. In the past he had hidden from his ethnicity, embarrassed and
ashamed. At Morris High he and his friends had eaten their lunches—
"crusty Italian bread heaped with salami, cheese or Italian sausage"—

---

[9]Russian schoolchildren achieved the highest graduation rate among immigrant groups, 16
percent.

before they even reached school, so that their classmates "of the white-bread-and-ham upbringing would not laugh" at them. In college Covello "finally came into contact with men of true intellectual caliber" who accepted him for what he was. Their frequent and lengthy discussions encompassed all subjects, including Italians and immigration. In the process, Covello discovered that his ethnicity was no longer something he needed to conceal. It was a liberating experience:

> Across the lunch table the ideas flew. What had been private thoughts and unexpressed ideas in me for years now found words. I could talk with non-Italians about being an Italian, about being an immigrant in America. Something in me was being set free.

Covello had come to recognize that being an American did not mean giving up his Italian heritage. But when he began teaching at DeWitt Clinton High School in 1913, he had difficulty transmitting this discovery to his students, many of whom were immigrants. Covello taught French and Spanish; no course in Italian existed, despite the city's population of more than 340,000 Italian immigrants. This omission conveyed to Covello's students the same message of inferiority and sense of shame that he had himself struggled with only a few years before. In 1914, he therefore sponsored establishment of *Il Circolo Italiano*, a student Italian club. In explaining its purpose to friends, Covello noted, "It must not be an isolated island interested only in the social or intellectual activities of a group of students of Italian parentage. . . . The *Circolo* must keep in mind that its members are American citizens in an American school and soon to be active citizens in an American city." The club would help bridge gaps which existed between young Italian-Americans and their parents as well as between the Italian community in the United States and the rest of American society. Within this project lay the seed of the community-centered school, a concept Covello would one day be credited with initiating.

At the same time that his career was being defined in terms of its direction, Covello's personal life was also undergoing significant change. Shortly before he entered Columbia his mother had died. Pietro Coviello had brooded about the loss for two years but then remarried, sending back to Avigliano for a wife. This was *campanilismo* with a vengeance—nearly 20 years had passed since Coviello had seen Italy, but tradition was hard to defy. As Leonard Covello explained, "If someone from Avigliano married a girl from even a neighboring town he was looked upon with disapproval, as if [he thought] the girls of his own *paese* were not good enough for him." These strictures applied not merely to the older generation: when Covello married in 1913 it was to Mary Accurso, long-time New York neighbor and native of Avigliano. Mary died the next year, following a lingering kidney ailment. And when Covello remarried after about 10 years, his new wife was Rose Accurso, Mary's younger sister.

Not long after Covello began teaching at DeWitt Clinton, World War I erupted. The intense anti-German feelings which built up in the United States even before America entered the conflict had a beneficial, if only temporary, impact upon the new immigrant groups from southern and eastern Europe. Objection toward them diminished as nativist passions found an outlet in hostility directed against German-Americans. Because the new immigrants came from Italy and Russia—Allied powers—or were former, unwilling subjects of Germany or Austria, they tended enthusiastically to support the Allied cause, which further raised their standing. When the United States entered the war in 1917, large numbers of immigrants offered tangible evidence of their patriotism by volunteering for military service. Leonard Covello watched with mixed emotions as some of his older students dropped out of school to enlist. Despite the fact that he was 30 years old, Covello concluded that he had to do the same, explaining that "if I sat back . . . and did not enlist I would not be living up to what I was taught to believe."

After a year overseas, Covello returned to New York. A wartime contact led to a job in advertising which paid considerably more than he had made as a teacher. But the emotional rewards were far less, so the beginning of a new school year in 1920 found Covello in the classroom once more, teaching what was perhaps the only Italian course offered by any public school in the nation. To his surprise, Covello and his class were the objects of considerable criticism. He was accused of insulating his students from American culture and retarding their assimilation. As Emma Goldman also discovered, the war had intensified feelings that immigrants should conform. Covello observed that "Americanization meant the casting off of everything that was 'alien,' especially the language and culture of national origin." The Red Scare was in full swing. An early and active leader of the Teachers' Union, Covello felt what he termed "the heavy hand of conformity" descend upon the classroom. Since "to express one's political opinions was sure to result in reprisals," he steered clear of political issues—but he refused to yield on his commitment to a theory of education which acknowledged the immigrant's ethnicity rather than seeking to destroy it.

One axiom which evolved from this line of thinking was that "the unit of education was not merely the child. The unit of education must be the family." Acting on this supposition, he helped organize the Italian Parent-Teachers Association which, in the words of one distinguished educator, "afforded a bridge between the schools and the Italian community." Covello also applied his considerable energy to a newly established East Harlem project called *La Casa del Popolo*—the People's House. Mustering the students from his Italian club at DeWitt Clinton, Covello oversaw the renovation of a building to serve as a center for *La Casa*'s activities. There his students published a weekly bulletin which noted neighborhood problems and items of interest, and organized an after-school recreational program for children. But the principal business of *La Casa del Popolo* was adult education—teaching English to Italian immigrants and preparing them to qualify for citizenship. "If we don't help them, who will?" Covello exhorted his students. "Are we going to allow them to be robbed of their rights as Americans?"

Covello's disciples faced an uphill battle, despite their evident commitment. The rate at which Italians, especially those from the southern provinces, became naturalized citizens was significantly lower than was true for immigrants as a whole. On the eve of World War I fewer than 18 percent of Italian immigrants opted for citizenship, whereas among the general immigrant population the proportion was nearly 46 percent. A dozen or so years later, when *La Casa del Popolo* became a center for the promotion of naturalization, the discrepancy was only slightly less. A major reason for their disinclination to become citizens was the tendency on the part of Italian immigrants to return to Italy. From 1906 through 1915 65 percent as many Italians returned to their homeland from the United States as came to America from Italy![10] This figure points to the fact that among Italians the "bird of passage"—the temporary immigrant—was a rather common phenomenon. These transients saw no need to become citizens, participate in politics, or even learn English.

But to those who intended to remain in America, Covello felt a sense of almost personal obligation. He rejected offers to teach at colleges, fearing that such a position might isolate him from the Italian-American community. Rather than seeking an escape from East Harlem, Covello immersed himself even more in its rich life. Outside the classroom his spare moments were spent founding, promoting, or otherwise involving himself in a variety of organizations designed to assist Italian immigrants adapt themselves to American life without sacrificing their ethnic identity or personal pride. Most notable in this regard was Covello's establishment in 1932 of the *Casa Italiana* Educational Bureau. Such an agency was needed, Covello claimed, because "where the Italian immigrant is concerned, the assimilative process has been retarded partly because of lack of intelligent handling on the part of the larger American community and partly by the Italian community itself." Expanding on this, he noted:

> The American community could not, or would not, see the problems that were being created. It is also reasonable to conclude that the Italian, because he considered himself a transient, failed to become conscious of his broader social responsibilities. There was no real development of an immigrant community—it was rather an agglomeration of numerous disjointed groupings. . . .
>
> The need for unification and coordination of all kinds of educational work in Italian-American communities is therefore a pressing matter.

In response to this need, Covello proposed that the *Casa Italiana* Educational Bureau pursue several objectives. It would collect and disseminate "social and educational facts for all agencies and individuals to whom

[10]During the years 1906–1915 2,109,974 Italians came to the United States, while 1,371,931 returned to Italy.

such information may be of value." In addition, the Bureau would function as a focal point of "efforts directed toward social and cultural advancement of the Italian-American." Finally, it would undertake "a promotional program of educational and social activities. To this end it will concern itself with the establishment and guidance of similar organizations throughout the United States."

In a very real sense, the Bureau represented the natural extension of the mutual benefit societies which were so prevalent within the Italian-American community at the time. Initially established to insure proper burial of deceased immigrants and furnish assistance for their survivors, these organizations rapidly enlarged their focus. Groups like the Society for Italian Immigrants, established in New York in 1901, offered their members help in a number of forms—maintaining a library, furnishing interpreters, locating jobs, conducting English classes, in addition to sponsoring a whole range of social and recreational activities. Obviously filling a widely felt need, mutual-benefit societies proliferated wherever Italians settled in the United States. In 1912 estimates placed the number of such societies in Chicago alone at 400, with even more serving New York's larger Italian population. One reason for the prevalence of mutual-benefit societies was the strong sense of *campanilismo* which continued to operate among America's Italians. Most societies were initially established on a regional or even local basis; often they were named for a particular village or for its patron saint.

It was precisely this sort of fragmentation that Leonard Covello hoped to combat when he established the *Casa Italiana* Educational Bureau. Within two years, the Bureau had managed to bring together more than 250 such groups in the Greater New York area to support educational programs, including sponsorship of a scholarship fund for Italian Americans. But his efforts had little lasting effect; the Bureau closed in the early 1940s. Partly the problem lay in the fact that, as Covello later conceded, "the Italian communities . . . never understood educational programs of this character. . . . Such things as educational research and educational programs even for the propaganda of the Italian language never had any financial support." A further explanation might be that another project—more of a mission—commanded increasing amounts of Covello's energy.

In 1934 Leonard Covello was named the principal of newly established Benjamin Franklin High School. His appointment gave Covello an opportunity to assist East Harlem's 90,000 first and second generation Italians more effectively than ever before. His aim at the time, he would note from the perspective of 35 years later, "was to bring the community into the school, so that our youngsters might better grow into understanding and participatory citizens." The community school concept, which had germinated inside Covello's head since he began teaching 20 years earlier, became a reality.

In addition to the standard educational fare, Benjamin Franklin High School offered night classes for adults, maintained an after-school recreational program for children, and functioned as an evening community center. Covello stayed late in his office one night a week, often with some of his teachers, where they "interviewed parents and people of the community who sought our advice on everything from citizenship to childbirth." The school was a beehive of activity:

> Young men and adults who for one reason or another had been unable to graduate from day school were now completing their high-school education at night. In other rooms immigrants of various ages and nationalities struggled with the complexities of the English language, sometimes taught by their own sons, while still others prepared for citizenship tests. In the gymnasium a basketball game was in progress. . . . In the library, the Parent-Teachers Association was holding a meeting, while from the auditorium might come the shrill sounds of an argument that meant that the Community Advisory Council was in session.

When Benjamin Franklin High School moved into a new structure in 1942, Covello carried his program one step farther, opening up the school to all members of the community on a 24-hour-per-day, 365-day-per-year basis. Growing with his school, Covello wrote and published articles on immigrants, communities, and schools in a number of educational and sociological journals. This process culminated with his doctoral dissertation, "The Social Background of the Italo-American School Child," for which he received a Ph.D. from New York University in 1944.

Covello's commitment to the community-centered school remained unaltered even as the community itself began to change. The passage of restrictive legislation in the 1920s had greatly reduced the number of new arrivals from Italy.[11] Instead, Blacks and Puerto Ricans flooded into East Harlem, taking over from Italians in much the same fashion that Italian immigrants had previously displaced the Irish. Other than the fact that they were American citizens, these newcomers differed little from the area's earlier occupants in terms of their needs and the problems they faced. Leonard Covello remained in business at Benjamin Franklin.

Upwardly mobile second and third generation Italian-Americans began to fulfill the dreams of their immigrant parents and grandparents by taking better jobs and moving to better neighborhoods. Not until his mandatory retirement in 1957 did the 70-year-old Covello join this exodus, moving to a New Jersey suburb. But he could not altogether sever his ties to the old neighborhood or its new inhabitants. He took the position of Educational Consultant to the Migration Division of the Puerto Rican Department of Labor, drawing upon his years of observation and experience to render valuable service. In 1972, following the death of his wife, Covello responded to the tug of something even more elemental. After more than three quarters of a century in the United States, he journeyed to Sicily where he joined Danilo Dolci, a social activist, at the Center for Study and

---

[11]Under the Immigration Act of 1924, an annual limit of 3,845 was placed upon Italian immigration. See Chapter 12 for a detailed discussion of this legislation and its effects.

Action. For a few years Covello assisted Dolci in a campaign against the poverty, unemployment, corruption, and crime that were so much a part of Sicilian life, but at last he retired. Remaining in Sicily, Leonard Covello died in 1982 at the age of 95.

FURTHER READING

CINEL, DINO. *From Italy to San Francisco: The Immigrant Experience.* Stanford: Stanford University Press, 1982.

CORDASCO, FRANCESCO, ED. *Studies in Italian American Social History.* Totowa, N.J.: Rowman and Littlefield, 1975.

COVELLO, LEONARD. *The Teacher in the Urban Community: A Half Century in City Schools.* Totowa, N.J.: Rowman and Littlefield, 1970.

————. *The Social Background of the Italo-American School Child.* Leiden: E.J. Brill, 1967.

FOERSTER, ROBERT F. *The Italian Emigration of Our Times.* New York: Russell and Russell, 1968.

KESSNER, THOMAS. *The Golden Door: Italian and Jewish Immigrant Mobility in New York City, 1880–1915.* New York: Oxford University Press, 1977.

NELLI, HUMBERT S. *From Immigrants to Ethnics.* New York: Oxford University Press, 1983.

PITKIN, THOMAS M. *Keepers of the Gate: A History of Ellis Island.* New York: New York University Press, 1975.

RIIS, JACOB A. *How the Other Half Lives: Studies Among the Tenements of New York.* Cambridge: The Belknap Press, 1970.

12

Frank Steiner, 1937

Photo courtesy of Lotte Haynes.

12

Frank Steiner

FRANZ STEINER STRAINED to hear his friend's voice above the roar of the motorcycle. "You had better make yourself scarce again," Fritz warned. "They're coming tonight." Steiner realized all too well that his friend knew what he was talking about: Fritz Schopf was a member of the S.A., the brown-shirted Nazi auxiliary.[1] And Steiner was a Jew.[2] Since the German army had taken uncontested control of Austria in March 1938, the Nazis had periodically swept up Jews and other "undesirables" and shipped them to forced-labor camps. Twenty-five years old, tall and strong, Steiner was a likely prospect for such slavery.

Riding back into town, each man was silent, absorbed in his own thoughts. "God, please wake me from this nightmare," Steiner fervently prayed. But he knew it would not be so simple. His only real hope for salvation lay in escape to the United States—and that hope was slim indeed. For months he had been haunting the American consulate in Vienna, seeking an entry visa—and for months an impersonal bureaucracy had kept him at bay. Nor could he foresee that it would be several months more before the precious visa would be granted and he could flee to America.

---

[1]The S.A., short for *Sturmabteilung*, was Hitler's corps of brown-shirted stormtroopers. Fritz Schopf, Steiner's companion since childhood, joined the S.A. in order to help his Jewish friends by providing them with information about the plans and movements of the Nazis. Following the war he served in the Austrian government in several capacities, most notably as *Obersenatsrat*, roughly the equivalent of Undersecretary of Commerce.

[2]Born of Jewish parents and raised in their faith until he was nearly ten, Steiner became a Protestant at that age when his mother remarried a Lutheran. Years later under the Nazis he would therefore officially be classified as a "non-Aryan," but in their view the difference between a non-Aryan and a Jew was purely one of nomenclature. Both groups were subjected to discrimination and terror, and both were ultimately earmarked for annihilation.

For tens of millions of immigrants who preceded him—for Johann Buettner, John Hughes and others—the major challenge had been adjusting to a new life in a new world. But for Franz Steiner and the rest of the refugees who flocked to America in the 1930s and 1940s, the main mission was much more basic than that—merely reaching safety in the United States. It was a task made difficult by America's new immigration policies, which dramatically restricted access to the United States, and by the bureaucrats who administered them. Despite desperate pleas from terror-stricken refugees, immigration officials interpreted their mandate so narrowly that as millions of souls perished in gas chambers, America's entry quotas were rarely filled.

In a very real sense, the refugee crisis which confronted the United States in the late 1930s and early 1940s was traceable to World War I. The burden of guilt and the enormous reparations which the victorious Allies had imposed on Germany at the conclusion of the struggle contributed to widespread resentment and economic distress among the German people, conditions which Adolf Hitler skillfully exploited in his rise to power. In the United States, the war had led directly to the passage of measures which, for the first time in American history, effectively curtailed immigration.

During the conflict, with transatlantic shipping menaced by submarine warfare, the volume of immigration had dropped off markedly from prewar levels. In 1918, the last year of the war, fewer than 111,000 immigrants arrived in America. Four years earlier, before the conflict erupted in Europe, more than 1,218,000 immigrants came to the United States. Once the war ended, the tide began to surge again. In 1920 about 430,000 immigrants entered the country; the following year approximately 805,000 came. To some Americans it seemed as though their country was on the verge of being engulfed by a flood of foreigners fleeing war-ravaged Europe.

Their fears were not totally unreasonable. Postwar Europe was in shambles, its industrial base shattered, twenty million of its people dead, many of the survivors existing in uncertainty and fear. To some of these, the United States offered the prospect of escape—but many more remained where fate had left them. In Vienna, capital of one of the vanquished Central Powers, the Steiner family coped with the unaccustomed discomfort of defeat. A coal shortage prevented them from heating more than one room of their apartment; insufficient food supplies forced them occasionally to go hungry. Making matters worse was the fact that just as the war ended Hugo Steiner, Franz's father, had succumbed to disease, leaving his widow, Elly, and her six-year-old son to carry on as best they could. Even so, it never occurred to her that a better life could be found in America—the Steiners stayed where they were.

Americans who hysterically claimed that their shores were being swamped by hordes of immigrants were reacting more to their own disillusionment than to fact. After all, even by 1921, immigration was still well below the prewar level. But in the isolationist mood which gripped the nation at war's end, that was still too much. President Woodrow Wilson's crusading rhetoric had inspired Americans to believe that they would "make the world safe for democracy" and that the war would "end all wars." When the postwar world failed to conform to their idealistic vision, they felt betrayed. Disillusioned with the idea of international involvement, Americans retreated into an isolationist shell. Many worried that merely seeking to avoid other nations' problems was not enough; those problems might find their way to the United States in the form of immigrants. Obviously isolationism and immigration restriction went hand in hand, and both were powerful forces in American life by the early 1920s. Restrictionist sentiment was further bolstered by the Red Scare and by economic concern arising both from a postwar depression and the labor glut caused by the demobilization of four million soldiers.

Mirroring the popular mood, in 1921 Congress passed a revolutionary law which established immigration quotas based on nationality. The annual quota for each national group was established at 3 percent of the number of foreign-born persons of that nationality counted in the 1910 census. Restrictionists were only partially satisfied by this measure; in their eyes it still allowed too many "inferior" southern and eastern Europeans to enter the United States. In 1924, therefore, Congress altered the formula by shifting the base year to 1890 and the quota figure to 2 percent. This achieved the dual purpose of reducing the aggregate number of immigrants allowed into the United States and severely curtailing entry by the "undesirable" ethnic groups whose numbers in 1890 had still been relatively small.

The Immigration Act of 1924 accomplished several other things. It barred further entry by Asians, thereby helping to poison relations with Japan. It required prospective immigrants to submit to examination by, and obtain visas from, American consular officials in their countries of origin before departing for the United States. Although this minimized the possibility of rejection by immigration officials in America, it effectively made American immigration policy more capricious, because it was thereafter subject to the interpretation, whim, or prejudice of individual consular agents. Most important, the 1924 law devised an even more restrictive quota system, to be put into effect whenever a special commission of experts from the Departments of State, Commerce, and Labor could manage to establish quotas under its complicated guidelines.

This new system, which proved even more limiting and discriminatory than that which had preceded it, did not take effect until 1929. An annual ceiling fixed the total number of immigrants allowed at 153,714, although America's hemispheric neighbors were exempted from this limitation.[3] National quotas were then proportionally assigned on the basis of each

[3]The hemispheric exemption reflected efforts by the government to mend fences with its Latin American neighbors. Theodore Roosevelt's "Big Stick" policy, William Howard Taft's "Dollar Diplomacy" and Woodrow Wilson's interference in the Mexican Revolution had all complicated inter-American relations. In the 1920s, however, the foundation was laid for

group's representation within the American population as a whole in 1920. According to one blunt Kansas congressman, the law was designed to keep out "Bolshevik Wops, Dagoes, Kikes and Hunkies." This it did with a vengeance. Nearly 80 percent of the quota openings it established were assigned to northern and western European immigrants, despite the fact that in the decade before the quota laws were passed immigrants from southern and eastern Europe had outnumbered them by a margin of well over three to one.

The national origins policy substantially reduced the volume of immigration. In 1930, its first year of operation, 241,700 immigrants entered the United States. That same year the United States plunged into the decade-long Great Depression, a development which amplified the restrictive effects of the immigration law. In fact, immigration was so reduced that for the entire decade those who departed the country exceeded arrivals by about 85,000! Much of this reduction was owing to a policy instigated by the Hoover Administration in 1930. To diminish the competition for jobs facing unemployed Americans, consuls were advised to restrict the numbers of visas which they issued. The device for accomplishing this was a clause in a 1917 immigration act which barred any person deemed "likely to become a public charge." That clause was now interpreted to permit entry only by those individuals with money or property substantial enough to insure their support for the indefinite future—that is, the United States would accept only wealthy immigrants. Within a few months the number of visas issued to European immigrants declined by 90 percent.

Shortly before leaving office, Herbert Hoover reflected upon the decrease in immigration, attributing it to the end of political oppression. "With the growth of democracy in foreign countries, political persecution has largely ceased," he declared. "There is no longer a necessity for the United States to provide an asylum. . . ." The irony of this statement lies less in the President's failure to recognize his own handiwork than it does in the fact that within a matter of weeks Adolf Hitler became Chancellor of Germany.

Almost immediately upon gaining power, Hitler's Nazis began a two-fold program aimed at the political and racial purification of Germany. They initiated a campaign to crush dissent, silencing or driving out opposition politicians, anti-Nazi scholars, labor leaders, and clergymen through a combination of economic harassment, physical violence, and even murder. In pursuit of their goal of racial purity, the Nazis focused their attention on Germany's 500,000 religious Jews and roughly equal number of "non-Aryans," which together constituted less than 2 percent of Germany's 65,000,000 inhabitants. Jews—including the non-Aryans—were an easy target, readily identifiable due to their geographical and

what would become the "Good Neighbor Policy" of the 1930s and preserving unrestricted entry for Latin American immigrants was considered an important aspect of this new direction. Besides, with the exception of Mexico, immigration from Latin America was statistically insignificant, so restrictionists saw no harm in making such an exception.

economic concentration. About three quarters of them lived in the dozen largest cities; over 60 percent of those who worked were engaged in commerce and trade, while many of the rest were professionals, especially doctors and lawyers.

The initial campaign against Germany's Jews began with an economic boycott of Jewish goods and services in April of 1933 and soon excluded Jews and non-Aryans from all civil service or governmental positions. Further proscriptions barred them from the radio, theater, and other cultural endeavors, and limited their enrollment in universities. These and similar measures produced the exodus desired by the Nazis. Within a year about 50,000 people fled Germany—after surrendering a flight tax constituting 25 percent of their property.

Over the next several years the measures directed against Jews became more stringent. The Nuremberg Laws of 1935 stripped them of their citizenship and barred intermarriage or sexual relations between Jews and Aryans. Jewish entrepreneurs were pressured (although not yet compelled) to sell their businesses, and in 1938 Jews were required to register all their property worth over 5,000 reichsmarks (about $2,000) with the government. In addition, the flight tax was progressively increased, becoming confiscatory by 1938.

In Vienna, Franz Steiner—now a young man in his early twenties— followed these developments with only the vaguest sense of concern. His maternal grandmother, an aunt, and several cousins were German Jews, and all were adversely affected by the growing discrimination against them. His uneasiness, however, was tempered by the belief that the Nazi program represented a wild aberration which could not long continue or progress further in a society as civilized as Germany's. This view, shared by many German Jews, helps account for the failure of such large numbers to seek safety in flight before it was too late.

While worried about his relatives, Steiner was not at all apprehensive about his own welfare. Despite the close cultural and historical links between Germany and Austria, Steiner was convinced that Naziism posed no threat to his country. In 1934, following the assassination of Chancellor Engelbert Dollfuss in an abortive attempt by Nazis to seize control of Austria, the government executed more than a dozen of the conspirators and exiled others to Germany. Naziism made only limited headway among Austrians, who prided themselves on being more sophisticated than their bumptious German cousins. Besides, Austria's Jewish community, being proportionally larger than that of Germany, seemed a less likely target for persecution. Steiner felt secure, socially and in every other respect. His mother's marriage in 1922 to Leo Weinmann had immediately improved the family's situation. Weinmann was a successful Jewish lawyer who had earlier converted to Lutheranism in order to advance his career. At the time of their marriage, his new wife and her son—not quite ten years old—converted as well. Continuing in his stepfather's footsteps, Franz Steiner later attended the University of Vienna and in the mid-1930s embarked upon a legal career of his own. His sense of well-being stemmed no less from the fact that in 1937 he became engaged to Moira Auner, the daughter of a cultural attaché at the Rumanian embassy in Vienna.

The bright promise which the future seemed to hold for Franz Steiner had already vanished for his counterparts in Germany. Many of them, in fact—perhaps 135,000 between the time of Hitler's accession to power in 1933 and the beginning of 1938—left the country in response to persecution. Only about 30,000 of those refugees were able to enter the United States, however, even though for the years in question the number allowable under the quota was nearly 130,000.[4]

Throughout this period the Roosevelt Administration adhered to a visa policy that was scarcely less restrictive than that which Hoover had advocated. In 1933 the "likely to become a public charge" clause was reinterpreted in such a way that only applicants who were wealthy or who could present "affidavits of support" from immediate relatives in the United States could hope to obtain visas. This latter requirement was so limiting that thousands of German Jews were discouraged from even applying for visas. In 1934 and 1935 the number of such applicants actually declined, despite the increasing persecution to which they were subjected by the Nazis. The escalating flight tax collected from refugees rendered ridiculous the notion that they could satisfactorily demonstrate the requisite means for supporting themselves. Not until 1939, when the State Department slightly relaxed its interpretation of the immigration code, was the German quota filled for the first time.

This policy clearly conflicted with the words of welcome engraved at the base of the Statue of Liberty, and it defied the American tradition of granting asylum. Historically, fugitives from oppression had not only found refuge in America, but often had been embraced in sympathy. John Winthrop's Puritans fled to Massachusetts, escaping religious persecution in England; the Germantown through which Johann Buettner passed had been established by German refugees invited to Pennsylvania by that colony's founder. Sometimes Americans suffered attacks of apprehension at an influx of foreign revolutionaries, as they did in 1848, but they erected no barriers to entry. In the 1930s, however, those seeking to escape the Nazis confronted a different situation—the welcome mat had been removed and the American people and their government were determined to keep it hidden.

Several explanations can be found for this. The Great Depression lingered on throughout the 1930s; even as late as 1940 some 9,000,000 Americans were still looking for work. With jobs in such short supply, many Americans questioned the wisdom of generating more competition in the form of immigrants. Anti-Semitism also played a considerable role in shaping America's response to the refugees. On the increase since the late 1800s when Russian Jews like Emma Goldman had poured into the United

[4]To this point, more refugees had gone to Palestine—a British-held League of Nations mandate—than to the United States. Argentina, Brazil and South Africa also absorbed significant numbers. Nearly 50,000 refugees remained in Europe, many of them hoping to emigrate overseas but frustrated in their attempts to do so.

States, anti-Semitism was a powerful force by the 1930s. A 1938 opinion poll revealed that 60 percent of Americans objected to those Jews who were already present in the country. A series of polls taken over the next three years showed that as much as one third of the American public was willing to approve an anti-Jewish campaign, approximately another third would not object to it, and only one third pronounced itself opposed. Virtually every survey on the subject prior to 1946 indicated that Jews were the group which Americans regarded as the greatest menace to the nation. These attitudes extended from the streets to the highest levels of government; Undersecretary of State William Phillips made no secret of his anti-Semitic views. Isolationism also militated against a more sympathetic refugee policy. Many Americans, still fearful of foreign entanglement, dismissed the problem as Europe's responsibility.

Those isolationist tendencies in fact increased during the mid-1930s, fed by the expansion of German power. In defiance of the Versailles Treaty which had ended World War I, Hitler in 1935 began to rearm Germany. The next year German troops reoccupied and fortified the Rhineland, while Hitler reinstituted conscription and began constructing an air force, again in violation of the Versailles settlement. Clearly trouble was brewing in Europe, but the American people meant to steer clear of it.

The unwillingness of the United States—or any other nation—to stand against him encouraged Hitler. On March 12, 1938 unresisted German troops occupied Austria, the country of his birth. The next day Hitler proclaimed the two nations formally unified. The *Anschluss*, as it was called, spelled disaster for Austria's 190,000 Jews as well as a somewhat smaller number of non-Aryans. The anti-Jewish program which had evolved over five years in Germany was now immediately applicable in Austria. Within hours of the takeover, hundreds of Jewish leaders were arrested. Jews were evicted from apartments, banished from schools, dismissed from jobs, prohibited from voting. Their businesses were plundered, their synagogues desecrated. Physical assaults upon them became commonplace and went unpunished. Within two weeks of the *Anschluss* the mortality rate among Viennese Jews increased more than 800 percent. The New York *Times* reported that as many as 170 committed suicide each day. Many more elected to try to save their own lives. In the five months following the German takeover, about 40,000 Austrian Jews lined up at American consulates to apply for visas.

Among the thousands besieging the consulate in Vienna in March of 1938 was Franz Steiner. His family, which now included a half sister, Lotte, as well as his parents, had quickly concluded that his flight to the United States represented their likeliest hope. If he could get in, he stood the best chance of finding the job that would enable him to furnish affidavits of support for the rest of them. At first Steiner had intended to stay relatively close to his homeland; England, then Cyprus, seemed likely possibilities—but he learned almost immediately that they would not accept him. But there was a slight chance that the United States would issue him a visa. He found his way impeded, however, by the multitude of forms and data which the United States required: birth certificate, passport, health clearance, financial records, affidavit of support, and more. Collecting and submitting the required documents was further complicated by the fact that Nazi bureaucrats could hardly be depended on to furnish Steiner the records he needed.

Deeply disturbed by the *Anschluss* and its turbulent aftermath, President Franklin D. Roosevelt responded by combining the small Austrian quota (1,413) with Germany's larger one (25,957) to facilitate the escape of Austria's Jews. He also invited 32 nations, primarily in Latin America and Europe, to a conference to address the refugee situation. Held at Evian-les-Bains, France in July of 1938, the conference accomplished very little. At the outset the United States made clear its determination to adhere to its quota system, pledging only that the quotas would be more fully utilized in the future. Western European nations were no less reluctant to make any commitment; most of them had already absorbed, in proportion to their numbers, many more refugees than had the United States.

Roosevelt hoped to promote resettlement of the refugees in underdeveloped areas of Latin America, Africa, or Asia; discussions suggested possible sites ranging from Madagascar to Mindanao. But the attitude which prevailed at Evian was that expressed by an Australian delegate who declared, "As we have no real racial problem, we are not desirous of importing one." Aside from creating the powerless Intergovernmental Committee on Refugees, the conference was a failure. Roosevelt dared not go further. A *Fortune* magazine poll published in the month of the Evian conference revealed that 66 percent of those surveyed believed the refugees should be kept out of the United States altogether; only 18 percent were, like the President, willing to admit refugees within the existing quotas; while under 5 percent advocated increasing the quotas if it were necessary to accommodate the refugees. Such figures were too dramatically one-sided for a politician as experienced as Roosevelt to ignore.

Still, the one technical change made by the State Department to fulfill the President's pledge to utilize the quotas fully did open the door wider for Franz Steiner. Affidavits of support for refugees would now be accepted from any willing and sufficiently well-endowed individual, not just from relatives. Because Steiner was not aware that he had any relatives in the United States, this modification greatly improved his prospects for a visa. Exploiting a business connection, Leo Weinmann was able to secure the necessary pledge of support from the daughter of one of his clients, who had married into New York's wealthy Astor family.

As the ponderous bureaucracy slowly digested the various documents which Steiner fed it, his position grew increasingly precarious. Barred from practicing law by the Nazis, Steiner attempted a crash course in ceramic work at his uncle's tile factory. His hope was that the knowledge he acquired would land him a job in America, but in the meantime it did not provide a living. And always there was the awful possibility of arbitrary arrest by the Nazis, followed by deportation to a labor camp or even death. Steiner's physical appearance offered him some limited protection—with his chestnut-colored hair, blue eyes, *lederhosen*, and duelling scars, he so resembled the archetypical Nazi that he was frequently greeted on the street with a cheerful "Heil Hitler!" Even more insurance came in the form of Fritz Schopf, his S.A. friend who several times took Steiner on motorcycle rides to warn him of impending raids. On those occasions Steiner hid in the home of his fiancée, which, as the residence of a Rumanian diplomat, afforded him sanctuary. Even there, however, he felt insecure—Moira's father, Dr. Michael Auner, was anti-Semitic and strongly objected to his daughter's engagement to Steiner. Dr. Auner had tried to break apart their relationship, and refused absolutely to speak with, or even to see, Steiner—but he also refused to denounce him to the Nazis.

Steiner's position—and that of all Jews—eroded further on November 7, 1938, his twenty-sixth birthday. On that day a Jewish youth—whose parents in Germany had been victimized by the Nazis—assassinated a German embassy official in Paris. Retaliation came two nights later on what became known as *Kristallnacht* ("night of crystal"—a reference to the shattered glass in Jewish homes and shops). Throughout Germany (including Austria) mobs of Nazi stormtroopers and civilians looted Jewish-owned businesses, burned synagogues, destroyed homes, and wrecked hospitals, terrorizing, beating and killing their Jewish occupants. Upwards of 50,000 Jews were arrested and shipped to concentration camps. The German government then imposed an "atonement fine" of $400,000,000 upon the Jewish population, to be paid by the confiscation of property. At the same time, the government issued a Decree for the Elimination of Jews from German Economic Life, requiring Jews to transfer their business enterprises to Aryans within seven weeks.

The savagery of the events associated with *Kristallnacht* stunned much of America. President Roosevelt demonstrated his anger by recalling the American ambassador from Berlin "for report and consultation." And, in a sympathetic gesture, he extended for at least six months the visitors' visas held by 12,000–15,000 German Jews, providing them temporary refuge. At the same time, however, Roosevelt rejected any suggestion to modify the quota system, and the State Department moved to restrict the granting of visitors' visas! This sort of schizophrenic policy reflected quite closely the attitude of the American people. Polls taken shortly after *Kristallnacht* showed that 94 percent of those surveyed disapproved of Germany's treatment of its Jews, but 77 percent of the public also opposed admitting more Jewish refugees.

The horror of *Kristallnacht* did stimulate immigration officials, for the time being at least, to exploit fully the quotas. Within about two weeks Steiner's visa—pending for more than eight months—was suddenly approved. But what remained for him to accomplish was even trickier—he needed to obtain an exit permit from the Nazis. This involved collecting more documents—financial records and the like—and presenting them at various offices. It meant lining up at three in the morning and waiting fourteen hours only to be denied service or sent elsewhere by a sneering official. Nazi stormtroopers preyed on the Jews standing in line, arresting them for shipment to concentration camps. But there was nothing else to do. The few days that this took seemed to last an eternity, but by the beginning of December Steiner was granted the permit. He booked passage on the next ship leaving Europe (the *Nieuw Amsterdam*, from Rotterdam), bid his family and fiancée a tearful farewell, and departed on the very day he had been ordered by the Nazis to report for transportation to a labor camp. Less than two weeks later he was in the United States, with a few items of clothing, ten dollars (all the money the Nazis would permit him to take), and a stamp collection whose value was more sentimental than monetary.

Two weeks before he left Austria, Steiner had learned from his uncle that he had a cousin in New York. Immediately upon arriving he made the most of this connection, temporarily moving into the Bronx apartment of Jesse Steiner. Over the next few days Franz discovered, to his amazement, that he had between 50 and 60 second and third cousins in New York City alone. Eight of his grandfather's ten siblings had immigrated to America years before, and their many descendants represented to the young refugee what he later would describe as an "unexpected asset." Few of them were financially secure, ranging as they did from the middle class downward, but almost all of them embraced him warmly—inviting him for meals, providing sympathetic company, and helping him look for work. The only relatives who refused contact with Steiner were the few who could make some claim to affluence; they were, he concluded, afraid that he "would touch them for money."

The response of Steiner's American cousins to his plight mirrored the reaction of America's Jewish community as a whole to the refugee problem. Some Jews, fearful that an influx of refugees might damage them personally by fanning the flames of anti-Semitism, opposed any special efforts to aid Hitler's victims. The great majority, however, felt a strong sense of kinship toward their European counterparts and offered them assistance. Although jurisdictional disputes and jealous factionalism did hamper some of their efforts, a number of agencies—the Hebrew Sheltering and Immigrant Aid Society, German-Jewish Children's Aid, The American Jewish Congress, and others—provided invaluable services to the refugees. Not all such agencies were strictly Jewish; the National Coordinating Committee, the largest assistance organization, was a nonsectarian coalition of these and many other groups established in 1934. Although largely trusting to his network of relatives for help in finding his way, Steiner did turn to several groups—the National Council of Jewish Women, the American Friends Service Committee (the Quakers), and Selfhelp—for advice on how to rescue his family and fiancée.

These organizations afforded many of the refugees an advantage that few of their immigrant predecessors in America had enjoyed. The assistance of such groups helped reduce the refugees' confusion and eased the trauma of what was always a disorienting experience. In addition to benefiting from external resources of this sort, many refugees could also draw upon substantial internal ones. The very nature of the refugees made them better equipped than traditional immigrants to deal with some of the demands which adapting to a new society imposes. The refugees tended, after all, to come from middle or upper class backgrounds. Like Franz Steiner, most had been city dwellers, many of them professionals. They were frequently well-educated; quite a few of them in fact (Steiner included) spoke English. In short, they were as a group more sophisticated and better able to deal with the complexities of an urban, industrial society than was the mass of immigrants who had preceded them to America.

In other respects, however, adjusting to life in the United States posed an unparalleled challenge to the refugees. Finding their proper niche in American society was often more difficult than it was for an unskilled peasant, simply because the refugees' expectations were greater. Several obstacles barred them, for example, from resuming the professional lives which the Nazis had disrupted. Lawyers like Franz Steiner found their training useless: America's legal system bore little resemblance to Austria's. Even physicians, the great majority of whom did eventually succeed in resuming their medical careers, discovered that their path was temporarily blocked by laws in a majority of states limiting medical practice to citizens. Nor was it easy even to find unskilled jobs. Steiner's first few days in New York were devoted to a search for employment—rendered unsuccessful by the judgment that he was "over-qualified." Only after he changed his approach, concealing his educational and professional background, was he able to land a job.

Their backgrounds haunted the refugees in another respect. Their lives in Europe had been, at least before Hitler, comfortable and secure. These were not the sort of people, in other words, who ordinarily immigrated to America. The typical immigrant who had come from a less privileged background could well view the prospect of starting over in the United States with less dismay and anxiety than might the representative refugee. For the typical immigrant America held out the possibility of improved status; for the refugee it offered the chance merely to hang on to what remained of his shattered life. The refugees' trauma was in many instances magnified by uncertainty over the fate of those left behind and by the weight of the knowledge that their ultimate salvation depended upon how well and how quickly they could establish themselves in America.

This latter burden bore heavily upon Steiner. Within a few weeks of his arrival he found a job with the June Dairy Company of Jersey City and moved to a rented room in New Jersey to save himself the cost of commuting. His duties at the dairy involved loading and unloading by hand 70-pound tubs of butter, totaling over 60,000 pounds for an 8-hour shift. An 8-hour workday was the exception, however, not the rule. Steiner put in as much overtime as he could, sometimes more than 30 hours beyond the normal 44 hour week. Entries in the diary which Steiner kept throughout his first year in America recorded the toll which his labor exacted: "I'm awfully tired."—"Tired!"—"It seems as if I would have to be tired all my life."—"Tired. When not?" He recognized, though, that complaint was out of order. "This week is bad," he wrote in February 1939. "But I should be grateful for every hour of overtime work instead of grumbling. Who knows how long this good occasion to earn a few extra dollars lasts on?"

Most of the money Steiner earned, he saved. A "meal" out consisted of ten cents worth of bread and butter at the automat; more often he secured a dinner invitation from a sympathetic relative. After six and a half months, his self-discipline wavered slightly—one hot June day he spent five cents on ice cream. Beset by guilt, he confessed in his diary to feeling "very mean," adding "but it was the first nickel I wasted on myself since I left Vienna."

Steiner's refusal to "waste" any money on himself indirectly thwarted his desire to be accepted by Americans. His European clothes made him conspicuous: "Children playing in [the] park have big fun when I pass by," Steiner wrote, "because my knickerbockers are an unusual view for them." His presence on the street was often announced by the children who ran after him yelling "Refugee! Refugee!" Others besides children reminded him of what he was. On his way to work one day someone shouted "refugee" at him, prompting the bitter observation in Steiner's diary that "Hitler might be satisfied!" For everyone who resented his presence, however, there seemed to be someone else willing to extend the hand of friendship. Steiner later remembered that "even the poor old corner grocery woman took pity on the refugee, and of whatever I needed [she] selected the best bargain and then gave me a price reduction."

What Steiner really wanted, however, was to be viewed as something other than a "refugee," even if that label elicited sympathy rather than contempt. When he filed his "first papers" in mid-1939, initiating the process of naturalization, he changed his name to Frank because it sounded more American—the sort of alteration which immigrants often made—and added a middle name because he understood most Americans had them. At the dairy he gritted his teeth and contributed an entire dollar to his fellow workers' baseball pool, even though he had no knowledge of, or interest in, the sport. But Steiner could not escape the fact that he *was* different, as an ironic entry in his diary indicated: "Today Sirkin said I was the only gentleman among them. Very sad, as I tried to be one of them." Because the men at work did seem to hold him at arm's length, Steiner was surprised when they asked him to join their union: "It seems I even am in."

His major concern, of course, lay not in winning friends, but in finding a means for bringing his loved ones to safety in the United States. Steiner's burden eased somewhat in March of 1939 when he learned that Lotte, his fifteen-year-old half sister, would soon be part of a group of children taken to safety in England by a Swedish relief organization. Similar efforts to rescue children were suggested in the United States, but virtually nothing came of them. The most ambitious proposal was the Wagner-Rogers Bill, introduced in early 1939 as an attempt to translate the angry American reaction to the events of *Kristallnacht* into effective action on behalf of the Nazis' most vulnerable victims. Their plight had been especially dramatized in newspaper accounts, which described how they were bullied, left homeless, and separated from parents who had been shipped to concentration camps. The outpouring of American sympathy convinced New York Senator Robert Wagner that special legislation on their behalf would win wide support.

The Wagner-Rogers Bill provided for the admission of 20,000 German children, beyond the numbers allowable under the quota and spread over a two-year period. To defuse any complaint that they would compete with Americans for work, they were limited to age fourteen or under. Not all would be Jewish, a provision designed to allay anti-Semitism. Public funds would not be required; private sources would be responsible for their care. Although the measure was endorsed by a broad cross-section of individuals and organizations, it also generated vehement opposition from patriotic societies like the American Legion and the Daughters of the American Revolution. They contended that the measure would subvert the ethnic balance of the United States, so carefully preserved by the national origins system. The American Coalition warned that within five generations the 20,000 children would produce 640,000 descendants. Other opponents declared that by making an exception to the quotas of the national origins system the Wagner-Rogers Bill would open the door for other exemptions, undermining altogether America's immigration laws. Crying "charity begins at home," spokesmen of the patriotic societies shed crocodile tears for the offspring of sharecroppers, slum dwellers, and other groups which had previously escaped their notice, and argued that assisting foreign children would mean depriving young Americans.

These arguments proved effective. A Gallup poll revealed that two-thirds of those surveyed opposed the Wagner-Rogers Bill; only one quarter favored its passage. Encouraged, restrictionist forces in Congress attacked the measure in committee, saddling it with amendments which rendered it meaningless. The most destructive addition charged the 20,000 children against the German quota, in effect permitting their rescue only at the sacrifice of 20,000 other would-be immigrants. This so warped the bill's purpose that even Senator Wagner voted against it; the Wagner-Rogers Bill, killed in committee, never reached the floor of Congress. While this sorry charade was acted out in early 1939, President Roosevelt remained studiously aloof. He had already been impressed by the political danger associated with refugee matters and refused to incur any risk on behalf of the Wagner-Rogers Bill.

Lotte's escape to England still left Steiner with the problem of rescuing his parents. Securing affidavits of support for them was absolutely crucial for accomplishing this. Steiner's many relatives were sympathetic, but their straitened circumstances prevented them from undertaking the commitment themselves, although they did help by introducing Steiner to individuals whom they hoped would be able to assist him. Virtually every moment that he was not working or sleeping Steiner spent in pursuit of these leads, explaining his situation and pleading for help. One frustrating problem which he encountered was skepticism on the part of many whom he approached. "Americans tended to consider the horror stories we [refugees] knew about as figments of our neurotic fears," Steiner later lamented. "Such atrocities appeared impossible in the twentieth century."

But Steiner knew they were not only possible, they threatened the lives of his parents, as occasional, desperate letters from home reminded him. This knowledge provided him with relentless resolution, as he continued to search for a benefactor. Late in March of 1939 he was introduced to a Mr. Cohn, who agreed to sign an affidavit of support. By mid-April the precious document was in his parents' hands. When Steiner received confirmation of this from his father he felt so relieved that, according to his diary, he "cried like a little boy." But in early May immigration officials disallowed the affidavit on a technicality, necessitating its resubmission. In the meantime, Cohn had had second thoughts and, to Steiner's dismay, refused to sign again.

Once more the search for a sponsor began. As it continued the pressure on Steiner built to almost intolerable levels. Letters from his parents described the escalating persecution in Vienna. In early August he learned that they had been ordered to leave their home and move into the ghetto. Even worse than such depressing news were the long intervals without any reports at all. "No news from home," Steiner noted at the end of June. "I really am worried." Finally, late in August, Edmond Uhry, a cousin of the wife of one of Steiner's cousins, was persuaded to sign an affidavit. The relief that Steiner felt at this development once again proved premature. He learned early in November that the document, incredibly, had been lost. By this time the situation was even more urgent than before. War had broken out in Europe and the Nazis were beginning to clear Vienna's Jewish ghetto by shipping its inhabitants to concentration camps.[5] "I'm perfectly desperate . . . the situation asks for immediate action," Steiner wrote. Uhry responded quickly to the crisis, completing the necessary forms, and within days a new affidavit was sent to Steiner's parents.

What followed then was an agonizing wait to see which bureaucracy— the deliberately unhurried State Department or the relentlessly thorough Nazis—would be the first to take action on the Weinmanns. Nothing more clearly illustrates the tenuous nature of their chances than the action taken by the President's Advisory Committee on Political Refugees to rescue a limited number of renowned figures.

The President's Advisory Committee was established early in 1938, following the *Anschluss.* One of its projects was to make a special effort

---

[5]Germany's invasion of Poland on September 1, 1939 triggered the Second World War. The principal Allied nations, Great Britain and France, entered the conflict on Poland's behalf. The Soviet Union remained neutral, under the terms of a non-aggression pact with Germany, until June 1941, when the Nazis launched a surprise attack against it. Six months later, following the Japanese assault on Pearl Harbor, the United States joined the Allied cause. Germany was supported by its Axis partners, Italy and Japan.

to identify and rescue refugees of "superior intellectual attainment, of indomitable spirit, experienced in vigorous support of the principles of liberal government, and who [are] in danger of persecution or death at the hands of autocracy." While some notable individuals were saved—including Franz Werfel, Marc Chagall, Max Ernst, and others—the Committee was so impeded in its efforts by America's restrictive policy and by the State Department's leisurely administration of it that of the 3,286 persons targeted for action, only 1,236 were rescued. Obviously if President Roosevelt's special commission could do no better than that, the odds that Frank Steiner would be able to save his parents—persons of no real distinction—were rather long. The prospects of rescuing more distant relatives—his grandmother, an uncle and cousins—were even dimmer.

Equally dear to him was his fiancée, Moira Auner. Securing entry into the United States for her posed an entirely different—and seemingly more difficult—problem. A Rumanian citizen, she was subject to an impossibly small annual quota of 377. Since tens of thousands of Jews were attempting to flee that country as well, the competition for visas was fierce. Steiner was stunned to discover in mid-1939 that the enormous logjam of applicants had created a 43-year waiting list! "Things look pretty desperate for Moira getting here," he worriedly wrote. Apparently unable to gain his fiancée's admission to the United States, Steiner next explored the possibility of her immigrating to a nearby country. Throughout the 1930s several Latin American nations had accepted a limited number of European refugees, although the immigrants were often required to bribe their way in. But by 1939 even those escape routes were being closed off, as Steiner learned from visits to the Cuban and Mexican consulates. Late in June he despairingly noted "the chances of going to Mexico . . . have gone, after first Cuba has failed. What shall we do?"

A fellow refugee, more familiar than Steiner with the intricacies of American immigration law, offered a suggestion which ultimately afforded the young couple a solution to their dilemma. If Moira were to enter the country on a visitor's visa, they could get married. Although she would then have to leave the United States in order to immigrate properly, as the spouse of an alien who had initiated the process of naturalization, Moira would gain preference over most other Rumanians seeking entry.[6]

This strategy was more easily conceived than executed. Even a visitor's visa required an affidavit and a bona fide invitation from an American relative or friend. The applicant was also required to purchase a round-trip ticket to the United States as a demonstration of the intent to leave when the visa expired. So during the summer of 1939, while he sought someone to sign an affidavit of support for his parents, Steiner also tried to secure an invitation to his fiancée for a visit. At the end of August, Eugen Boissevain, husband of poet Edna St. Vincent Millay and a second cousin of Moira's, wrote to volunteer his help. But its timing gave Boissevain's

[6]Under the National Origins Act parents and husbands of American citizens were given first preference for quota openings; wives and unmarried minor children of resident aliens were accorded secondary preference.

offer a bittersweet quality—it arrived on September 1, the day that Hitler's invasion of Poland plunged Europe into World War II. Steiner's diary reflected his gloom: "Coming home I found Eugen's charming invitation. Too late, probably." Unwilling to give up, however, he forwarded the invitation to Moira.

Steiner's spirits gyrated wildly over the next ten weeks as news from his fianceé and the front alternately raised and dashed his hopes. Her cable requesting a return ticket and suggesting her imminent departure sent Steiner, "crazy with joy," to the bank to withdraw his precious savings. A few days later, however, the spreading war threatened to upset their plans. "I don't know how I would stand this one more disappointment," he lamented. "I have no idea what to do . . . and feel like near madness." The next day another cable from Moira indicated she would soon be underway. "I literally stood on my head in bed and laughed and shouted," an exuberant Steiner exclaimed. "I am optimistic again and think the critical two weeks will pass by fortunately, and even Ellis Island had no dreads for me." But at the end of October, just four days before Moira was scheduled to sail from Trieste, he wrote, "O God, shall this start again? Trouble in Rumania, German offensive, the *Saturnia* [her ship] stopped in Gibraltar. . . . God, let everything go its normal way!"

On the morning of November 17 the *Saturnia* steamed into New York harbor, bringing Moira Auner to the United States. But fate had reserved one last torment—suspicious immigration officials held her in quarantine at Ellis Island while they decided whether to permit her entry. Their deliberation reflected a deeply rooted fear of foreign "subversives," a concern magnified by the recent outbreak of hostilities in Europe. This anxiety was not limited to federal officials—a Roper poll taken in mid-1940 would reveal that nearly three-quarters of those surveyed believed that the Nazis were organizing a "fifth column" of spies and saboteurs in the United States. Moira's presence aroused some official suspicions; she was not, after all, a refugee who had been forced to flee Europe, but rather a "visitor." Yet why would anyone hazard the submarine-haunted sea lanes for the sake of a vacation? If not a spy, she at the least appeared to be someone bent on short-circuiting the immigration laws. It took three days of argument and red tape before immigration officials were persuaded to let Moira leave Ellis Island.

Clearly the outbreak of fighting in Europe had a dampening effect on America's already restrictive policy. To the limited extent that the United States continued to accommodate refugees, that willingness to do so was tempered by a determination to safeguard the nation against any security risk which they might pose. Beginning in 1940 the State Department shifted its focus away from those Jews still trapped in Germany, out of concern that they could be compromised by the Nazis. Instead, American consuls were instructed to issue visas only to those German refugees who had already found sanctuary in other nations.

Fortunately for his parents, their visas were issued just as this shift in policy was taking place. In February of 1940 they hastily left Vienna for

Italy, booked passage on the first available steamer, and within a few weeks had joined their son, who had moved back to New York. In the meantime, he and Moira had been married. Then Frank Steiner, overcome with relief at having arranged the rescue of those people he loved most dearly, collapsed from physical and emotional exhaustion. Unable to work for several weeks, he was fired from his job at the dairy. Survival then became even more of a struggle as Steiner attempted to earn a living by peddling light bulbs, scouring powder, and kitchen supplies from door to door.

The marriage of Frank and Moira Steiner provided her with the means to gain legal access to the United States as an immigrant, but in order for her to comply with the law it was necessary to leave the country and obtain the proper visa from an American consul. So Steiner took the last of his savings, spending them on a round-trip ticket to Havana and the bribes needed to obtain a Cuban visitor's visa.

While his wife was in Cuba, Steiner found work as a gardener on an estate in Wheaton, Illinois. Leaving New York was a daring step for him— it was all he knew of America. More than half his fellow refugees settled permanently in and around New York, where they provided each other with consolation and support. At the same time, however, the extremely high level of their concentration and interaction with each other tended to retard their integration into American society. In venturing off to the Midwest, on the other hand, Steiner was furthering the process he had already initiated by applying for American citizenship. After a few months in Wheaton, Steiner located a more permanent position at a door factory in Cincinnati, Ohio. Back from Cuba, Moira joined him there and the young couple began to build a new life.

America's entry into the war in December of 1941 created some problems for the Steiners, but these problems also hastened their assimilation. Steiner's coworkers reacted to the declaration of war by demanding that their employer fire the "enemy alien." Although the demand was rejected, the sentiments behind it affected the way the Steiners lived. By now the parents of one child and planning to have more, they decided to make English the language of their household in order to spare their children any embarrassment that might arise from speaking the language of the enemy. "I didn't want to do anything that would expose them to ridicule," Steiner explained many years later.

The involvement of the United States in the Second World War, of course, had a much broader impact on refugee matters. The trickle of immigrants allowed to enter the country was reduced even further; in 1942 the United States accepted only about half as many immigrants as it had admitted in 1941. The 23,725 who arrived the following year represented the second lowest annual total in more than a century.[7] Paralleling this development was a horrifying alteration in German emigration policy. Up to this point the Nazis had attempted to solve their "Jewish prob-

---

[7] In 1941 the United States admitted 51,776 immigrants; in 1942 28,781 entered the country.

lem" by forcing Jews to flee the country. But the effectiveness of their efforts was limited due to the reluctance of the United States and other nations to accept refugees. Consequently, in 1941 the Nazis opted for a "final solution" to the matter and embarked upon a campaign of mass extermination.

Initially the nations engaged in the fight against Germany were ignorant of the Nazis' program of genocide. But even after the State Department in late 1942 gained credible evidence of what was taking place, it suppressed the information. Top officials feared that if the American public understood the full extent of the tragedy unfolding in Europe it would demand more effective measures to rescue those Jews who could still be saved, regardless of the immigration quotas. Other agencies of the Roosevelt Administration were similarly kept in the dark by the State Department—and for much the same reason. At last, in January of 1944, Treasury Secretary Henry Morgenthau, Jr. forwarded to President Roosevelt a document titled "Report to the Secretary on the Acquiescence of This Government in the Murder of the Jews." According to the report, certain members of the State Department had "hidden their gross procrastination" in addressing the refugee issue, "suppressed reports . . . on German atrocities," and "utterly failed to prevent the extermination of Jews in German-controlled Europe." The report further suggested that more than "simple incompetence" was responsible for this policy, hinting that "plain anti-Semitism" lay at its heart.

Roosevelt responded by immediately shifting responsibility for refugee matters away from the State Department to a newly created War Refugee Board; but it was a case of too little, too late. Not until the war ended a year and a half later was the full extent of the tragedy known. The Nazi efforts at racial purification had resulted in the systematic slaughter of six million people. The members of Steiner's family who survived the holocaust were far outnumbered by those who didn't—his grandmother, uncles, aunts, and cousins perished among the anonymous masses.

The record of the United States in the face of this enormous tragedy was ambiguous at best. Although America accepted many more refugees than any other country—perhaps 250,000 between 1933 and 1945—it did considerably less than what might have been accomplished.[8] During that same period the United States took in over a million *fewer* immigrants than were permitted under the quota system. For its efforts the United States was richly rewarded. Those refugees who reached America repaid the nation with their intellectual, cultural and scientific achievements—a partial list includes Albert Einstein, Bruno Bettelheim, Paul Tillich, Enrico Fermi, Hannah Arendt, Sigmund Freud, Bertold Brecht, Erich Fromm, Walter Gropius, Edward Teller, and many others.

[8]No other country came close to matching the number of refugees which the United States absorbed during this period. Palestine totalled 50,000, the next highest figure. In proportion to overall capacity to help, however, many countries—from Holland to the Dominican Republic—compiled a better record than the United States.

Although less distinguished than these, Frank Steiner nevertheless contributed what he was able. He devoted time and energy to a variety of civic organizations, became a Boy Scout leader, and after long years of advanced study in night school became a professor at the University of Cincinnati. As the end of his career there approached, he explained his motivation in terms that were almost universally applicable to the rest of those refugees favored with entry to the United States: "After the first few weeks here the shock of . . . upheaval had partly worn off, I pledged myself to whatever service I would be able to render to this new land, which so magnanimously had promised its citizenship in the future, and allowed me to raise a family, so that my children could grow up as free people and without fear."

FURTHER READING

COSER, LEWIS A. *Refugee Scholars in America: Their Impact and Experiences.* New Haven: Yale University Press, 1984.

DINNERSTEIN, LEONARD. *America and the Survivors of the Holocaust: The Evolution of a United States Displaced Persons Policy, 1945–1950.* New York: Columbia University Press, 1982.

DIVINE, ROBERT. *American Immigration Policy, 1924–1952.* New Haven: Yale University Press, 1957.

FERMI, LAURA. *Illustrious Immigrants: The Intellectual Migration from Europe, 1930–1941.* Chicago: University of Chicago Press, 1958.

FRIEDMAN, SAUL. *No Haven for the Oppressed: United States Policy toward Jewish Refugees, 1938–1945.* Detroit: Wayne State University Press, 1973.

WYMAN, DAVID S. *The Abandonment of the Jews: America and the Holocaust, 1941–1945.* New York: Pantheon Books, 1984.

————. *Paper Walls: America and the Refugee Crisis, 1938–1941.* Amherst: University of Massachusetts Press, 1968.

Magdalena and Jose Reveles, 1952

Photo courtesy of the Reveles family.

13

Jose Reveles

hundreds of *braceros* milled about in the glaring sun. Jose Reveles glanced anxiously at the buses and cattle trucks parked outside.[1] Uncertain of his immediate fate, Reveles nonetheless understood the symbolic importance of the waiting vehicles. He intuitively knew that somehow, if he were to board one of the buses, it would be better. "It bothered me to see those cattle trucks," he reflected many years later. "I was afraid, in that moment, that the *Americanos* thought we were no better than the cows that had ridden in them before us." The men were organized into smaller groups and marched out of the stadium. With every step Jose Reveles' apprehension increased. But when his group veered off toward the buses, a sense of relief flooded through him. America might not be so bad after all.

Because he was a *bracero*, Reveles' stay in America was only temporary. But it was also a prelude. He would return two years later, once more a *bracero*, and after that Reveles would live for a time in Mexico, crossing the border each day to work in the United States before finally immigrating permanently. The frequency and ease with which Jose Reveles moved back and forth across the border between Mexico and the United States are indicative of the unique quality of Mexican immigration, in comparison to the experience of other ethnic groups. The physical proximity of their homeland to the United States has had a profound effect on both the movements and the culture of Mexican immigrants. Huie Kin, Frank Steiner, and millions of other immigrants were to a large degree discon-

---

[1] *Bracero* literally means "arm," but has the connotation "worker" as well. With the establishment of the *Bracero* Program in 1942, the latter meaning became more sharply defined, to indicate those workers who entered the United States under that program.

nected from their past in America; Jose Reveles and other Mexican immigrants in many respects found their life in the United States to be a continuation of their Mexican past.

This is not surprising, given the fact that the American Southwest, where the great majority of Mexican immigrants to the United States settled, was once a part of Mexico. Texas separated from Mexico in 1836; a dozen years later, following a war, Mexico ceded to the United States the territory comprising the present states of California, Arizona, New Mexico, Utah and Nevada, as well as part of Colorado and Wyoming.[2] In addition to this territory, the United States acquired the inhabitants—an indeterminate number of Indians and about 80,000 Mexicans. Perhaps 3,000 of these repatriated to Mexico, but the vast majority chose to remain in the United States, their civil rights and property supposedly protected under the terms of the Treaty of Guadalupe Hidalgo, which had ended the war. Only in Texas were Mexicans immediately in the minority. There the *Tejanos* were outnumbered by Anglo-Americans by a margin of about 30,000 to 5,000. In southern California, *Californios* would remain numerically and culturally dominant until the 1870s when completion of the transcontinental railroad brought a flood of American settlers. In New Mexico, *Hispanos* would constitute a majority well into the twentieth century.[3]

Physically, culturally, and economically, the American Southwest was a continuation of Mexico. The ill-defined and often invisible border between the two countries posed no obstacle to movement or trade. Economic patterns continued as before, linking Santa Fe to Chihuahua as well as to St. Louis. Travelers and settlers passed easily from one country into the other. America's imposition of border controls in the twentieth century had only a limited effect on this traffic—and absolutely none on the transmission of culture. Mexican-Americans continued to cross the border to shop, visit relatives, or work, revitalizing their ethnic roots at the same time. If anything, twentieth century technology helped to reinforce Mexican culture in the American borderlands, where Mexican radio and television broadcasts are readily received and Mexican books, magazines, and newspapers are widely circulated.

The traditional ease with which the border was crossed, particularly in the nineteenth century, makes it difficult to discuss the volume of immigration from Mexico in any but the most general terms. Between 1850 and 1910, federal officials recorded fewer than 65,000 immigrants from Mexico, but that figure is certainly low. Nevertheless, it does indicate the relatively slight nature of immigration from Mexico, in contrast to the

[2]The Treaty of Guadalupe Hidalgo also settled the Texas-Mexico boundary at the Rio Grande, provided for an American payment of $15,000,000 to Mexico, and obligated the United States to assume the debts which Mexico owed American citizens, up to the amount of $3,250,000.

[3]*Tejanos* were the Texas Mexicans, *Californios* the Mexican inhabitants of California before its conquest by the United States, and *Hispanos* the pre-Anglo New Mexicans.

flood of arrivals from Europe. Beginning in 1910, however, the number of Mexicans coming to the United States increased tremendously. In that year, a revolution broke out against the dictatorial government of Porfirio Diaz, who had ruled Mexico since 1877. What followed was more than a decade of political chaos: assassination, rival generals battling for power, and skirmishes with the United States. All of this had enormous economic and social implications. The lives of millions of Mexicans were disrupted or lost. Many fled north, seeking safety in the United States. From 1911 through 1920, federal officials tallied 219,000 Mexican immigrants, not counting many more undocumented arrivals. Estimates of the total range up to a million.

Their flight from Mexico was further encouraged by a great demand for unskilled labor in the United States. The recent widespread introduction of irrigation to the arid Southwest produced a spectacular increase in farm acreage under cultivation. Simultaneously, western railroads extended their tracks throughout the region, while new restrictions on Chinese and Japanese immigration reduced the availability of unskilled labor from the Orient.[4] The outbreak of World War I in 1914—and especially America's entry into the conflict three years later—contributed to the labor shortage. As immigration from Europe was reduced, American workers were siphoned off from the factory to the front, while industry struggled to meet the demands of war.

During the 1920s, continued turmoil in Mexico and the passage of laws restricting European immigration prompted even greater movement from Mexico. Some American employers, particularly western railroads, actively recruited Mexican workers. In response to such efforts, Ignacio Reveles, Jose's father, came to California. For two years he worked in the northern part of the state, laying track near Colusa and laboring at a lumber camp on Mt. Shasta. He then went back to Mexico. Even though he never returned to the United States, Ignacio Reveles would retain his passport for half a century, keeping it safe in a metal can as though it were a talisman. He would keep, too, his memories of America, passing on to his children his impression of the United States as a land of opportunity.

Back in Mexico, Ignacio Reveles settled down to the life of a rancher. One of the consequences of the Mexican Revolution had been a partial redistribution of land, as *haciendas* were broken up and peasants given title to the land they worked. Ignacio Reveles was awarded a small land grant near San Luis de Cordero in the state of Durango. In order to obtain horses and wagons, however, he was forced to sacrifice some of his holding. The land was good, but there were many mouths to feed. Jose, born in 1927, was one of eight children. Circumstances dictated that all who were

---

[4]For a discussion of the measures pertaining to Chinese immigrants see Chapter 9. Japanese immigration was held in check by the Gentlemen's Agreement of 1907. Under its terms, the Japanese government voluntarily halted emigration by Japanese laborers in return for the promised withdrawal of discriminatory policies in the United States.

able had to contribute to the support of the family. After just three years of school, Jose quit in order to help his father care for their livestock. But he had acquired a taste for learning; with hard-earned *pesos* he bought books from an occasional peddler.

As the years passed, the Reveles family engaged in a ceaseless struggle for survival in a world indifferent to their fate. As he grew to manhood, Jose was increasingly torn between the restless yearnings of youth and a sense of duty to his parents. His restlessness was reinforced by a curiosity about the United States fed not only by his father's tales but by articles which Jose read in newspapers. Ironically, as his interest in it grew, the United States became for a time less, not more, accessible. During the 1920s, in a reflection of the same mentality which produced the National Origins restriction plan and other restrictive measures, the Border Patrol was established and a barbed-wire fence constructed in a futile attempt to check the increasing flow of immigrants from Mexico. Far more effective in accomplishing that end was the decade-long Depression which gripped the United States throughout the 1930s. With unemployment painfully high among Americans and the agricultural sector especially plagued by Dust Bowl conditions, the job opportunities which had attracted Mexican immigrants in the past evaporated. From 1931 until 1940 only slightly more than 22,000 entered the country, a figure dwarfed by the exodus from the United States to Mexico. Many of those who went back to Mexico did so in response to the American government's Repatriation Program. Supposedly aimed at Mexican aliens illegally in the United States, the program in fact affected many whose presence was permitted. American authorities at all levels of government pressured Mexican nationals to return "voluntarily" to their homeland, at times deporting those who resisted. Naturalized citizens and even native-born Americans were also forced to leave the country in order to keep their families intact as Mexican-born spouses or parents were repatriated!

The end of the Depression and the outbreak of World War II created a labor shortage in the United States, which led to the establishment in 1942 of the *Bracero* Program, under which the Department of Agriculture assumed the role of a labor contractor, recruiting and supplying temporary workers from Mexico to satisfy the needs of American employers. By mutual agreement of the two governments, Mexican workers were guaranteed transportation to and from the United States, work for at least three-quarters of the term of their contract, a minimum hourly wage of thirty cents, and adequate housing. The two countries found the arrangement mutually beneficial. The United States was able to relieve an acute labor shortage; western growers particularly benefited from having a dependable, readily available and artificially cheap workforce. Mexico in turn was able to reduce its labor surplus while at the same time gaining an important source of foreign exchange. By the time the program ended in early 1947 about 200,000 *braceros*, working primarily on farms and railroads, had been shipped to 21 states. Under pressure from western growers, a series of annual agreements extended this system through 1950. In 1951, ostensibly in response to the Korean War, Congress re-established the *Bracero* Program on a much larger scale, continuing it until 1964. Its importance to America's agricultural sector was undeniable. By 1960 more than a quarter of the seasonal farm workers in the United States were *braceros*! The *Bracero* Program, particularly in its second phase, attracted Mexicans to the United States in greater numbers than ever before. It provided Jose Reveles and millions of his countrymen with the chance to sample—and perhaps adopt—a different way of life.[5]

By the time the expanded *Bracero* Program was instituted, Jose Reveles was a young man with dreams of setting out on his own and starting a family. In love with Magdalena Ortiz, a young woman he had grown up with, Jose felt he could not approach her empty-handed and propose marriage. Satisfied that his younger brothers could help his father run the farm, Jose bade his family farewell in 1952 and set out for Chihuahua, where he had heard *braceros* were being recruited. Walking and hitching rides on trucks, he covered the more than 300 miles to Chihauhua. There he found so many men with the same idea that he worried that there might be too many applicants. His army record and letters of recommendation worked to his advantage, but even more important was Reveles' physical condition. Each applicant was subjected to a hasty medical examination. "The doctor was an *Americano* who checked our bodies quickly, and yet took a long time looking at our hands," he remembered later. "It was like this was another test, to see if we were people of agriculture. The *Americanos* wanted to see if we had calluses to prove we had experience working in the fields."

Reveles and the other *braceros* were then led on foot to the railroad station and packed aboard a train for the 8-hour trip to the border. The location of recruiting stations at such a distance from the border was a point of real contention between the United States and Mexico. American growers complained about the increased expense which this entailed for them, but the Mexican government recognized that hiring at the border would merely deplete the workforce of the commercial farms occupying Mexico's northern fringe. As it was, the growers' expenses could not have been too oppressive—for the entire trip Reveles and his fellow *braceros* were each given only a sandwich. Reveles registered the same appreciation that Huie Kin had exhibited for applesauce: "I could not understand how the *Americanos* could get full on one little piece of meat inside of two breads."

At Juarez the train stopped. Numb from the long ride, the men scrambled off, formed a ragged line, and walked to the border station. There they were checked one more time, sprayed with insecticide, and marched into the United States.

[5]From 1942 through 1964 nearly 5,000,000 *braceros* entered the United States. However this figure does not take into account the fact that some individuals, like Jose Reveles, were counted more than once.

Farm Laborers

Photo by Arthur Sirdofsky/Art Resource.

After assembling at the stadium in El Paso, the *braceros* were divided into two groups, one of which boarded buses and the other cattle trucks. Reveles and the others aboard buses were destined for New Mexico; those in the cattle trucks would work in Texas. Their respective means of transportation had symbolic significance: The intense discrimination against Mexicans in Texas at first prompted the Mexican government to prohibit any *braceros* from being sent there. Even though this ban was later rescinded, the cattle trucks eloquently attested to the degraded status of Texas *braceros*.

The long bus ride from El Paso to Carlsbad, New Mexico, the destination of Reveles' group, was interrupted only once for a rest and meal stop. The sandwiches which were distributed filled him with dread, as he wondered if this was the only food he would ever eat in America! No less of a problem than the Americans' food was their language. Only one of the workers aboard the bus understood any English—his ability to translate instructions and relay information automatically made him the leader of the *braceros*, who called him *El Capitan*.

In Carlsbad the men were divided into smaller groups. Reveles and about 20 others were assigned to a grower named Harrison Martin. Reveles would remember his employer as a good man, one "who did not make us feel bad because we were *braceros.*" But he also remembered the work as being very hard. Each morning before sunrise the men headed out to the fields to pick cotton. The sun was hot and the days were long. Their workweek averaged 60 hours. In this respect, however, Reveles was more fortunate than many *braceros* whose most frequent complaint was about the lack of work. Despite the fact that *braceros* were supposedly guaranteed a certain amount of work, that commitment was often ignored by employers. In such instances, the worker's earnings were usually inadequate. Even Reveles, although he was given all the work he wished, earned "just barely enough to eat and buy small things." He was also spared the sort of unfortunate treatment to which many other *braceros* were subjected—unauthorized deductions from their pay, food that was spoiled or insufficient in quantity, ramshackle housing, even physical abuse. Where Reveles worked the *braceros* were able to order their own food and lived in an old house that was crowded but adequate.

One experience which Reveles did share with other *braceros* was resentment on the part of many Mexican-Americans who feared their economic competition. Such fears were not unjustified. At mid-century about a third of all adult male Mexican-Americans were employed in agriculture. The introduction into their midst of tens of thousands of *braceros* not only undercut them economically, it also left the Mexican-American workers more vulnerable to exploitation by their employers. Indeed, an implicit purpose of the *Bracero* Program was to neutralize the growing militancy and independence of farm workers brought on by the shortage of labor.

Although Mexican-Americans were often mistreated and exploited in the same fashion as their *bracero* cousins, their mutual experience did not create a community of interest between the two groups. In addition to the economic rivalry that separated them, there was the matter of social acceptability. Some Mexican-Americans viewed the newcomers as embarrassingly unsophisticated, even inferior. Jose Reveles and the other *braceros,* therefore, had little contact with the local Hispanic population. As he noted, "*Mexicanos* born in the *Estados Unidos* [United States] . . . look[ed] down on us." Such intra-ethnic rivalry was not, of course, unique to Mexicans. Similar divisions existed between Jews from Germany and Russia, northern and southern Italians, as well as other ethnic groups.

Far more overt was the hostility which came from Anglo-Americans. Reveles discovered this almost immediately as he and some of his comrades went to town on the weekends. They learned that some saloons were off limits to them simply because of their ethnicity. Even in bars which catered to a Mexican clientele, their sanctuary was not completely secure. On one occasion "many *Americanos*" invaded Reveles' favorite hangout, looking for a fight. Finding more than they had bargained for, they made their exit aboard stretchers. But Reveles learned that not all Americans were bigots. His employer escorted Reveles and the other *bra-*

ceros to a restaurant that had refused service to Mexicans and forced its proprietor to serve them all chili.

The clarity with which racial lines were drawn in the United States deeply troubled Reveles. A few years later, while living in Texas, he would encounter the institutionalized racism of the Jim Crow system which mandated segregation of blacks from whites.[6] Typical of this code was the requirement which restricted blacks to the back of buses, reserving the front seats for whites. Although Mexicans were themselves often the targets of racial discrimination, they were in this situation expected to ride in the front. Rebelling against the cruelty of such practices, Reveles registered his protest by sitting with *"los Negros"*. In other instances, segregation policies applied to Mexicans, barring them from some restaurants, preventing them from attending public schools with whites, limiting their access to swimming pools and other recreational facilities, and prohibiting their residence in certain neighborhoods.

His varied experiences left Reveles with mixed feelings about the United States. But they also affected his view of Mexico. When his contract expired and Reveles returned to his parents' ranch, he saw it in a new light. "I was happy to see my family again, but I also saw now, more clearly, the poorness of my people and my country," he remembered later. "It brought a sadness that grew more and more." Determined to create a different sort of life for himself, in September of 1952 he moved to Juarez, married Magdalena, and tried his hand at a variety of jobs from selling razors to playing records at a dance hall. But the limited opportunities and low wages failed to keep pace with his growing responsibilities. A daughter, Cristina, was born in 1953, and a son, Francesco, followed the next year. Reluctantly, Reveles decided that his only recourse was to become a *bracero* again.

Having heard that *braceros* were being recruited in Guadalajara, Reveles traveled there only to find himself among thousands of applicants. Joining the line, he waited all day and night, sleeping on the ground so he wouldn't lose his place. The following morning it all proved to be for nothing—the last worker permitted to apply was the man immediately in front of him. Frustrated and angry, Reveles considered his next move. Completely broke, he realized that going back to Juarez was out of the question. "To return to your home with no food, not even a bag of bread or tortillas, and to eat what they have, is the worst thing you can do," he reasoned.

Hitching a ride on a truck, Reveles traveled all night to Chihuahua, where he managed to sign up as a *bracero*. But his relief at being hired yielded quickly to misgivings as he and the other workers were loaded into cattle cars. The journey proved to be as grim as their accommodations

---

[6]Formalized racial segregation hung on throughout much of the South many years after the 1954 Supreme Court decision in the case *Brown v. the Board of Education of Topeka, Kansas* ordered the integration of public institutions "with all deliberate speed."

promised. Following a circuitous route, the train took three days to reach California. During that entire period the *braceros* were neither fed nor let off the train. At the border they were at last given food and allowed to rest before being transferred to trucks and buses. Reveles was part of a contingent taken to a huge labor camp at Cutler, about 25 miles southeast of Fresno in the fertile San Joaquin Valley. California's giant agribusiness absorbed *braceros* at a rate second only to Texas, in order to insure that growers had a sufficient labor supply—and to maximize their leverage over domestic farm workers. But what benefited the growers penalized Reveles and his fellow *braceros* who had to take turns working. While they waited to pick grapes or cotton they had to eat, and for their food— even though it was only boiled potatoes—they paid a premium price. "Even before you had any money, you had bills to pay," Reveles bitterly recalled. He could hardly wait for the contract to end.

When it did expire after three months, Reveles attempted to return directly to Juarez, but Program officials insisted on shipping him back to Guadalajara. This was the crowning indignity, for it meant that he would have to spend most of what he had saved traveling from Guadalajara to Juarez. Confined once more in a cattle car, Reveles and the other *braceros* vented their rage at such treatment by breaking out the wooden slats of the car.

As poorly as the *braceros* were sometimes treated, their situation was not as bad as that of their countrymen who entered the United States illegally. Paralleling the expansion of the *Bracero* Program was a rise in the number of *mojados* (wetbacks) and *alambristas* (wire-jumpers)— illegal immigrants. No reliable statistics exist to indicate the scope of the problem, although deportation figures, which approached 1,100,000 in 1954, offer some indication. Many growers in California and elsewhere regarded illegals as more than a source of low-cost labor; they were also viewed as an instrument for holding down wages and enforcing labor discipline. Because *braceros* who complained about working conditions or pay would not have their contracts renewed, their places taken by illegals, complaints were kept to a minimum. Employers also appreciated the fact that illegals, who labored without benefit of contracts, were more flexible than other farm workers. And of course their illegal status made the wetbacks all the more vulnerable to exploitation. Some unscrupulous growers even made a practice of calling in Immigration and Naturalization Service agents at the end of the harvest to arrest and deport the illegal workers before they could collect their pay.

The physical proximity of Mexico to the United States encouraged not only an increasing traffic of illegals, but a rising tide of legitimate immigrants as well. During the 1940s about 56,000 documented Mexican immigrants entered the United States; in the next decade the figure rose to nearly 274,000, including Jose and Magdalena Reveles and their two children. Returning from his second stint as a *bracero*, Reveles had decided to obtain a "green card"—a legal immigrant visa which confers resident alien status—enabling him to live and work in the United States. He assembled the required documentation and received a card, although first it was necessary to wrestle with an unsympathetic bureaucracy. But like tens of thousands of other green-card Mexicans in border towns like Juarez, Nogales, and Tijuana, he decided to continue living in Mexico while working in the United States.

El Paso lay just across the Rio Grande from Juarez, but finding a job there was not easy. Reveles was rejected by Anglo- and Mexican-American employers alike. Finally he decided to seize the initiative. After the foreman of a roofing company told him there was no job available, Reveles began to work anyway, busily moving equipment and materials around the yard. As the foreman watched, astonished, Reveles kept up his charade all afternoon. At the end of the day, having demonstrated both an ability and a will to work, he was given a job. For several months Reveles continued to live in Juarez while working in El Paso, but at last he brought his wife and children across the river to live. Thirty years later the memory of his family's first home in America remained indelibly, and painfully, imprinted in his mind—a run-down, two-room apartment without electricity or plumbing in a building that looked like it had been abandoned.

Reveles' transition from his parents' ranch to an American city reflected the increasingly urban nature of Mexican settlement in the United States. As late as 1940, Mexicans remained the most rural major ethnic group in the country; 30 years later they were among its most urban. In some southwestern cities—El Paso, for example—they constitute an absolute majority of the population, while in others they make up a substantial minority. In the cities they tend to congregate in *barrios*, neighborhoods which are largely or exclusively Mexican in composition. Other immigrant groups exhibited similar, culturally uniform patterns of settlement. (Most of Leonard Covello's neighbor's in East Harlem were Italian.) But few groups carried this exclusivity to the extent which Mexicans did. For one thing, most European immigrants in the United States seldom were exposed to the degree of racial prejudice or discrimination as that directed against Mexicans. In contrast, that discrimination—sometimes in the form of restrictive covenants on real estate—often left Mexicans with no alternative to settlement in a *barrio*. In addition, despite the fact that most immigrants attempted to live among people whose language, customs, and origins were similar to their own as they adjusted to American life, such ethnic clustering tended to diminish as the passage of time eroded connections to their homeland. For Mexicans, on the other hand, the proximity of their homeland to the United States has continually revitalized their traditions, preserving their cultural distinction and prolonging their residence in the *barrio*.

The Reveles family settled in an El Paso *barrio*, where Jose worked hard to improve their station. After two years, he moved his family to a better home—one with electricity and a bathroom. Not long after that, the family moved again, this time into a house Reveles bought rather than rented. This upward movement did not represent an attempt to escape the *barrio*; rather, it occurred within the *barrio's* familiar and comforting context.

And when the family did move from the *barrio*, they settled in another Mexican neighborhood.

But the urban setting in which he and many other Mexicans lived brought problems as well as opportunities. The El Paso *barrio*, like those of a number of other cities, had a few years earlier given rise to the *pachucos*—organized gangs of young toughs. *Barrio* gangs gave their members a sense of identity and importance, helping to combat feelings of alienation in a society which kept them on its fringes. In this regard they were little different from the street gangs which had formed among communities of Irish, Italian, and other immigrants. In the early 1940s, however, *barrio* gangs gained particular public notoriety because of the flamboyant "zoot suits" affected by their members. Police harassment of *pachucos* and "zoot suiters," coupled with newspaper ridicule, both concealed and legitimized anti-Mexican feelings in general. The resultant tensions reached a bloody climax in Los Angeles with the Zoot Suit Riots of 1943.

The Zoot Suit Riots were preceded by, and directly related to, the Sleepy Lagoon murder case. In that case, 17 *pachucos* were convicted of various charges arising from the death of a Mexican-American youth who belonged to a rival gang. The trial made a mockery of judicial standards of fairness and impartiality, clearly turning instead on racial prejudice. The verdict was such a miscarriage of justice that in 1944 it was overturned by an appellate court. Before that occurred, however, American servicemen, egged on by the anti-Mexican climate, went on a rampage. Mobs halted streetcars and invaded movie theaters in search of zoot suiters, tearing off their distinctive clothes and cutting their long hair. Police declined to intervene in the violence; in some instances, they even arrested its victims.

One consequence of such police behavior, as well as the callous actions of authorities who had administered the Repatriation Program of the 1930s, was a strong and persistent distrust of government agencies by Mexican-Americans. Their contact with the government frequently resulted in some minor indignity, humiliation, irritation, or inconvenience—or sometimes in real and lasting harm. In 1954, shortly before Jose Reveles moved his family to the United States, the federal government had lanched "Operation Wetback," a campaign to identify and deport illegal Mexican aliens. In the process, the lives of legitimate residents were sometimes disrupted as the shadow of suspicion fell upon anyone of Hispanic appearance.[7] Within this context, a Border Patrol officer confiscated and shredded Reveles' green card, proclaiming it a fake. Loss of the card left Reveles unable to cross the border and return home that night, and forced him into the inconvenience of obtaining a replacement.

---

[7]Nearly 30 years later the Reagan Administration launched a highly publicized campaign against illegal aliens called "Operation Jobs." Ill-conceived and even more poorly executed, "Operation Jobs" resulted in the improper detention and harassment of American citizens of Latin origin, but created few employment opportunities. Widespread protests and Administration embarrassment brought the campaign to a mercifully quick end.

Despite his rude introduction to life in the United States, Reveles was able to carve out a comfortable existence for his family in El Paso. In the early 1960s, however a shortage of work caused his roofing business to falter. Striking out in a new direction, he decided to try California, where friends had told him "life . . . was good . . . [with] plenty of work [and] . . . good pay." In 1963 Reveles left his wife and three children—another daughter, Magdalena, had been born in 1960—and drove to Colusa, California, where his father had worked 40 years before. There he found employment as a farm laborer and, after establishing himself, sent for his family.

Although their migration from Texas to California represented a big move in geographical terms, its enormity was considerably less in a cultural sense. After all, both states were formerly Mexican territory and lie within the area of the United States in which Mexican population is concentrated. In fact, about 90 percent of Americans of Mexican descent live in the Southwest. Because of their tightly focused pattern of settlement, as well as the region's proximity to Mexico, Mexican culture tends to be well-established and reinforced throughout the area.

That heritage was evident within the Reveles household, in California no less than in Texas. Jose and Magdalena consciously preserved and conveyed to their children the traditions and culture of their homeland. Despite the fact that each family member was capable of communicating in English, they only spoke Spanish at home. Their diet was also strictly Mexican. The songs which their parents sang not only acquainted the Reveles children with Mexican music, they also provided information about Mexico itself.

Such efforts at cultural preservation received a measure of official support in the 1960s and 1970s with the implementation of a number of bilingual programs. These programs were a direct outgrowth of the civil rights movement of the 1950s and 1960s. As black Americans asserted a claim for equal rights and protection under the law, they also proclaimed themselves proud of their race and its African background. Their example stimulated the ethnic consciousness of other groups, inspiring them to make similar proud declarations. All of this was then reflected in policies which repudiated the traditional image of American society as a "melting pot," replacing it with one in which the nation's various ethnic elements were viewed as distinct, vital, and legitimate components of the American whole. Consistent with this line of thought, the federal government adopted legislation designed to guarantee that deficiencies in speaking, reading, or understanding English would not limit opportunities for acquiring an education or exercising voting rights.

Bilingual education was hardly a novel concept. Immigrant parents like Gro Svendsen had often tried to ensure that their children were educated in their traditional culture, parallel to their exposure to the English language and American customs. What was new was the official support given this concept in measures like the Bilingual Education Act of 1967. Historically, public school had been regarded as a mechanism for breaking the hold which foreign institutions and cultures exerted over immigrants and their children, leading immigrant activists like John Hughes to campaign vigorously against them. In the 1960s, advocates of bilingual education successfully offered pedagogical and sociological arguments in support of their ideal. They contended that children with limited ability to speak English inevitably fell behind their contemporaries in school because, while they concentrated on overcoming their deficiency in English, their peers were improving skills in other areas, such as arithmetic. Moreover, it was argued, bilingual education would shield impressionable children against being made to feel inferior because they were not competent in English.

Not everyone accepted these arguments. Some opponents of bilingual education contended that it hindered, rather than advanced, the prospects of integration into society by Mexican-American and other ethnic children. Reinforcement of their traditional culture merely locked them into their *barrios* and ghettos, rather than liberating them. Others argued simplistically that, as English was the language of common usage in the United States, everyone ought to use it—or get out. Some organized groups campaigned actively against bilingualism, supporting a Constitutional amendment to make English the official language of the United States. These attacks became more strident in the late 1970s and early 1980s, a period of increasing immigration and high unemployment.

No less controversial was the concept of bilingual ballots. Proponents insisted that any device which contributed to a more informed electorate was worthwhile, and since bilingual ballots tended to broaden political participation, they were consistent with America's democratic ideals. Objections centered on the inconvenience and expense engendered by bilingual voting, the same arguments made against bilingual education. Some opponents also contended that people who were unable to understand the language in which the government transacts its business did not deserve to play a role in the selection of its officials.

The debate over bilingualism had particular importance for Hispanics. They are the second largest ethnic minority in the United States, behind blacks, whose native language is English. The language barrier which bilingual voting was designed to overcome is only partially responsible for the fact that Mexican-Americans are under-represented in the political process, both as voters and especially as officeholders. Not only are they excluded from that process, they often, in effect, exclude themselves, either by failing to register to vote or by refusing even to become American citizens. The naturalization rate of Mexican immigrants is markedly lower than that of immigrants from other countries. Among Mexicans eligible for citizenship between 1959 and 1966, just 2.4 to 5.0 percent naturalized per year. Other immigrants with a comparable length of residence in the United States naturalized at an annual rate of 23 to 33 percent.

This disparity appears to be rooted in a widespread intention to return someday to Mexico, a desire strengthened by the proximity of the border.

Thirty years after coming to the United States, Jose Reveles remained a resident alien. Although he admitted that "in many ways I think of *los Estados Unidos* as my home," he retained strong emotional ties to the country of his birth. But going home is never easy. "All that is left behind changes," Reveles explained. "People die and places fall and all that remains is a sadness and the memory." For many years he contemplated returning to Mexico to visit his parents, but something indefinable always held him back. Yet, until he made such a visit, his life seemed incomplete. "To leave one's country and to try to make a life somewhere else is like leaving your soul behind and hoping to one day find it again. There is a great emptiness," Reveles observed.

Finally in 1975, more than 20 years after he had left Mexico, Jose Reveles made the trip with his wife and children. Crossing the border once again was a strange experience—it almost seemed as if he had never left Mexico. "The mountains still looked the same," he noted. "I was not sure of what had changed until I got to my *pueblo*. Everything there was different. . . . The ranch was older than I remembered. It seemed like the desert was eating up the land. The wind tore the adobe buildings. It was then I saw my father coming. He surprised me because he was still very tall and straight."

Father and son later went together to collect a few treasured items—old army clothes and some faded photographs—which Ignacio had saved for Jose. "I felt shivers as I touched my things again," Jose acknowledged afterward. "I looked at the old pictures and I knew that I had found my soul again." When the time came to leave, his memory transported him back 20 years, to another departure: "I said good-bye to my mother . . . and pretended, for a moment, that I was young again and that I was just leaving for *los Estados Unidos*." With an aching heart, he drove away.

The emotion—the tenderness and tears—which characterized the reunion did not imply regret on Reveles' part. "I am very happy I came to America," he subsequently declared. "I think that it has a system of life that gives the poor man a chance to . . . have a better life." The one regret that he continued to harbor related not to himself but to his brothers and sisters—a wish that they too lived in the United States. Only one brother followed Reveles—legally—across the border. The rest, he observed, "missed their chance." A law passed in 1965 abandoned the 1924 National Origins plan, the quota restrictions of which had not applied to immigrants from America's hemispheric neighbors, and replaced it with a system which imposed a total annual ceiling of 120,000 immigrants from western hemispheric countries. A 1976 modification established a maximum of 20,000 immigrants from any single nation.[8]

---

[8]Other provisions of the Immigration and Naturalization Act of 1965 established an overall annual limit of 170,000 for immigrants from the eastern hemisphere, with a ceiling of 20,000 from any one country. Preferential consideration was accorded spouses and immediate relatives of American citizens, as well as professionals or persons having particular artistic abilities or job skills.

This limitation fell far short of accommodating the growing desire among Mexicans to flee the terrible economic and social problems which gripped their country. By 1984 Mexico owed American banks in excess of eighty billion dollars, and struggled unsuccessfully in the face of a world oil glut to find a means of payment. Dissatisfied, hungry peasants sought relief in the cities, only to confront an unemployment rate exceeding 40 percent. Eager to escape such desperate conditions and frustrated by the restrictive immigration policy of the United States, many Mexicans crossed the border illegally. Hysterical estimates placed the number of illegals resident in the United States as high as twelve million in the 1970s; more reasonable calculations during the next decade indicated at most half that many. Not all, of course, were Mexican; nevertheless many more illegals came to the United States from Mexico than from any other country.

This situation spawned a vigorous debate in the early 1980s concerning the impact of immigration upon the United States and what should be done about it. Neo-restrictionists argued that the nation was being overrun by unprecedented numbers of immigrants who undercut wages and "stole" jobs from native-born Americans. In addition, immigrants were accused of abusing government services, burdening society with their welfare claims, and draining Social Security funds. Opponents of further restriction noted that the immigrant "flood" was significantly *less* than at the turn of the century: in the first decade of the twentieth century the arrival rate of immigrants was 10.4 per thousand Americans; in the 1970s the rate was only 2.1 per thousand. More to the point, they contended, immigrants do not always compete directly with native workers for employment; instead they often perform tasks spurned by Americans as too demeaning or unrewarding. Further, immigrants create jobs—their purchases generate demand for production and labor. As for government services, the argument continues, immigrants—especially illegal ones—more than pay their own way. A 1970s Labor Department study indicated that 73 percent of illegals had federal income taxes withheld from their pay; 77 percent contributed to Social Security. But only 4 percent dared collect unemployment insurance, 1 percent obtained food stamps, 1 percent accepted welfare payments, and virtually none received Social Security, because to utilize government services was to risk detection.

One outgrowth of this debate was the 1982 introduction in Congress of the Simpson-Mazzoli Bill, which contained two major—and extremely controversial—provisions. One attempted to check illegal immigration by making it unprofitable through the imposition of stiff penalties on the employers of illegal aliens. Although this provision had the backing of organized labor, among other groups, it was vehemently opposed by Hispanics, who claimed that such penalties would reduce employment opportunities for Mexican-Americans, since some employers—wary of violating the law—might simply refuse to hire anyone who looked Latin. Agribusiness spokesmen added their objections, contributing to the deletion of this item from the final form of the Bill. The other main provision, amnesty for illegal aliens who had lived in the United States for a given period and who met certain other qualifications, excited even more protest, particularly from those who asserted that rewarding past violators of immigration laws would only encourage future violations. Due to these objections, as well as the political pressures of a presidential election campaign, the Simpson-Mazzoli Bill was defeated in 1984.

The issues addressed in the debates over the Simpson-Mazzoli Bill were immensely important to Jose Reveles. It raised, for a time at least, the possibility that two of his sisters, illegal residents of the United States, might have their status legitimized. In addition, the elimination of penalties for those who employ illegal immigrants would have made his job considerably easier. As the foreman managing operations of four Sacramento Valley ranches, Reveles was responsible for hiring and supervising work crews.

From *bracero* to foreman—a hard road, yet a rewarding one. But Reveles was determined to secure an even better future for his children. With the encouragement and support of both their parents, Cristina, Francisco, and Magdalena Reveles all graduated from college and pursued advanced degrees in teaching or law. In his children's success, even more than in his own, Jose Reveles could see the truth of what his father had told him so many years before: the United States was indeed a land of opportunity.

FURTHER READING

ACUNA, RODOLFO. *Occupied America: A History of Chicanos.* New York: Harper and Row, 1981.

BARRERA, MARIO. *Race and Class in the Southwest: A Theory of Racial Inequality.* South Bend, Ind.: University of Notre Dame Press, 1979.

CARDOSO, LAWRENCE R. *Mexican Emigration to the United States, 1847-1931: Socio-Economic Patterns.* Tucson: University of Arizona Press, 1980.

CRAIG, RICHARD B. *The Bracero Program: Interest Groups and Foreign Policy.* Austin: University of Texas Press, 1971.

GALARZA, ERNESTO. *Merchants of Labor: The Mexican Bracero Story.* Santa Barbara: McNally and Loftin, 1964.

McWILLIAMS, CAREY. *North From Mexico.* New York: J.B. Lippincott Co., 1949.

STEINER, STAN. *La Raza: The Mexican Americans.* New York: Harper and Row, 1968.

14

Indochinese "Boat People"

© *Jacques Pavlovsky/Sygma.*

14

Jamie Nguyen[1]

THE SMALL GIRL WATCHED impassively as the old man's body was cut down. Over a year in the refugee camp had robbed him of any hope that he would ever leave; in despair he had hanged himself. His death aroused more curiosity than sorrow in Nguyen Tuyet Lan. Because of her size, Lan appeared younger than her 14 years, but inside, having already endured much cruelty and grief, she was far from young. Without changing expression Lan turned away. In the world of the Vietnamese refugee horror had become routine.

In the 40 years since Franz Steiner had come to America, the United States had failed to develop a coherent policy toward refugees. Instead it had responded to a series of crises by adopting a number of stopgap measures. Where consistency did prevail it was furnished by the demands of a foreign policy which was increasingly defined by America's Cold War confrontation with the Soviet Union. The necessity of defeating Nazi Germany had forced the United States and the Soviet Union into a marriage of convenience, but when World War II ended relations between the two Allies reverted to prewar patterns of suspicion and hostility.

Not only did conclusion of the war fail to secure stability and world peace, it did not spell an end to the refugee problem either. In many respects the situation became even more acute. Millions of people—survivors of the Nazi death camps, forced laborers taken to Germany from occupied countries, refugees from eastern Europe who had fled before the advancing Soviet armies—had been displaced by the war, and collectively they were a burden so heavy as to threaten any attempt to repair the war-

[1]"Jamie Nguyen" is an alias. Because her father remains in Vietnam, where he is vulnerable to reprisal, Jamie insisted that steps be taken to prevent his identification. Consequently the names of family members, places where they have lived in the United States, and other information as well, have been changed. Their experiences, however, occurred as described.

shattered economy of Europe. The United States responded, despite considerable domestic opposition, with the Displaced Persons Act of 1948, which authorized admission of 202,000 displaced persons over a two-year period. Reflecting Cold War tensions, the Act specifically reserved 40 percent of the available positions for refugees who had fled territory annexed by the Soviet Union.[2] In the competitive atmosphere of the Cold War anyone who left a communist-controlled country, legally or illegally, was viewed, *ipso facto*, as a refugee. When Soviet troops suppressed a 1956 revolution in Hungary, the United States responded with a special program for admitting 38,000 Hungarian refugees. The success of Fidel Castro's 1959 revolution prompted establishment of the Cuban Refugee Resettlement Program and the admission of 675,000 Cuban refugees between 1959 and 1973. And by the time Nguyen Tuyet Lan became a refugee in 1978, the United States had already adopted another emergency measure—the Indochina Migration and Refugee Assistance Act, which provided a haven to 300,000 of her countrymen.

World War II not only precipitated the Cold War, it also broke the hold which western colonial powers had exercised over southeast Asia since the late nineteenth century. Before their defeat in 1945, the Japanese had driven the Americans out of the Philippines, the British from Malaya, the Dutch from Indonesia, and the French from Indochina. After the war the United States fulfilled its wartime pronouncements supporting self-determination by conferring independence on the Philippines. The British and Dutch, facing vigorous nationalist movements in their Asian colonies, followed suit, albeit somewhat reluctantly. But France unwisely attempted to reverse the tide of events by reasserting its control over Indochina—Vietnam, Cambodia, and Laos.

The United States initially frowned upon France's efforts, but as the Cold War deepened American policy changed. With the seizure of power in China by communists in 1949 and the outbreak of war in Korea the next year, the United States reversed its policy completely. Convinced that communism posed a serious threat to southeast Asia, the United States came to regard the French presence there as a valuable source of stability rather than a betrayal of ideals. The fact that Vietnamese resistance to French control was spearheaded by communists led by Ho Chi Minh seemingly confirmed this view. Despite considerable American support—the United States supplied its ally with money and military equipment—the French failed. In 1954 they suffered a major defeat at Dien Bien Phu and decided to withdraw. Under the terms of an agreement reached at Geneva later that year, Vietnam was temporarily divided along the seventeenth parallel. The northern half of the country was ruled by Ho's communists and in the south a native regime established by the French held sway. All parties agreed that for a limited period refugees

[2]The Displaced Persons Act did not disrupt the ethnic quotas established under the 1924 law. Displaced persons who entered the United States were charged against the annual quotas of future years.

would be permitted to move freely from one part of the country to another. About 800,000 northerners, many of them reflecting France's influence in their Catholic beliefs, moved south. The Geneva agreement also provided that within two years an election should be held to determine under whose auspices the nation would be reunited. A further stipulation prohibited the presence of foreign military personnel in Indochina.

Although this arrangement was acceptable to the Vietnamese and the French, the United States viewed it as an opportunity for future communist expansion. So in 1954 the United States took up the struggle in Vietnam where the French had abandoned it. With American approval the Republic of Vietnam, as the south came to be called, cancelled the election scheduled for 1956 and attempted to crush its opponents, communist and non-communist alike, through the application of force. As insurgency against the government spread, the United States began to supply South Vietnam with money, arms, and several hundred military advisors. By the early 1960s American advisors numbered in the thousands and began to carry out combat missions. On the other side, the South Vietnamese insurgents, known as the Viet Cong, received increasing amounts of aid from North Vietnam. The conflict escalated rapidly. By late 1965 there were 200,000 American soldiers in Vietnam, engaged directly, but unofficially, against soldiers from North Vietnam as well as Viet Cong guerrillas.

Despite an ever-increasing application of force—550,000 soldiers by 1968, and heavier bombing than occured in World War II—the military effort failed. As American casualties mounted, public protest against the war grew proportionally, making its continuation politically impossible. By the early 1970s American troops were being slowly withdrawn as the Nixon administration began "Vietnamizing" the war, a policy designed to turn over responsibility for fighting to the South Vietnamese army. At the same time, the intensity of aerial attacks was increased and the war expanded to include previously neutral Cambodia and Laos. In early 1973 the last American troops were withdrawn, although the United States continued to back the South Vietnamese with enormous amounts of equipment and aid. For a short time South Vietnam appeared to hold its own against its adversaries, but in April of 1975 its armies were routed and the government collapsed abruptly.

The long war exacted a terrible toll from all its participants. Over 58,000 American soldiers were killed, many times that number wounded or exposed to life-threatening chemical weapons. In Vietnam—a nation of 50,000,000 people—the war claimed over 3,000,000 lives and uprooted another 12,000,000 from their homes. Whole villages were destroyed, once-lush jungles were given a lunar look by chemical defoliants and bomb craters, and an entire society was warped by the presence in its midst of a huge army of occupation. Yet for all the disruption which it caused, many Vietnamese were surprisingly insulated from the conflict. In the cities, away from the battlefields, the war touched them only indirectly through the inflated economy, the draft, and the presence of a large number of foreigners. The South Vietnamese government suppressed news of the war, since so much of it was bad. The 1968 My Lai massacre, in which an American infantry company slaughtered over 300 unarmed civilians, was given widespread publicity in the United States, but was scarcely reported in South Vietnam. Some whose lives were affected by the war immigrated to the United States from Vietnam, but these constituted a mere handful. In fact, prior to 1965 there were so few Vietnamese immigrants that the Immigration and Naturalization Service did not even maintain a separate designation for them in its statistics. During the last ten years of the war, from 1966 to 1975, a total of 20,038 Vietnamese entered the United States, most of them the wives or children of American servicemen who had been stationed there.

In the South Vietnamese capital of Saigon, Nguyen Tuyet Lan was scarcely aware that a war was going on at all. Her father's clothing factory provided the family with a life that was more than comfortable; their large house was staffed by four servants. Because Lan's only brother was well below the age of military service, the draft posed no immediate threat. As 1975 began, her interests were the same as those of her ten-year-old playmates: clothes and school. But when South Vietnam collapsed a few months later, it was no longer possible to remain insulated—and the trickle of immigrants to America became a flood.

The speed with which South Vietnam fell caught American officials by surprise. Neither the embassy staff in Saigon nor the State Department in Washington had devised in advance any program for the evacuation of those Vietnamese whose close association with the United States might jeopardize their lives in the event of a communist victory. There were many: high-ranking civil and military officers; employees of various government agencies (like the CIA) and private corporations; national policemen, and more. Not until early April, as the North Vietnamese advanced rapidly on Saigon, were plans made even for the evacuation of American personnel. And although President Gerald Ford declared on April 10 that the United States intended to evacuate Vietnamese associated with the Americans, events in Saigon suggested otherwise. Top embassy officials refused to prepare for departure for fear that it would precipitate panic in Saigon; at lower levels, however, secret arrangements were made. Lists of "high risk" individuals were drawn up; land, air, and sea transportation was secured. But because these arrangements lacked official support they were incomplete and proved only partially effective.

On April 21 government troops making their last stand 26 miles from Saigon were beaten and President Nguyen Van Thieu resigned. Not until four days later was the embassy in Saigon granted authority by the State Department to undertake a full-scale evacuation. The next four days were chaotic. Although Saigon had been sealed to prevent an influx of hundreds of thousands of panicky civilians and soldiers, the city's population was already swollen by refugees.[3] They jammed the streets, clogging escape

[3]Saigon's population in 1961 was about 300,000; by 1975 it had reached nearly 4,000,000.

routes to the airport and disrupting the evacuation. Vietnamese soldiers forced women and children off airplanes to make room for themselves. The confusion culminated on April 29 when the American embassy closed. Thousands of desperate Vietnamese collected outside the embassy compound, begging to be rescued. Some threw money to the Marine guards, trying to buy their way out. A few even attempted to toss their babies over the compound wall, only to see them caught in the barbed wire at its top. When helicopters arrived early the next morning to remove the remaining staff and guards, the terrified mob roared in rage as the Americans abandoned it. That same day Saigon fell and the war ended.

The panic which some South Vietnamese exhibited at the prospect of victory by the communists stemmed from their conviction that a "bloodbath" would accompany it. Predictions of a wholesale slaughter by the communists had been a staple of American propaganda in Vietnam for 20 years, obviously with some effect. But many Saigonese remained relatively calm. They were weary of war, ready for an end to the fighting. Nguyen Van Minh, Lan's father, viewed the communist victory with equal parts of relief and apprehension. The war had threatened to destroy Vietnamese society altogether; peace, even under the communists, had to be better. Besides, he had little to fear personally from the victors. Nguyen Van Minh had no connection with the South Vietnamese government, nor with the Americans, or even with the French who had preceded them. His family was from the south, not one of those who had already fled the communists once before in 1954. Nor were the Nguyens Catholic, a numerically small, but conspicuously anticommunist group.

Initially Minh's decision not to flee seemed sound. Far from embarking upon the sort of bloodbath anticipated by Americans, the triumphant communists pursued a moderate, conciliatory policy. There were few reprisals, no wholesale massacres. Instead emphasis was placed on winning the confidence of the South Vietnamese and restoring the nation's ravaged economy. Saigon was renamed Ho Chi Minh City, but few substantive changes were undertaken immediately. To keep economic disruption to a minimum private enterprises like Nguyen Van Minh's clothing factory remained in the hands of their owners. Although North and South Vietnam were now unified, they continued to use separate currencies.

In contrast, those Vietnamese who fled faced serious problems at first. Lack of organization caused severe hardship for some. Families were separated—often permanently—in the confusion. At Da Nang about 15,000 people crowded aboard barges for transfer to American ships and waited four days in 90-degree heat without food or water. At least 75 of them, mostly women and children, died. All told, the United States managed to evacuate about 65,000 Vietnamese. An approximately equal number escaped on their own, flying military aircraft to American bases, or putting to sea in fishing boats for pick-up by American ships. Although a few continued directly to the United States, most were transferred to military bases in the Philippines or Guam for processing.

While they waited a storm of protest swept over the United States. California's governor complained bitterly over Camp Pendleton's designation as the site of a refugee resettlement center. A member of the state's Congressional delegation urged rejection of the refugees altogether, exclaiming, "Damn it, we have too many Orientals!" In Florida neighbors of Eglin Air Force Base, site of another resettlement camp, circulated petitions demanding that the refugees be sent elsewhere.[4] By a seven-to-one vote the Seattle city council defeated a resolution welcoming the refugees to the United States. Overall, a Harris Poll found that only 36 percent of those surveyed favored admitting Vietnamese refugees, while 54 percent objected.[5] In view of the Congressman's remark, racism was clearly a factor in this reaction. So was the economy. With the United States in the middle of a recession, 8,000,000 Americans were unemployed, nearly 9 percent of the workforce. And perhaps because the refugees reminded Americans of a war that most wished to forget, they were resented all the more.

Such resentment notwithstanding, the federal government moved quickly to implement a refugee resettlement program. Even before Saigon fell an Interagency Task Force, combining elements of 12 different federal agencies, was created to oversee the effort. By the end of May a total of four resettlement centers had been opened and Congress had passed the Indochina Migration and Refugee Relief Act, providing $405,000,000 for the program. In the camps the refugees were photographed, fingerprinted, and extensively interviewed. Personal information relating to age, family size, religion, education, and occupation was noted. Thorough medical examinations were carried out. Each refugee was assigned social security and alien registration numbers and registered with one of the nine voluntary agencies affiliated with the program.

The resettlement camps provided a mechanism for finding groups or individuals to sponsor Vietnamese while preparing them culturally for American life. That preparation had as its objective reducing the possibility of their becoming public burdens. Most adult refugees therefore spent several hours each day studying English as well as taking classes designed to shape their expectations and behavior. Camp schools for children had a similarly dual purpose, but because they stressed values that were alien to Vietnamese culture, such as independence and assertiveness, parents sometimes objected to their children's attendance. Bilingual newspapers provided practical advice as well as useful glimpses at American life; news from Vietnam was virtually ignored. The principal activity in camp, however, was waiting, waiting to leave.

For the handful who had the $4000 per individual needed to demonstrate a capacity for self-support, the delay was brief. But nearly 90 percent

---

[4]Other resettlement camps were located at Fort Chaffee in Arkansas and Fort Indiantown Gap in Pennsylvania.

[5]Although most of the 130,000 refugees were from Vietnam, a small proportion came from Cambodia and Laos, where communists had seized control at virtually the same time as in Vietnam.

of the 130,000 refugees were required to find sponsors before they were permitted to depart. Matching refugees with sponsors was the major task of the nine voluntary agencies. Although larger groups like the United States Catholic Conference and the Lutheran Immigration and Refugee Service had extensive experience with refugee placement, a few of the organizations lacked either the proper background or sufficient personnel. In addition, all the agencies were subjected to considerable pressure by the federal government, which was determined to close the camps before the year ended. As a result, refugees and sponsors were often matched rather arbitrarily. Because a major goal of the government was to minimize the refugees' impact on American cultural and economic life, they were deliberately and widely dispersed across the country, even though this process frequently fragmented extended families. This meant that although the Vietnamese refugees received an unprecedented amount of assistance from the government, they were also deprived of the sort of comfort and support which Jose Reveles found in the El Paso *barrio*, or which had benefited Leonard Covello in East Harlem's Little Italy.

Comfort and support were also increasingly rare in Indochina. The communist triumph in Vietnam had resounded throughout the region, echoed by communist takeovers in Laos and Cambodia, which was renamed Kampuchea. And while the South Vietnamese had been spared the long-predicted bloodbath, their neighbors were not so fortunate. In Laos the Hmong, hill tribesmen who had worked with the CIA during the war, were marked for extermination, while in Kampuchea the ruling Khmer Rouge went on a senseless rampage that destroyed their nation's economy, emptied its cities, and ultimately claimed the lives of at least 2,000,000 of its 7,000,000 inhabitants.

In Vietnam the postwar readjustment was less drastic, but nonetheless harsh. The communists launched a massive indoctrination campaign in the schools, on the job, at neighborhood meetings. Nguyen Tuyet Lan later recalled that at school "the whole system changed." She could no longer select the classes she wanted, and all courses were given a political thrust. There was a wholesale dismissal of teachers. Their replacements, she noted, "mostly came from the North." Lan and her schoolmates "had to join clubs," in which communist principles were preached. The process of indoctrination was even more rigorous for former military and civilian officials. Thousands of them were sent to "re-education camps" where they performed hard labor, listened to political lectures, were physically abused, and in some cases were even killed.

The implementation of a Five Year Development Plan in 1976 produced further hardship. Reflecting the Plan's emphasis on agricultural production, 1,400,000 people from South Vietnam's cities were forced back into the countryside. Most returned to their home villages, but nearly a third were sent to "New Economic Zones," raw new villages carved out of the jungle or established in areas depopulated by the war. The harsh environment of the New Economic Zones often represented little improvement over the re-education camps. The importance of Nguyen Van Minh's factory insured that his family would not be sent away from Ho Chi Minh City, but it could no longer guarantee them a comfortable life. On one hour's notice they were ordered to vacate their home. "We couldn't take anything out," Lan later remembered. "Guards watched us. . . . We only had the clothes we wore." With nowhere else to go, the Nguyens moved into the home of cousins.

Not all the problems facing the Vietnamese stemmed from their government's policies. Drought, devastating typhoons, and protracted cold spells resulted in crop failures in 1976 and 1977. The amount of rice which each person was allowed to purchase at a controlled price was reduced, while the cost of other foods increased. As economic problems became more severe, the government grew even more harsh in its treatment of dissidents.

The deteriorating conditions in Vietnam stimulated a steadily increasing flow of refugees, although the overall number was small in comparison to the exodus that had occurred when the war had ended. In 1976 over 5,200 Vietnamese, mostly fisherfolk, fled by boat; the next year nearly 15,700 escaped. Most sailed west across the Gulf of Thailand, landing either in Thailand itself or in Malaysia. Because of the horrible slaughter taking place in Kampuchea and the lesser but still considerable disruption in Laos, few Vietnamese dared risk overland flight. By the end of 1977 about 150,000 Laotian and Kampuchean refugees had gathered in Thailand; ironically, even more Kampucheans had sought refuge in Vietnam, demonstrating that, in the words of one relief official, "there is a pecking order even in hell."

The Vietnamese government reacted to its problems by exerting more control over its economy. In March of 1978 it abolished "all trade and business operations of bourgeois tradesmen" in the South. This resulted in the abrupt closure of more than 30,000 large private enterprises. Many businessmen and their families were banished to villages or to New Economic Zones. Some luckier ones were permitted to enter into a kind of partnership with the state: Nguyen Van Minh's factory was taken over by the government, but because of his expertise he was retained as its manager. The next month volunteer youth brigades and soldiers forcibly shut down open air markets, wiping out thousands of small merchants. In May the introduction of a new currency for the whole country represented another severe blow to the once-prosperous middle class; at a single stroke their savings were destroyed. "We were only allowed to have a limited amount of the new money," Lan explained, no matter how much of the old currency they had turned in.

One group particularly hard hit by these developments was Vietnam's 1,500,000 ethnic Chinese. Although they represented only 3 percent of the country's population, the Chinese were disproportionately active in its commercial life. Their position quickly became even more tenuous as Vietnam engaged in a series of border skirmishes with China, its neighbor to the north. The two countries were historic antagonists; China had ruled Vietnam for more than 1,000 years of its early history. That ancient score had not been settled by the aid which China had furnished North Vietnam during its war with the United States, and now new differences arose to aggravate further their relations. Beginning in 1977 the Khmer Rouge in Kampuchea carried their campaign of terror into Vietnamese villages along their border—torturing, raping, and killing. Because the Kampucheans enjoyed steadfast support from China, Vietnamese attempts to assert control over the region caused friction with China. In December of 1977 a large-scale Vietnamese incursion into Kampuchea precipitated border problems with China as well.

These events coincided with a spectacular increase in the number of "boat people" fleeing Vietnam. Just over 5,000 washed ashore in neighboring countries during April of 1978, twice the total of the previous month and about one third as many as in all of 1977. The numbers continued to grow. In July over 6,200 arrived; in September nearly 8,600. During the same period about 160,000 Sino-Vietnamese fled over the border into China. In addition 150,000 Kampucheans sought sanctuary in Vietnam, while another 195,000 fled to Thailand.

In part, the increased volume of refugees from Vietnam reflected worsening conditions there, including imminent war with China and another crop failure in the summer of 1978. But to a large extent it also indicated a change in the government's policy. Up to this point those attempting to leave Vietnam had been punished harshly when caught, given stiff prison sentences, or even killed. But by Spring of 1978 the government appeared not only to have relaxed its vigilance, it actually began to organize "escapes" and charge refugees for the privilege of fleeing! The government's purpose was two-fold. Practically all of the refugees going to China and over one half the boat people were ethnic Chinese. Just as the Nazis had at first tried to rid Germany of its Jews by applying social and economic pressure, so Vietnam sought to solve its minority "problem." And, like the Nazis who had collected an "exit tax" from departing Jews, the economically hard-pressed Vietnamese government saw in those who wished to leave a source of foreign exchange—and required from them payment in gold.

One indication of the degree to which the refugee traffic was officially organized was the establishment of a number of transit camps along the southern Vietnamese coast. These camps served as staging areas for departure; would-be refugees gathered there after surrendering their gold. The whole process was controlled and directed by a division of the Public Security Bureau, a secret police force. A well-justified fear of the Bureau persuaded many Vietnamese to avoid the official machinery of escape and instead make their own arrangements. Those who dealt with the Bureau took fewer risks, but nonetheless embarked upon a course fraught with danger. Bureau officers sometimes insisted on unexpected bribes; on occasion they arrested or shot those who had already paid. Refugees betrayed in such a fashion had no recourse; they were, after all, breaking the law by attempting to flee. Because of the peril involved in leaving Vietnam, those who planned to do so kept their arrangements as secret as possible. Lan

*Indochinese Refugees, Awaiting a
Host Country, 1978*

© J.P. Laffont/Sygma.

was therefore surprised one night late in 1978 when her mother informed her, "We're leaving tomorrow." "Where?" the young girl asked. "Don't ask where," she was told.

Before the fall of South Vietnam some members of the middle and upper classes had kept their savings in gold as a hedge against their country's rampant inflation. Just before the communist capture of Saigon, they had hidden or buried their gold to prevent its confiscation. This, apparently, is what Nguyen Van Minh had done as well, for he was now able, miraculously, to produce enough of the precious metal to purchase their freedom. But not all of them. Fearful of betrayal by the Public Security Bureau, or of some other disaster along the way, he and his wife, Nguyen Xuan Thu, reached a heart-rending decision. To insure that at least part of the family survived, Minh and his son would remain behind. Only when he heard that Thu, Lan, and her younger sister, Nguyen Thi Hue, had reached safety would Minh and the boy attempt to leave.

The next evening, carrying only a few bags of food, Minh set out grimly with his wife, their two daughters, a cousin, and her two young children. They travelled to a farm where several hundred other people waited breathlessly in the darkness. "Everyone was so scared," Lan noted. After two agonizing hours an authoritative voice called out, "Get in line!" Out of nowhere a convoy of buses appeared and the crowd scrambled aboard. They were driven to a harbor where they were lined up once more. Their names were read from a list and checked off. Lan began to cry, as it dawned on the 14-year-old girl that she might never see her father again. At a signal from an official, the crowd surged forward into several fishing boats. Clinging to both her mother and sister, Lan looked around frantically for her father. "I didn't say 'good-bye' to my father," she regretfully remembered later. "I couldn't see him." In the confusion Lan's bag of food was lost or stolen. The boats were so overloaded that one began to sink immediately; some of its passengers were transferred to the other boats.

Even after the boats cast off, "we were still crying," Lan recalled, "because we were so scared." With good reason. Ahead loomed a lighthouse; its guards might not have been bribed to let the refugees pass unmolested. For safety's sake the boats spread out and sneaked quietly out to sea. As dawn broke Lan's little boat, packed with about 200 grieving but hopeful people, was alone on the South China Sea. The nearest safe landing lay about 250 miles west, across the Gulf of Thailand. The voyage was short in comparison to those taken by Johann Buettner and other early immigrants to America. But in terms of the hardship they endured and the danger they encountered, the experience of the boat people exceeded anything which Buettner could even have imagined.

Yet an increasing number of Vietnamese willingly risked those hazards in order to be free. The volume of boat people arriving in neighboring countries reached 12,500 in October of 1978 and exceeded 21,500 the following month. By the Spring of 1979 they would constitute a flood—51,100 in May, 57,000 in June. In all, between the time that South Vietnam fell in April of 1975 and July of 1979, when large-scale sea escape was sharply curtailed, about 293,000 boat people arrived in other southeast Asian countries from Vietnam.[6] A small percentage of them travelled aboard large freighters: the *Hai Hong* brought 2,500 to Malaysia in November of 1978; the *Huey Fong* arrived at Hong Kong in December carrying over 3,300. Modified to transport human cargo in a manner reminiscent of ships engaged in the African slave trade, some of the vessels were barely seaworthy. The *Seng Cheong,* run aground by its 1,400 passengers after they were abandoned by the crew, was so rusty that there were holes in its sides. Masters of these larger vessels steadfastly denied participation in the refugee trade, insisting unconvincingly that their ships had somehow been overrun by flotillas of boat people on the high seas. Investigation proved, however, that the ships deliberately waited at prearranged coordinates in order to "rescue" the refugees. But most boat people travelled, like Lan, in smaller vessels, usually fishing boats. These craft were often so flimsy that they could not be relied upon to survive an open-sea crossing.

---

[6]The boat people represented less than 14 percent of the total number of Indochinese refugees seeking sanctuary outside their homelands.

The human tide washing out of Vietnam threatened to swamp neighboring countries, which reacted with an alarm bordering on panic. The generosity with which Malaysia had accepted the early boat people diminished precipitously in late 1978. By the end of November there were 45,000 of them crowded into Malaysian refugee camps. Nearly half were confined on a desert island in crude facilities designed to accommodate 2,000. The beleaguered government announced that no more boats would be permitted to land as long as they were seaworthy or capable of repair and movement to other countries. In the immediate aftermath of the order, dozens of boats were turned away; at least five capsized in the process, drowning hundreds of refugees. Angry villagers attacked the survivors stoning and beating them, as they struggled in the surf. Yet compared to that of several of its neighbors, Malaysia's policy was humane. At the initial appearance of the boat people, Singapore had steadfastly refused to permit any to land. Even boats that were sinking were towed far out to sea. In defense of such actions, Singapore Premier Lee Kuan Yew asserted, "You must grow calluses on your heart . . . otherwise you will bleed to death."

The Premier had a point. The countries of "first asylum," where the refugees initially landed, were mostly underdeveloped and poor. Even though the United Nations High Commission for Refugees, or UNHCR, shouldered the cost for feeding and sheltering the refugees, the host countries inevitably faced additional expense. The dimensions of the problem in Hong Kong, destination of many of the boat people fleeing northern Vietnam, were quite clear. With a population of 5,000,000 crowded into an area of only 404 square miles, Hong Kong was hard pressed to accommodate the nearly 42,000 boat people who arrived during just two months early in 1979. Not only did refugees tax the resources of the first asylum countries, they posed political problems as well. Natives resented the attention and aid given them, meager though it was. The government of Thailand actually rejected millions of dollars in United Nations refugee relief so that the standard of living in the camps would not surpass the miserable conditions in which many Thai peasants lived.[7] A further factor in the reaction against the boat people was the fact that so many of them were ethnic Chinese. In both Malaysia and Indonesia, considerable prejudice and frequent violence were directed against Chinese already residing in those countries; the government of each was wary of upsetting the ethnic balance even further.

But the nature of the reception awaiting them was far from the minds of Lan and other Vietnamese when they took to the sea. Their initial concern was simply to survive the voyage. The danger posed by the often unseaworthy condition of their vessels was multiplied by the fact that the exodus began to swell to a peak late in 1978, at the height of the monsoon

---

[7]Relief officials frequently apprehended Thais attempting to sneak into refugee camps; the daily food allowance of twenty-five cents per refugee exceeded the living standards of many peasants.

season. No less deadly were the Thai pirates who preyed mercilessly on the boat people—robbing, raping, or killing them, sometimes disabling or even sinking their boats. Some luckless refugees were attacked several times by different gangs of pirates. Nor could those adrift at sea be certain that the standard humanitarian practice of rescue by passing vessels would be observed. When Malaysia and other first asylum nations prohibited landing by refugees, some ships began to ignore desperate boat people whose vessels were crippled or sinking. All told, although 293,000 boat people managed to survive, anywhere from 10 to 70 percent that many— 29,000 to 205,000—died anonymously at sea.

For a time it seemed as though Lan and her shipmates might join them. Initially she was too stunned by grief to grasp fully their situation. Missing her father and her brother as well as their home, she asked herself, "What am I going to do now?" Lan found no comfort among the others, who were filled with as much despair as she. Poorly supplied, the refugees ran out of food and water after just two days. Most lay listlessly in the sun: "I had no energy," Lan would recall. When the boat began to take on water, panic swept the entire vessel. "Oh my God," Lan thought, "we'll all die!" Hope surged when a large ship appeared. Everyone screamed and waved, but it sailed past, ignoring them. Finally a merchant vessel stopped. The refugees climbed up the side of the ship on cargo nets. Weak from hunger and fear, Lan despaired, "I cannot make it." But somehow she arrived safely on deck with the rest.

The bigger ship represented a major improvement in safety, but a somewhat lesser one in terms of comfort. Supplies and facilities stretched thin and broke under the strain of unanticipated demand. Food was available, but in small quantities, and the refugees could get it only after waiting in a long line. Water supplies ran low and toilet facilities ceased to function altogether. For two weeks the ship sailed the South China Sea, seeking vainly to unload its human cargo. "We weren't allowed in Malaysia," Lan remembered; Singapore turned them away as well. Finally the captain put his unwanted passengers ashore on a remote island in the Indonesian archipelago, leaving authorities no choice in the matter.

Although the ship sent out a radio signal for help, the refugees were in a state of panic. Without food, they survived on wild fruit. "We didn't know what it was," Lan admitted. "It was tested first by an old lady before the others ate it." Fresh water was found in a nearby stream. At night the frightened refugees slept on the beach. They built a huge fire for warmth and as a signal, but torrential rains drowned it out. Several ships were sighted; Lan and the others waved frantically, but to their disappointment all sailed past. After nearly two weeks one ship halted; its captain sent supplies ashore and promised to radio Indonesian authorities as well. A few days later a small Indonesian patrol boat arrived. Several refugees who appeared desperately ill were taken aboard; the rest were told to expect rescue within two days. Four more days passed, however, before another naval vessel evacuated them.

Their next stop was a UNHCR-run camp elsewhere in Indonesia. The accommodations which awaited them there were scarcely better than what they had scraped together for themselves on the beach. A small ration of food was allotted each inmate: three eggs a week, a few cups of rice, some cabbage, and occasionally fish which Lan found to be uniformly "terrible." Her hunger nonetheless compelled Lan to consume it all, until she heard that one refugee had found a human finger inside his fish. Years afterward she still grimly insisted, "I'll never eat fish again." Their meager food allotment was supplemented by whatever the refugees could buy or steal. If they had any money they could purchase what they wished from vendors who appeared on a weekly basis. Others, less fortunate, sometimes tried to take what they needed. As a precaution against thieves, what remained of Lan's family slept in shifts, guarding their possessions. It hardly seemed worth the bother; their worldly goods were so few. Camp inmates had not been issued any blankets, cooking utensils, or water vessels. Instead they had been forced to improvise, using tin cans, gourds, or whatever else they could find.

As the oldest of the four children in her party, Lan bore a special responsibility. "I had never cooked in my life," she admitted later, but there was no alternative then. "I had never carried water in my life. It was so heavy." Somehow Lan did what had to be done. Less resilient than their offspring, many adults had difficulty adjusting to their new circumstances. "In the camp you saw the kids cry a lot," Lan noted, because adults sometimes took out their fear and frustration upon their children. Weeks dragged into months. Under their collective weight Lan's "whole person changed." Once energetic and lively, she became extremely passive, sitting quietly for hours and watching the others, or standing stoically in line six hours for a shower.

Her family's transfer to another camp after three months meant no real change in their circumstances—one was depressingly like the other. But little more could have been expected. When Malaysia had begun to turn the boat people away late in 1978, their focus had shifted quickly to Indonesia. Within a few months, more than 45,000 arrived there. The UNHCR was caught completely unprepared. It had only one official in all of Indonesia; its undersubscribed operating fund permitted only a week-to-week effort. The United States supplied over 50 percent of the UNHCR's budget, although a half dozen other nations, from Australia to Sweden, furnished more on a per capita basis. But as Malaysia's Home Minister angrily observed in December of 1978, "Conscience money is not the answer." He asserted that "countries who contributed toward the creation of this problem cannot turn their heads and wish it away." Yet that is exactly what the rest of the world attempted to do.

That same month a UNHCR-sponsored "Consultative Meeting with Interested Governments on Refugees and Displaced Persons in Southeast Asia" was held in Geneva. The results were sadly similar to the Evian Conference held 40 years earlier to address the problem of Jewish refugees from Germany. None of the 38 nations in attendance appeared willing to extend itself. With over 200,000 Indochinese refugees in camps awaiting resettlement, the conferees added only 3,500 new admissions pledges to the ones which they had already made, and promised the bankrupt relief organization eight more weeks of operating funds.

The United States was among the conferees in Geneva. Despite the havoc caused by its 20-year war in Indochina, the United States refused to acknowledge any special responsibility for the refugees. It was, even at this point, still without any sort of policy for their admission. The initial surge of 130,000 Indochinese refugees accepted in 1975 had been taken in as "parolees". That meant that they were admitted without reference to limitations in existing immigration law, but were also denied the resident alien status which could eventually permit them to become citizens.[8] Since then the United States had accepted more Vietnamese parolees, but relatively few and very slowly: 11,000 in 1976, 15,000 in 1977, and 32,500 in 1978. Moreover, these later admissions were required to meet normal American immigration criteria relating to job skills and the like, a policy which infuriated the first asylum nations. "It seems they are taking only the better educated [refugees]," one Malaysian official complained. "What will happen to the residue? . . . No one wants them. They will take away the cream and leave us the crumbs."

The caution with which the United States approached the Indochinese refugee issue reflected several fears. Public opinion was by this time even less sympathetic than it had been three years earlier. In addition, the Carter Administration worried that if the United States made too great an effort at resettlement it might actually inspire more boat people to flee Vietnam, exacerbating the refugee problem. Little evidence suggested any basis for this concern, nor did America's caution stem the tide of refugees. In fact, in the six months following the Geneva conference on refugees, mounting pressure in Vietnam drove another 167,000 boat people onto the sea. Yet even as the problem became more acute, American policy-makers stumbled about in confusion. Delays in funding by Congress reduced America's monthly refugee intake to less than one half of what was authorized.

Most developed nations were even less willing to accept the refugees. Just four countries—the United States, Australia, Canada, and France—provided over 91 percent of the resettlement pledges received by the UNHCR by mid-January, 1979. In the camp where Lan waited for an opportunity to begin life anew, she observed only American, Australian, and Canadian representatives collecting information and processing applications. In the face of American immigration restrictions, Lan hoped initially for eventual resettlement in Australia. But in early 1979 the focus of her aspirations shifted as the United States undertook several measures that at last defined a cohesive American refugee policy. In February, Pres-

---

[8]The refugees were later granted resident alien status, retroactive to the time of their arrival in the United States.

ident Jimmy Carter created a new, high-level position in his administration: Coordinator for Refugee Affairs. The following month, Carter recommended legislation which would emerge from Congress a year later as the Refugee Act of 1980.[9] In April, he expanded America's annual refugee intake to 84,000; two months later he doubled it again.

But all of these advances would have counted for little had the flow of boat people from Vietnam continued unabated. In an effort to stem the tide, the United States pressured its allies to withhold the economic aid desperately needed for Vietnam's reconstruction until it agreed to stop exporting its people. Although Vietnam had consistently and vehemently denied it was abetting the refugees, it issued the desired declaration at another UNHCR-sponsored conference in July of 1979. Within a half year, the number of Vietnamese boat people seeking sanctuary in neighboring nations dropped by more than 96 percent.[10] As the volume of Vietnamese refugees substantially diminished, the developed countries more than doubled their resettlement pledges.

These developments had mixed implications for Lan. They increased the likelihood of her departure from the camp, but they also vastly decreased the possibility that her father and brother would ever rejoin their family. The door permitting exit from Vietnam was now virtually closed. Under its new "Orderly Departure Program," only a relative handful would be permitted to leave. Moreover, in America's view, their status had changed from "refugee" to "emigrant," in effect nullifying the special machinery which had been constructed to expedite their entry into the United States.

For those in the camps, however, that machinery continued to operate. Officials of various American relief organizations interviewed the inmates, recording family histories and other personal data. A thorough medical examination signalled the imminence of resettlement. Every day following her health check, Lan studied the bulletin board on which the names of those refugees departing for the United States were listed. Her mounting sense of excitement contained an element of what Lan later described as "terror" at the prospect of leaving. As depressing as the camp was, it had been her home for nearly a year; upon departing she would leave behind her cousins and friends that she had made. Ahead of her lay an uncertain future in a strange and distant country.

Late in 1979 Lan, her mother, sister and about two dozen other refugees from the camp flew to the United States. Upon their arrival in Seattle the group separated. As it had since 1975, the government continued to adhere to a policy of dispersing Indochinese around the country. From Seattle the

[9]Under the Refugee Act of 1980, the United States finally abandoned its Cold War-related definition of "refugee," replacing it with one adopted by the United Nations in 1951. In addition, the law established a "normal" refugee influx of 50,000 per year, and granted the President emergency authority to accept more.

[10]Ironically, the UNHCR in effect encouraged Vietnam to violate the right of free emigration which was contained in the Universal Declaration of Human Rights adopted by the United Nations General Assembly in 1948.

Nguyens proceeded to Chicago and finally to Oshkosh, in east central Wisconsin. Awaiting them at the airport was a large and enthusiastic reception committee from the Lutheran church which was sponsoring the Nguyens. Disoriented by the abrupt transition from refugee camp to middle America, and unable to understand any English, Lan became alarmed when several members of the congregation pressed forward, welcoming the Nguyens with kisses and hugs. They were then taken to the church, where a dinner in their honor was held. Lan quickly discovered that not only did Americans behave differently, they ate strange food. "There was Swiss cheese," she remembered later. "It was yucky!" To their relief, a Vietnamese refugee who had already lived in the United States for a short time had been brought from another town to translate.

The church group which sponsored the Nguyens saw to their immediate physical needs. It provided them with clothes, furnished a house, and stocked its refrigerator. At night members of the congregation sometimes visited, checking on the Nguyens and helping them study English. Many of the boat people resettled in the United States were not so fortunate; groups and individuals who sponsored the refugees often had fewer resources. Moreover, in comparison to the first wave of refugees which had arrived in 1975, the newcomers received far less in the way of government assistance. There were no longer refugee camps on American soil to help cushion the culture shock which they inevitably suffered. There were no government-sponsored English language classes. Yet many of the newer arrivals were less prepared for American life and more needy of help than those who had preceded them. A considerable proportion of the 1975 refugees had been people with connections to the American diplomatic, military, or commercial presence in Vietnam, a familiarity that aided in their adjustment in the United States. This is not to suggest that the 1975 refugees adapted readily to their new home. Many faced enormous difficulty; few were truly well-acquainted with American customs or thought. But according to a 1983 report from the General Accounting Office, the more recent arrivals were even "poorer, less able to speak English, and less exposed to urban life than the earlier wave of refugees."

There had certainly been little in Lan's experience to prepare her for life in America. Due to her inability either to speak or understand English, school proved especially nightmarish for Lan. "I hated it so much, because I didn't know what [the teachers and students] were talking about," she recalled. Lan's failure frustrated her; it was a new experience. "In Vietnam I was always first in my class," she explained. Lan sometimes suspected that her classmates made fun of her, although she was uncertain of what they said. School was also the scene of racial problems. Fights between Anglo and Indian students occasionally broke out, dividing her classmates into two camps. Different from both groups, Lan was accepted by neither. Discouraged and lonely, she told her mother, "I want to go back," realizing even as she spoke that she had no place to return to.

The earlier wave of Indochinese refugees had likewise encountered prejudice. In 1975 high school students in one Florida town spoke of organizing a "Gook Klux Klan" to protest refugee resettlement. In Texas violence erupted between shrimp fishermen and Vietnamese refugees who attempted to compete with them. That sort of reception had been one factor which prompted many of the widely scattered refugees to undertake a secondary migration. For the most part they moved from isolated, often rural, areas to urban centers like Los Angeles, where they could begin to establish their own communities. Another factor in their movement was the physical environment. Conditioned to a subtropical climate, few Vietnamese were prepared for the severe cold characteristic of winter in the northern states. Consequently the secondary migration which did occur tended to take the form of resettlement in states like Florida, Louisiana, Texas, and especially California.

The Wisconsin winter took its toll on Lan and her younger sister, Hue. Both caught frequent colds and missed many days of school. Lan felt that watching television at home probably benefited her more anyway, in terms of learning English. But sometimes she was too sick even to manage that. A bout with pneumonia early in 1980 convinced Lan's mother than remaining in Wisconsin threatened her daughter's health. Over the protests and warnings of their sponsors, the Nguyens prepared to leave.

Nguyen Xuan Thu's decision to move was reinforced by her discovery that a friend from Saigon lived in the northern California town of Santa Rosa. Thu hoped her friend would help ease the family's sense of isolation as well as assist her in finding a job. Identical considerations would account for the movement to California of one third to one half of America's 700,000 Indochinese refugees by late 1984. The state's booming, high-technology economy and already large Asian population seemed to promise an easier adjustment than anywhere else.

When the Nguyens arrived in Santa Rosa in April of 1980, Lan was stunned to find a small town defined largely by surrounding farms and a state university. Her television-shaped conception of California had led her to expect that the whole state would be like Los Angeles. Lan's disgust mirrored her mother's disappointment: Thu was at first unable to find work. Thu's inability to speak or understand English and her lack of occupational skills posed formidable obstacles to securing employment. A century earlier, unskilled immigrants like Emma Goldman had been readily able to locate work in America's factories, but in an increasingly service-oriented economy the demand for such labor was declining. Like the majority of Vietnamese refugees, Thu eventually found a job, although, as in most such cases, it was of the blue collar variety and paid only the minimum wage.

Although it was an obvious improvement over life in a refugee camp, in comparison to what they had known before 1975, such a situation represented a step down for many Vietnamese in America. However, other refugees, not merely those from Indochina but earlier ones like Frank Steiner, had experienced a similar initial decline in their circumstances. Often, however, downward mobility was temporary, rather than a permanent pattern. Indeed, by the time the Nguyen family arrived in America members of the first wave of Indochinese refugees had already begun to improve their position in terms of family income. In part, this was due to their broader conception of family than that which prevailed among most Americans. A Vietnamese family extends beyond the nuclear unit; it includes cousins, grandparents, and other relatives. Families which had become fragmented while fleeing from Vietnam, or had been dispersed by American resettlement policy, reunited as soon as possible. This process created households with a larger than usual number of workers, albeit with more people to support. Still, because of their tendencies to crowd together and live frugally, such families could often raise their income level markedly. Similarly, Lan supplemented her mother's minimal earnings by working after school and during the summer.

In many respects the key to advancement by the refugees was education. Some adults attended English language classes or signed up for job training programs; their children enrolled in public schools. Nearly 16 years old upon her arrival in Santa Rosa, Lan was placed at the sophomore level in high school. While improving rapidly in terms of her English skills, Lan still had trouble with some of her schoolwork, especially classes in literature, government, and American history. But in mathematics, bookkeeping, and to a lesser extent science, she did quite well. In these areas, of course, mastery of the English language was far less important than in her other subjects. Her success at school encouraged Lan to study over the summer and enroll in extra classes the following year. By the time she graduated in 1982, Lan was earning A's in all her subjects. The accessibility of a state university in Santa Rosa enabled Lan to continue her education at relatively little expense, although it was necessary for her to balance her studies with part-time work. Continuing in the direction which her last years in high school had pointed, she decided to major in computer science.

College offered Lan her first opportunity in nearly three years for extensive contact with other Vietnamese immigrants; more than three dozen attended Sonoma State University. In high school she had been the only Indochinese student. Nevertheless, since her classmates there had already been familiar with other Asians, and because Lan had become more self-confident as her English improved, she had felt less isolated than she had in Wisconsin. "I had a lot of friends," she reported, and was invited to parties and other social activities. As Leonard Covello, Frank Steiner, and many other immigrants had done before her, Lan changed her name to one which sounded more "American" and was easier for her schoolmates to master: Jamie Nguyen.

At college Jamie discovered that most of the other Vietnamese students—almost all of whom were from large ethnic communities in Los Angeles, Orange County, or San Francisco—had not made all of the adjustments required of her. Somewhat insulated from American society, they remained "old-fashioned" in her view. "They tease me," she acknowledged ruefully. "They say, 'Jamie is not even a Vietnamese girl; she's totally American.' But I say, 'What's wrong with that?'" These differences, however, posed no obstacle to Jamie's acceptance by the others, who elected her an officer of the campus Vietnamese Student Association.

Jamie's Americanized ways did produce friction at home, however. Adjustment to a new way of life proved harder for her mother, who remained rooted in Vietnamese traditions. Nguyen Xuan Thu, disturbed by her daughters' easy abandonment of their past, frequently chided them, "You're so Americanized now, but you must still remain Vietnamese." Thu preserved what she could of their native culture, speaking Vietnamese around the house and preparing traditional food. But Jamie and Danielle (as Hue began calling herself) conversed together in English, and when they cooked for the family, Jamie admitted, the menu is "strictly American: hamburgers or casserole. And cheesecake!"

Generational differences of this sort are hardly unique; Leonard Covello and many other immigrant children experienced similar tension with their parents. Nor is it surprising that the conflict was greater between Thu and her younger daughter. Five years Jamie's junior, Danielle brought even less in the way of cultural baggage from Vietnam than her sister did. As a result, Jamie noted, "Danielle has no accent. . . . She is a typical American teenager. She is always on the phone, talking about boys." Nor was Thu, in her reluctance to shed the past, any less typical of her generation. Despite her daughters' encouragement to learn English, she was slow to do so. "I want her to see the way that things are different than before," Jamie declared, but her mother refused to accept some changes. Thu resisted taking any steps toward obtaining American citizenship. "She is waiting for my father," Jamie explained, "to see what he thinks."

In contrast, Jamie became a United States citizen in February of 1985, as soon as she was eligible. Shortly afterward she reflected upon her new home and her changing view of it. When her family first came to America, Jamie recalled, "We had been through so much, we didn't care what it was going to be like. . . . We just wanted to be somewhere safe." Later she came to believe that "America is a pretty good place. You can do whatever you want. . . . It is a free country." Jamie would one day like to visit Vietnam, if it were safe. But she recognizes that, as have millions of other immigrants from John Winthrop to Jose Reveles, "my future is here."

FURTHER READING

GRANT, BRUCE. *The Boat People.* New York: Penguin Books, 1980.

KARNOW, STANLEY. *Vietnam: A History.* New York: Viking Press, 1983.

KELLY, GAIL P. *From Vietnam to America.* Boulder, Colo.: Westview Press, 1977.

MONTERO, DARREL. *Vietnamese Americans: Patterns of Resettlement and Socioeconomic Adaptation in the United States.* Boulder, Colo.: Westview Press, 1979.

MURFIN, GARY D. *War, Life and Stress: The Forced Relocation of the Vietnamese People.* Honolulu: University of Hawaii Press, 1975.

ST. CARTMAIL, KEITH. *Exodus Indochina.* Auckland, New Zealand and Exeter, N.H.: Heinemann Publishers, 1983.

WAIN, BARRY. *The Refused.* New York: Simon and Schuster, 1981.

Index